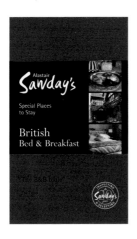

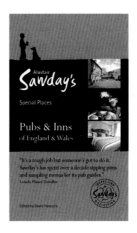

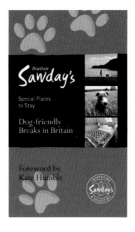

D0027666

Alastair

Sawday's

Special Places to Stay

Sixteenth edition
Copyright © 2014
Alastair Sawday Publishing Co. Ltd
Published in September 2014
ISBN-13: 978-1-906136-70-3

Alastair Sawday Publishing Co. Ltd,
Merchants House, Wapping Road,
Bristol BS1 4RW, UK
Tel: +44 (0)117 204 7801
Email: info@sawdays.co.uk
Web: www.sawdays.co.uk

The Globe Pequot Press,
P. O. Box 480, Guilford,
Connecticut 06437, USA
Tel: +1 203 458 4500
Email: info@globepequot.com
Web: www.globepequot.com

Series Editor Alastair Sawday
Editor Tom Bell
Assistant to Editor Lianka Varga
Senior Picture Editor Alec Studerus
Picture Editor Ben Mounsey
Production Coordinators Lianka Varga,
Sarah Frost Mellor
Writing Tom Bell
Inspections Tom Bell

Marketing & PR
0117 204 7801
marketing@sawdays.co.uk

*We have made every effort to ensure the accuracy
of the information in this book at the time
of going to press. However, we cannot accept
any responsibility for any loss, injury or
inconvenience resulting from the use of information
contained therein.*

Production: Pagebypage Co Ltd
Maps: Maidenhead Cartographic Services
Printing: Advent Print Group, Andover
UK distribution: Travel Alliance, Bath
diane@popoutmaps.com

Cover photo credits.
Front 1. The Scarlet, Cornwall, entry 22 2. The Swan Hotel & Spa, Cumbria, entry 46
3. The Manor Town House, Pembrokeshire, entry 308
Back: 1. Artist Residence London, London, entry 155 2. The Kings, Dorset, entry 99
3. La Fosse at Cranborne, Dorset, entry 93

4 Contents

Alastair Sawday's

Special Places to Stay

British
Hotels & Inns

the place lies in its stillness, with very human devotion and a gorgeous garden and chapel – an oasis in an urban wilderness.

These vital small hotels need more independent visitors, willing to book directly rather than through Booking.com or the other predators. The best and brightest are flourishing, but some of the very best are struggling too, partly because they ARE so decent, honest and generous. There is immense pressure from the giant booking sites to slash prices, but hotels can't survive by discounting up to 70% and many have lost the fight. The cold fact is that if you want your favourite hotel to survive, you need to pay the right price, so please use these pages to support the commitment and devotion of our wonderful owners.

Don't you love it when someone re-defines an old idea? The owners of Brooks Guesthouse Bristol must, over a long drink, have asked themselves what a hotel IS. The answer came loud, clear and astounding: Four Rockets (like Airstreams, those silver American 'motor-homes') on the roof. Clients book into them as easily as they book into the bedrooms below. They are going like a rocket.

St Katharine's Royal Foundation offers another definition of 'hotel': slap in the middle of the Limehouse district of London's East End, it is a religious retreat, or 'Royal Peculiar', as the vicar answers directly to the Monarch. (He describes himself, now that it is open to a wider public, as a Holy Hotelier.) The genius of

A personal weakness is to slip in to a hotel for a drink, or a winter cream tea, just to wallow in the sheer bravura of the owner's ideas. On the occasions when I stay, the rewards are great. To idle by a vast fire with the papers, at Combe House in Devon, is irresistible. To settle in for a drink at the bar of The Pier, in Harwich, is to meet the glitterati and the locals in happy mingle. To potter upstairs to bed, after a magnificent dinner, is the stuff of fantasy – and split infinitives.

Give yourself a treat, book direct, and enjoy a few nights in some of these inspiring special places.

Alastair Sawday

Photo above: Tom Germain
Photo right: Hammet House, Pembrokeshire, entry 311

It's simple. There are no rules, no boxes to tick. We choose places that we like and are fiercely subjective in our choices. We also recognise that one person's idea of special is not necessarily someone else's so there is a huge variety of places, and prices, in this book.

Those who are familiar with our Special Places series know that we look for comfort, originality, authenticity, and reject the anonymous and the banal. The way guests are treated comes as high on our list as the setting, the architecture, the atmosphere and the food.

Inspections

We visit every place in the guide to get a feel for how both hotel and owner tick. We don't take a clipboard and we don't have a list of what is acceptable and what is not. Instead, we chat for an hour or so with the owner or manager and look

Photo: The Hoste, Norfolk, entry 164

round. It's all very informal, but it gives us an excellent idea of who would enjoy staying there. If the visit happens to be the last of the day, we may stay the night. Once in the book, properties are re-inspected regularly, so that we can keep things fresh and accurate.

Feedback

In between inspections we rely on feedback from our army of readers, as well as from staff members who are encouraged to visit properties across the series. This feedback is invaluable to us and we always follow up on comments.

So do tell us whether your stay has been a joy or not, if the atmosphere was great or stuffy, the owners and staff cheery or bored. The accuracy of the book depends on what you, and our inspectors, tell us. A lot of the new entries in each edition are recommended by our readers, so keep telling us about new places you've discovered too. Please use the forms on our website at www.sawdays.co.uk.

However, please do not tell us if your starter was cold, or the bedside light broken. Tell the owner, immediately, and get them to do something about it. Most owners, or staff, are more than happy to correct problems and will bend over backwards to help. Far better than bottling it up and then writing to us a week later!

Subscriptions

Owners pay to appear in this guide. Their fee goes towards the high costs of inspecting, of producing an illustrated book and of developing our website. We only include places that we find special: it is not possible for anyone to buy their way onto these pages. Nor is it possible for the owner to write their own description. We will say if the bedrooms are small, or if a main road is near. We do our best to avoid misleading people.

Disclaimer

We make no claims to pure objectivity in choosing these places. They are here simply because we like them. Our opinions and tastes are ours alone and this book is a statement of them; we hope you will share them. We have done our utmost to get our facts right but apologise unreservedly for any mistakes that may have crept in.

You should know that we don't check such things as fire alarms, swimming pool security or any other regulation with which owners of properties receiving paying guests should comply. This is the responsibility of the owners. At some of our smaller places – particularly our inns – you should request a contact number for emergencies if staff are not present overnight.

Do remember that the information in this book is a snapshot in time and may have changed since we published it; do call ahead to avoid being disappointed.

Photo: Gilpin Lake House & Spa, Cumbria, entry 49

Finding the right place for you

All these places are special in one way or another. All have been visited and then written about honestly so that you can take what you want and leave the rest. Those of you who swear by Sawday's trust our write-ups precisely because we don't have a blanket standard; we include places simply because we like them. But we all have different priorities, so do read the descriptions carefully and pick out the places where you will be comfortable.

Maps

Each property is flagged with its entry number on the maps at the front. These maps are a great starting point for planning your trip, but please don't use them as anything other than a general guide – use a decent road map for real navigation. Most places will send you detailed instructions once you have booked your stay.

Symbols

These are explained at the very back of the book. They are based on the information given to us by the owners. However, things do change: bikes may be under repair or a new pool may have been put in. Please use the symbols as a guide rather than an absolute statement of fact and double-check anything that is important to you – owners occasionally bend their own rules, so it's worth asking if you may take your child or dog even if they don't have the symbol.

Wheelchair access ♿ – Some hotels are keen to accept wheelchair users into their

hotels and have made provision for them. However, this does not mean that wheelchair users will always be met with a perfect landscape. You may encounter ramps, a shallow step, gravelled paths, alternative routes into some rooms, a bathroom (not a wet room), perhaps even a lift. In short, there may be the odd hindrance and we urge you to call and make sure you will get what you need.

Limited mobility – The limited mobility symbol 🚶 shows those places where at least one bedroom and bathroom is accessible without using stairs. The symbol is designed to satisfy those who walk slowly, with difficulty, or with the aid of a stick. A wheelchair may be able to navigate some areas, but in our opinion these places are not fully wheelchair friendly. If you use a chair for longer distances, but are not too bad over shorter distances, you'll probably be OK; again, please ring and ask. There may be a step or two, a bath or a shower with a tray in a cubicle, a good

distance between the car park and your room, slippery flagstones or a tight turn.

Children – The 🧒 symbol shows places which are happy to accept children of all ages. This does not mean that they will necessarily have cots, high chairs, etc. If an owner welcomes children but only those above a certain age, we have put these details at the end of their write-up. These houses do not have the child symbol, but even these folk may accept your younger child at quiet times. If you want to get out and about in the evenings, check when you book whether there are any babysitting services. Even very small places can sometimes organise this for you.

Pets – Our 🐕 symbol shows places which are happy to accept pets. It means they can sleep in the bedroom with you, but not on the bed. It's really important to get this one right before you arrive, as many places make you keep dogs in the car. Check carefully: Prince's emotional wellbeing may depend on it.

Owners' pets – The 🐈 symbol is given when the owners have their own pet on the premises. It may not be a cat! But it is there to warn you that you may be greeted by a dog, serenaded by a parrot, or indeed sat upon by a cat.

Hotel Awards

This year, we have picked those places that deserve a special mention. Our categories are:

Hotels of the Year
(England, Scotland, Wales);
Favourite newcomers;
Old favourites;
Nicely priced;
Fabulous food.

More details are given on pages 16-21 and all the award winners have been stamped.

Photo: Drakes, Brighton & Hove, entry 10

Types of places

Hotels can vary from huge, humming and slick to those with only a few rooms that are run by owners at their own pace. In some you may not get room service or have your bags carried in and out. In smaller hotels there may be a fixed menu for dinner with very little choice, so if you have dishes that leave you cold, it's important to say so when you book your meal. If you decide to stay at an inn remember that they can be noisy, especially at weekends. If these things are important to you, then do check when you book.

Sawday's Canopy & Stars CANOPY&STARS

Take a peek at two of our Canopy & Stars entries – they are highlighted with a green logo. Then visit www.canopyandstars.co.uk to see more of our outdoor places. They could be anything from palatial treehouses to rustic wagons and everything in-between. The same standards of inspection and selection apply, but you might find things delightfully different to what you're used to. You could be clambering up a ladder to bed, throwing another log on the wood-burner or wheeling your luggage in a barrow, so have a look and keep your mind open to the outdoors.

Rooms

Bedrooms – These are described as double, twin, single, family or suite. A double may contain a bed which is anything from 135cm wide to 180cm wide. A twin will contain two single beds (usually 90cm wide). A suite will have a separate sitting area, but it may not be in a

different room. Family rooms can vary in size, as can the number of beds they hold, so do ask. And do not assume that every bedroom has a TV.

Bathrooms – All bedrooms have their own bathrooms unless we say that they don't. If you have your own bathroom but you have to leave the room to get to it we describe it as 'separate'. There are very few places in the book that have shared bathrooms and they are usually reserved for members of the same party. Again, we state this clearly.

Meals

Breakfast is included in the room price unless otherwise stated. If only a continental breakfast is offered, we let you know.

Some places serve lunch, most do Sunday lunch (often very well-priced), the vast majority offer dinner. In some places you can content yourself with bar meals, in others you can feast on five courses. Most offer three courses for £25-£35, either table d'hôte or à la carte. Some have

Photo: Plas Dinas, Gwynedd, entry 300

tasting menus, very occasionally you eat communally. Some large hotels (and some posh private houses) will bring dinner to your room if you prefer, or let you eat in the garden by candlelight. Always ask for what you want and sometimes, magically, it happens.

Prices and minimum stays

We quote the lowest price per night for two people in low season to the highest price in high season. Only a few places have designated single rooms; if no single rooms are listed, the price we quote refers to single occupancy of a double room. In many places prices rise even higher when local events bring people flooding to the area, a point worth remembering when heading to Cheltenham for the racing or Glyndebourne for the opera.

The half-board price quoted is per person per night and includes dinner, usually three courses. Mostly you're offered a table d'hôte menu. Occasionally you eat à la carte and may find some dishes carry a small supplement. There are often great deals to be had, mostly mid-week in low season.

Most hotels do not accept one-night bookings at weekends. Small country hotels are rarely full during the week and the weekend trade keeps them going. If you ring in March for a Saturday night in July, you won't get it. If you ring at the last moment you may. Some places insist on three-night stays on bank holidays.

Booking and cancellation

Most places ask for a deposit at the time of booking, either by cheque or card. If you cancel – depending on how much notice you give – you can lose all or part of this deposit unless your room is re-let.

It is reasonable for hotels to take a deposit to secure a booking; they have learnt that if they don't, the commitment of the guest wanes and they may fail to turn up.

Some cancellation policies are more stringent than others. It is also worth noting that some owners will take the money directly from your credit/debit card without contacting you to discuss it. So ask them to explain their cancellation policy clearly before booking so you understand exactly where you stand; it may well avoid a nasty surprise. And consider taking out travel insurance (with a cancellation clause) if you're concerned.

Arrivals and departures

Housekeeping is usually done by 2pm, and your room will usually be available by mid-afternoon. Normally you will have to wave goodbye to it between 10am and 11am. Sometimes one can pay to linger. Some inns are closed between 3pm and 6pm, so do try and agree an arrival time in advance or you may find nobody there.

Closed

When given in months this means for the whole of the month stated. So, 'Closed: November–March' means closed from 1 November to 31 March.

Sawday's British Hotel Awards 2014/15

After 15 years we thought it was time to throw a gong or two at some of our hotels, so here are 15 very special places that typify the Sawday ethos.

Award categories

Hotels of the Year

Favourite newcomers

Old favourites

Nicely priced

Fabulous food

Killiecrankie House Hotel   Entry 274
SCOTLAND
Killiecrankie, Perth & Kinross

Langar Hall   Entry 173
ENGLAND
Langar, Nottinghamshire

Hotels of the Year

We love small, intimate hotels and inns where the art of hospitality is practiced with flair – these three wonders of our world have mastered that art in spades.

The Felin Fach Griffin   Entry 313
WALES
Felin Fach, Powys

Ffin Y Parc Entry 294
Llanrwst, Conwy

Favourite newcomers

New hotels are hard to find in tough economic times, but that hasn't stopped creative owners bursting onto the scene with beautiful new places that delight us.

Mhor 84 Entry 281
Balquhidder, Perth & Kinross

The Packhorse Inn Entry 199
Moulton, Suffolk

The Inn at Whitewell   Entry 145
Whitewell, Lancashire

Old favourites

Jeake's House   Entry 222
Rye, Sussex

Like a good red wine, some hotels get better with age – these places have a clear instinct for great hospitality and have been delighting guests for years.

Combe House Devon   Entry 86
Gittisham, Devon

The King's Head Inn   Entry 178
Bledington, Oxfordshire

Nicely priced

There's nothing like washing up at a lovely small hotel and finding it has a lovely small price, too – here are three that do that with ease.

Cnapan Restaurant & Hotel Entry 309
Newport, Pembrokeshire

The Pheasant Inn   Entry 170
Stannersburn, Northumberland

The Great House   Entry 201
Lavenham, Suffolk

Linthwaite House Hotel   Entry 50
Bowness-on-Windermere, Cumbria

Fabulous food

From hot kitchens come small miracles to delight our tastebuds – here are three places where your pleasure receptors will delight in ambrosial food.

Little Barwick House   Entry 193
Barwick, Somerset

Photo: Belle Tout Lighthouse, Sussex, entry 220

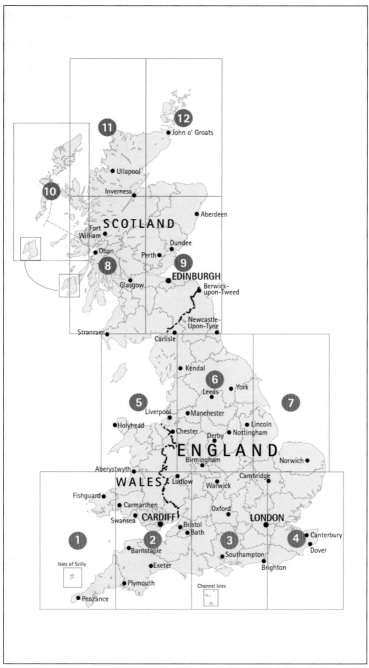

© Maidenhead Cartographic, 2014

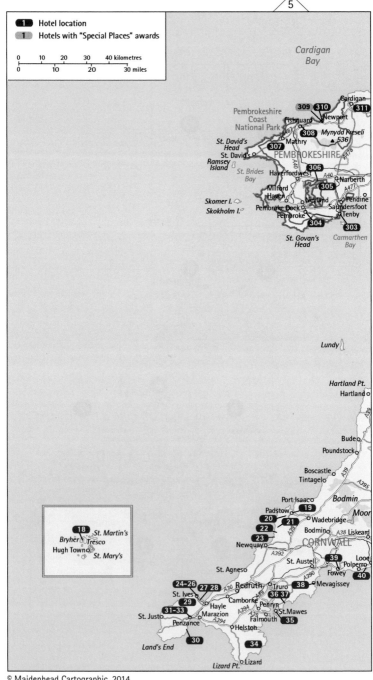

© Maidenhead Cartographic, 2014

Map 2   25

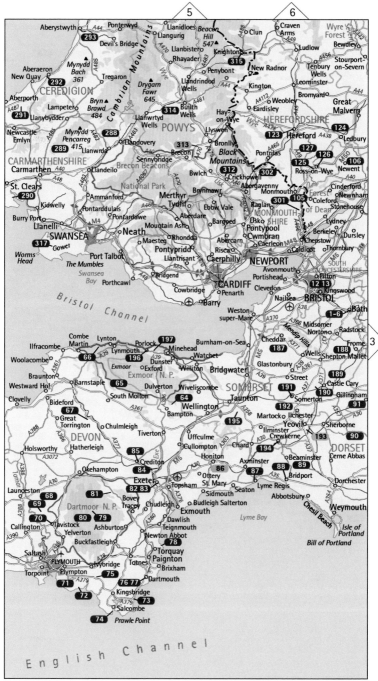

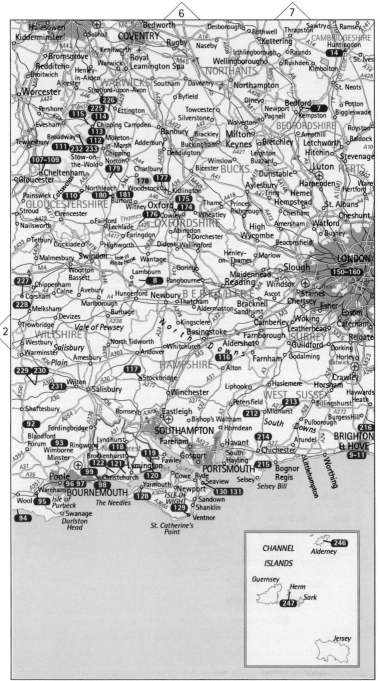

Map 4   27

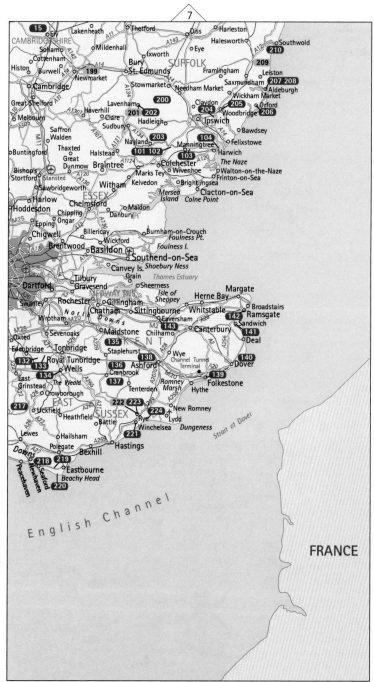

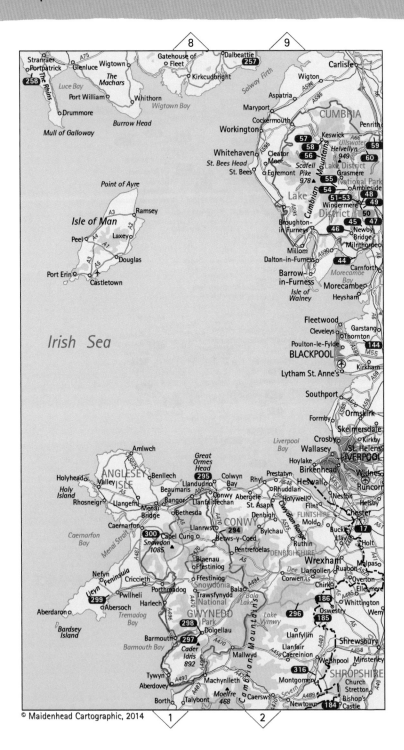

© Maidenhead Cartographic, 2014

Map 6   29

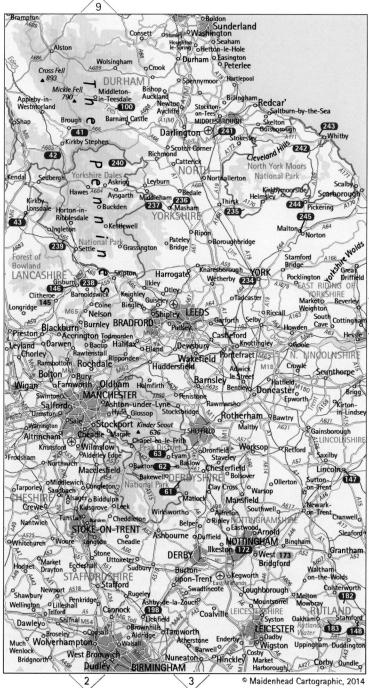

© Maidenhead Cartographic, 2014

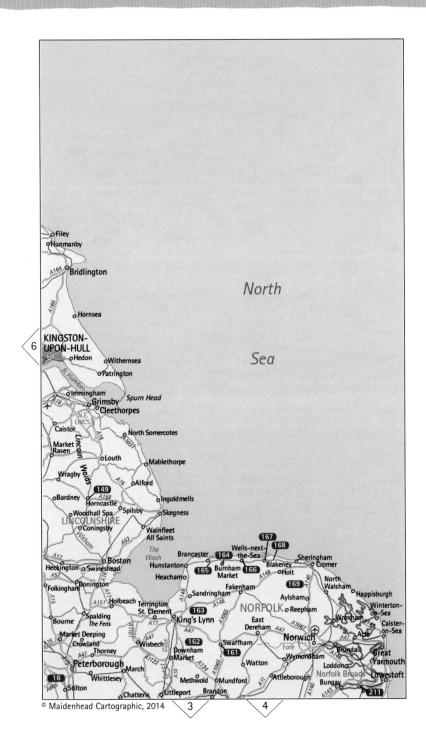

Map 8   31

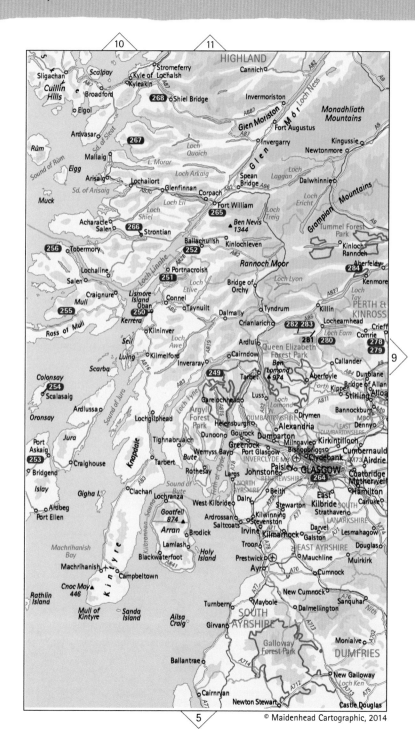

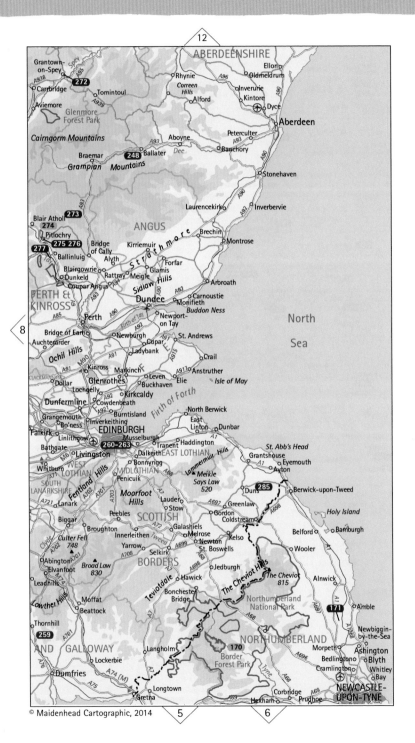

Map 10

33

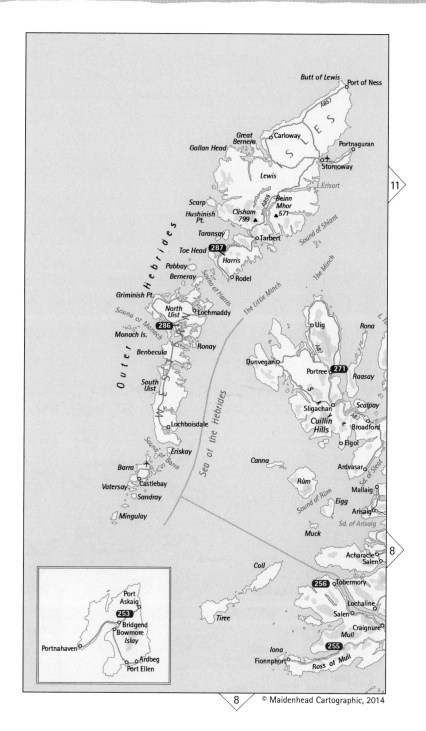

© Maidenhead Cartographic, 2014

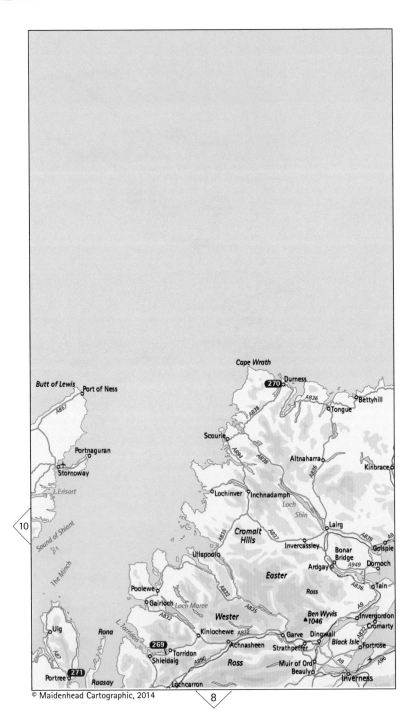

Map 12

35

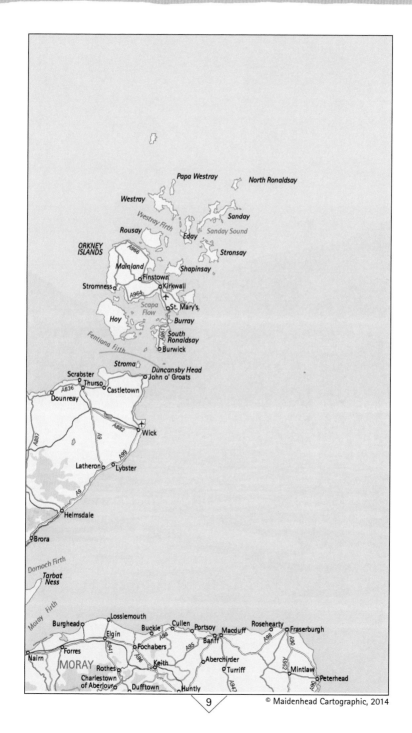

Papa Westray

North Ronaldsay

Westray

Westray Firth

Sanday

Rousay

Sanday Sound

Eday

ORKNEY
ISLANDS

A966

Stronsay

Mainland

Shapinsay

Finstown

Stromness

Kirkwall

A964

Scapa
Flow

St. Mary's

Hoy

Burray

South
Ronaldsay

Fentland Firth

Burwick

Stroma

Duncansby Head
John o' Groats

Scrabster

Thurso

Castletown

A836

Dounreay

A897

A9

A882

Wick

A9

A99

Latheron

Lybster

A9

Helmsdale

Brora

Dornoch Firth

Tarbat
Ness

Moray Firth

Lossiemouth

Burghead

Buckie

Cullen

Portsoy

Macduff

Rosehearty

Fraserburgh

Elgin

A98

Banff

A96

Fochabers

A95

A90

A941

Forres

Nairn

MORAY

Rothes

Keith

Aberchirder

Turriff

Mintlaw

Peterhead

A952

Charlestown
of Aberlour

Dufftown

Huntly

A941

A90

© Maidenhead Cartographic, 2014

England

Abbey Hotel

It's hard to think of a better position in Bath – you're behind the abbey, away from the traffic, in one of the prettiest quarters in town, with Parade Gardens across the road, the river approaching Pulteney Bridge and the rugby club on the far bank. As for the hotel, it's just as good. Ian and Christa are past masters at breathing new life into old hotels and The Abbey, their latest project, is no exception. In summer you take to the terrace café for a recuperative gin and tonic; in winter it turns into an après-ski bar for mince pies and mulled wine. Inside, the cocktail bar doubles as a sitting room and comes with fabulous art, not a bad spot for afternoon tea. Then there's Allium Brasserie, where Chris Staines, ex-Mandarin Oriental, conjures up seriously good food (Jay Rayner loved his), perhaps quail glazed in chilli caramel, fillet of stone bass with crispy squid, apple mille feuille with cider jelly. Airy bedrooms have vast bedheads, colourful throws, iPads for room service, a sofa if there's room. Bath waits on your doorstep: festivals, theatres, the Christmas market, the Thermae Spa. *Minimum stay: 2 nights at weekends.*

Rooms	55 doubles: £99–£257. 5 family rooms for 4: £150–£300.
Meals	Lunch from £15.95. Dinner, 2-3 courses, £17.50–£23.50. À la carte dinner, 3 courses, about £40.
Closed	Never.
Directions	In central Bath, 100m south of the abbey, 100m west of the river Avon. Parking in Southgate car park £13 a day.

Ian & Christa Taylor
Abbey Hotel
North Parade,
Bath BA1 1LF

Tel	+44 (0)1225 805615
Email	reception@abbeyhotelbath.co.uk
Web	www.abbeyhotelbath.co.uk

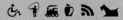

SACO Bath – St James's Place

Bath is one of England's loveliest cities, Georgian to its bone. It's built of mellow golden stone, so wander its streets for elegant squares, beautiful gardens, pavement cafés, delicious delis and the imperious Roman Baths (there's a spa if you want to take a dip). Close to the river, bang in the middle of town, these serviced apartments bask behind a Regency façade. Inside you find a collection of airy studios and apartments, all of which come with sparkling kitchens fully stocked with ovens, dishwashers, washer/dryers, microwaves, fridges and freezers. Some are small, some are big, but if you need a bolthole for a night, a base for a fun-filled weekend or a cool pad for a week, you'll find one here. You get white walls, Italian designer furniture, flat-screen TVs, CD players and good-sized bathrooms. Rooms at the back are quieter at night, there's a lift to whisk you about, 24-hour reception, and high-speed broadband throughout. Supermarkets are close, but there are masses of great restaurants on your doorstep. Don't miss the Christmas market in the first two weeks of December.

Rooms	5 apartments for 4, 29 apartments for 2: £125–£192. 9 studios for 2: £106–£120.
Meals	Self-catered. Restaurants within 0.5 miles.
Closed	Never.
Directions	In centre of town, 5-minute walk from station. Full directions on booking.

Karen Sheppard
SACO Bath – St James's Place,
37 St James's Place, Bath BA1 1UH

Tel	+44 (0)1225 486540
Email	bath@sacoapartments.com
Web	www.sacoapartments.com

Brooks Guesthouse Bath

Carla and Andrew and their lovely staff go out of their way to make your stay here special. Add to this comfy rooms, lovely prices, excellent breakfasts and a central position and you have a great base from which to explore the city. The house is close to Victoria Park (hot-air balloon rides, children's playground, botanical gardens) and just below the stupendous Royal Crescent. Inside, an easy style flows. You'll find lovely art, a fire in the sitting room, an honesty bar if you fancy a drink, then a breakfast room for eggs Benedict, homemade pancakes or the full cooked works; there are daily specials, free-range eggs, the meat is reared in Somerset. Bedrooms are split between two Victorian townhouses. A couple are small, a couple are huge, most are somewhere in between. All have the same lovely style: warm colours, papered walls, good beds, excellent shower rooms (two have baths). A map of the town, compiled by guests, shows the top ten sights: don't miss the Roman Baths or the Thermae Spa. One of the best pubs in Bath is around the corner and serves great food. Expect a little noise from the road.

Rooms	7 doubles, 10 twin/doubles: £75-£150. 2 family rooms for 4: £120-£160. 2 singles: £70-£90.
Meals	Restaurants close by.
Closed	Christmas Day.
Directions	Head west on A4 from centre of town. On right before Victoria Park, below Royal Avenue.

Carla & Andrew Brooks
Brooks Guesthouse Bath
1 Crescent Gardens,
Bath BA1 2NA

Tel	+44 (0)1225 425543
Email	info@brooksguesthouse.com
Web	www.brooksguesthouse.com

Grays Boutique Bed & Breakfast Hotel

Welcome to Grays, a Victorian villa on Bath's southern slopes, with 12 luscious bedrooms and the city a skip down the hill. The moment you enter the hall – high ceilings, gilded mirrors, sweet sofa – you feel you've arrived somewhere special. It's family run and the service is second to none: a mix of impeccable and warm-hearted. Smart coir carpeting brings you up to serene bedrooms with harmonious colours, beds (some French-retro, one modern four-poster) with sumptuous mattresses and heaps of pillows, fresh flowers, lavender bags, sweets, treats and chandeliers, limestone touches in the bathrooms and drenching showers. Rooms with the best views are at the front, the most peaceful at the back, and the most fun up in the attic – slopey-ceilinged but spacious. Saunter into town to take a guided dusk stroll around 'Bizarre Bath', swim, steam and soak at Britain's only natural spa. Then wake to breakfasts at gingham tables in the peaceful conservatory at the back, where eggs from Benedict to Florentine are announced on the board and the vegetarian option sounds delicious. *Minimum stay: 2 nights at weekends. Children over 12 welcome.*

Rooms	10 doubles, 2 twin/doubles: £100–£195.
Meals	Pubs/restaurants 15-minute walk.
Closed	Rarely.
Directions	A36 into Bath, then A367 south for Wells. Up hill and first right at sharp left hand bend. On left after 200m.

Jamie Grundy
Grays Boutique Bed & Breakfast Hotel
9 Upper Oldfield Park,
Bath BA2 3JX

Tel	+44 (0)1225 403020
Email	hello@graysbath.co.uk
Web	www.graysbath.com

Bath Paradise House Hotel

The view here is hard to beat, a wide sweep across the city that's best observed on a sunny afternoon while tucking into afternoon tea in the garden. Not that you will spend your time looking out of the windows, even if most of the rooms do have the view: what you find inside is just as special. This is a hugely welcoming house with owners and staff who go out of their way to help you make the most of Bath. Downstairs, a smart sitting room has three arched windows framing the city and an airy breakfast room with Lloyd Loom furniture. Bedrooms are lovely, even the smallest, coveted by returning guests for its doors onto the terrace. Others are more substantial, especially those with bay windows that look the right way. You'll find four-posters, beautiful fabrics, warm colours, no clutter at all. Some have vast bedheads, others travertine bathrooms; bigger rooms have sitting areas, perhaps a claw-foot bath. Menu Gordon Jones, a very short stroll, is a top spot for dinner, while the occasional peal of bells comes from a nearby church. The Thermae Spa with its rooftop pool is a must. *Minimum stay: 2 nights at weekends.*

Rooms	3 doubles, 3 twins, 4 four-posters: £120–£175. 1 family room for 3: £130–£185. Singles £75–£120.
Meals	Restaurants in Bath 0.5 miles.
Closed	24 & 25 December.
Directions	From train station one-way system to Churchill Bridge. A367 exit from r'bout up hill; 0.75 miles, left at Andrews estate agents. Left down hill into cul-de-sac; on left.

David & Annie Lanz
Bath Paradise House Hotel
86-88 Holloway,
Bath BA2 4PX

Tel   +44 (0)1225 317723
Email   info@paradise-house.co.uk
Web   www.paradise-house.co.uk

Villa Magdala

Villa Magdala is one of those lovely places that scores top marks across the board. You're pretty much in the middle of town, but nicely hidden away on a side street opposite a park. Then, there's a batch of lovely bedrooms, all recently refurbished in great style. Add to this staff on hand to book restaurants, balloon flights or day trips to Stonehenge and you have a perfect base. You're a five-minute stroll from magnificent Pulteney Bridge; the station isn't much further, so leave your car at home and come by train; you can hire bikes in town, then follow a towpath along the river and into the country. Back home, there's tea and cake on arrival, buck's fizz for breakfast, even bats and balls for children who want to go to the park. Breakfast is served in an airy dining room: smoked salmon and free-range scrambled eggs, buttermilk pancakes, the full cooked works. Smart rooms have big beds, pretty wallpaper, small armchairs and lovely sparkling bathrooms. Excellent restaurants wait close by. Don't miss the Christmas market or the magnificent Thermae Spa. *Minimum stay: 2 nights at weekends.*

Rooms	9 doubles, 11 twin/doubles: £99–£195. Singles from £89. Extra bed/sofabed available £45 p.p. per night.
Meals	Restaurant within 500 yds.
Closed	Christmas.
Directions	West into Bath on A4. Left into Cleveland Place (signed Through Traffic & University). Over bridge, 2nd right and on right opposite park.

Amanda & John Willmott
Villa Magdala
Henrietta Street,
Bath BA2 6LX

Tel	+44 (0)1225 466329
Email	enquiries@villamagdala.co.uk
Web	www.villamagdala.co.uk

d'Parys

This is one of those lovely places that give little idea of the marvels that wait within. You cruise up a leafy avenue of grand Victorian houses and wonder if you're in the right place. Moments later you step inside and your jaw drops in sheer delight. You don't often walk into a bar and spot an old-world sweet shop next to a vintage ice cream parlour, but that's what happens here. So welcome to the pleasure dome – a fine old house beautifully renovated in spectacular style. Fires roar, tram-seat benches wait at long tables, ceilings are clad in coloured shutters, even the air vents are works of art. But while nothing here is ordinary, it all fits together seamlessly, an open-plan world you drift through with ease. There's a mirrored bar for local ales, a library with leather booths, hanging lamps in the restaurant with the kitchen on display, then walls of glass that open onto a sail-shaded terrace. Sweep up the grand staircase and find chic bedrooms with boarded floors, cool colours, coffee makers and fabulous bathrooms. Tasty food waits below, helpful staff go the extra mile. *Extra beds for children (no charge).*

Rooms	11 doubles, 1 twin, 2 four-posters: £95.
Meals	Lunch from £5.95. Dinner, 3 courses, £25–£30. Sunday lunch from £12.95.
Closed	Never.
Directions	A1, then A421 and A4280 into Bedford. Right at lights after A6 x-roads; right again, then 3rd left (straight ahead). Immediately left and on right after 400m.

	Kasper Bedford
	d'Parys
	De Parys Avenue,
	Bedford MK40 2UA
Tel	+44 (0)1234 340248
Email	info@dparys.co.uk
Web	www.dparys.co.uk

The Queen's Arms

You're in the Lambourne valley, prime English horse racing country, with 80 stables in a five-mile radius – get up early, head to the gallops, watch the horses fly by. As for this lovely inn, it sits on the edge of the village, bordered by a couple of paddocks. Outside, there's a vine-shaded terrace for barbecues in summer (and a telly on race days), then a small lawned garden for lazy afternoons in the sun. Inside, rustic chic has conquered all quarters – pale olive panelling, armchairs in front of the fire, stripped floorboards and mismatching tables, old photographs on the walls. You'll find carafes of wine, bourbon cocktails, local ales, chilled champagne. As for the food, it's the sort of stuff lots of us want, perhaps chilli crab linguine, lemon sole with brown shrimps, steaks and ribs from the grill, build-your-own burgers; there's a good menu for children, too, and Sunday lunch is a treat. Bedrooms hit the spot – comfy wooden beds, bold colours and coir matting, white robes and REN oils for big walk-in showers; one has a sofa, another a claw-foot bath. There's local fishing too.

Rooms	8 doubles: £100–£130. Singles from £90 (not Friday/Saturday).
Meals	Lunch from £5.50. Dinner, 3 courses, £25–£35.
Closed	Never.
Directions	M4 junc. 14, then A338 north. Left at Great Shefford for East Garston. On right after 3 miles.

Zdenka Antoniazova
The Queen's Arms,
Newbury Road, East Garston,
Newbury RG17 7ET

Tel	+44 (0)1488 648757
Email	info@queensarmseastgarston.co.uk
Web	www.queensarmseastgarston.co.uk

Artist Residence Brighton

At the top of a square, looking down to the sea, a cute hotel with an arty vibe. You're bang in the middle of Brighton with all the stuff you'd want on your doorstep: galleries and good restaurants, the pier and the Brighton Pavilion. As for the hotel, a recent facelift has brought a fresh, cool feel. You get stripped boards, exposed brick walls, then an old garage door on rails which you roll back to reveal a rather chic dinning room. Cool art hangs on the walls, there are cushions made from coffee sacks, then fresh flowers on a table that doubles as reception. You can eat at the front under high ceilings with big windows looking down to the sea, or hide away at the back with planks of wood nailed to the walls and ferns erupting from gutter spouts. Some bedrooms have Pop Art murals, others come in Regency colours with polished wood beds. Most have compact shower rooms, one has a decked terrace. There's a cute bar for cocktails, then local restaurants for a good meal – try 64 Degrees for excellent Asian tapas or Riddle & Finns for great seafood. *Minimum stay: 2 nights at weekends in high season.*

Rooms	12 doubles, 5 twins: £60–£155.
	1 suite for 6: £125–£240.
	5 family rooms for 3: £100–£160.
Meals	Restaurants within 500 yds.
Closed	Rarely.
Directions	A23 south into Brighton. Right at pier along seafront. Right after 1 mile into Regency Square. Hotel in northeast corner. Car park below square.

Charlie Newey & Justin Salisbury
Artist Residence Brighton
33 Regency Square,
Brighton BN1 2GG

Tel	+44 (0)1273 324302
Email	brighton@artistresidence.co.uk
Web	www.arthotelbrighton.co.uk

Drakes

Drakes has the lot: cool rooms, a funky bar, big sea views, the best restaurant in town. It stands across the road from the beach, with the famous pier a three-minute walk and the big wheel even closer. Inside, a chic style has conquered every corner. Bedrooms are exemplary. Eleven have free-standing baths in the room, all have waffle bathrobes and White Company lotions, but what impresses most is the detail and workmanship. Handmade beds rest on carpets that are changed every year, contemporary plaster mouldings curl around ceilings like mountain terraces, Vi-Spring mattresses, wrapped in the crispest linen, are piled high with pillows. Don't worry if you can't afford the best rooms; others may be smaller and those at the back have city views, but all are fantastic and the attic rooms are as cute as could be (Kylie loved hers). As for the food, it's the best in town, perhaps cauliflower soup with a smoked quail egg, honey-glazed duck with cassis sauce, pears poached in sweet wine with a chocolate and hazelnut mousse. The Lanes are close and packed with hip shops. Don't miss the Royal Pavilion. *Minimum stay: 2 nights at weekends.*

Rooms	16 doubles, 1 twin/double: £135-£275. 1 suite for 2: £295-£345. 2 singles: £115-£145.
Meals	Breakfast £5-£12.50. Lunch from £20. Dinner from £39.95.
Closed	Never.
Directions	M23 & A23 into Brighton. At seafront, with pier in front, turn left up the hill. Drakes on left after 300 yds.

Richard Hayes
Drakes
43-44 Marine Parade,
Brighton BN2 1PE
Tel   +44 (0)1273 696934
Email   info@drakesofbrighton.com
Web   www.drakesofbrighton.com

brightonwave

A small, friendly, boutique B&B hotel in the epicentre of trendy Brighton. The beach and the pier are a two-minute walk, the bars and restaurants of St James Street are around the corner. An open-plan sitting room/dining room comes in cool colours with big suede sofas, fairy lights in the fireplace and ever-changing art on the walls. Bedrooms at the front are big and fancy, with huge padded headboards that fill the wall and deluge showers in sandstone bathrooms. Those at the back have been recently renovated in great style; they may be smaller, but so is their price and they come with spotless compact showers; if you're out more than in, why worry? All rooms have fat duvets, lush linen, flat-screen TVs and DVD/CD players; the lower-ground king-size has its own whirlpool bath and garden. Richard and Simon are easy-going and happy for guests to chill drinks in the kitchen (there are corkscrews in all the rooms). Breakfast, served late at weekends, offers pancakes, the full English or sautéed tarragon mushrooms on toast. Fabulous Brighton waits. *Minimum stay: 2 nights at weekends.*

Rooms	3 doubles, 1 four-poster, 4 twin/doubles: £95-£185. Singles from £65.
Meals	Restaurants nearby.
Closed	Rarely.
Directions	A23 to Brighton Pier roundabout at seafront; left towards Marina; 5th street on left. On-street parking vouchers £9 for 24 hours.

Richard Adams & Simon Throp
brightonwave
10 Madeira Place,
Brighton BN2 1TN

Tel	+44 (0)1273 676794
Email	info@brightonwave.co.uk
Web	www.brightonwave.co.uk

Brooks Guesthouse Bristol

When you have a flat roof at the top of your hotel, what do you do with it? For Carla and Andrew the answer was simple: make it home to four rooftop Rockets – rather cool vintage caravans, similar to American Airstreams. They're very cute, have comfy beds, compact showers and rooftop views. All of which makes this a funky launch pad for England's loveliest city. You're close to the harbour, St Nicholas market stands directly outside, there's a sun-trapping courtyard for inner-city peace. Inside, airy interiors, leather sofas and walls of glass that open onto the courtyard. Free WiFi runs throughout, a computer is on hand for guests to use, and you can help yourself to drinks at the honesty bar. Breakfast is served leisurely – you can eat outside in good weather. Stylish bedrooms aren't huge, but nor is their price; you get comfy beds, Cole & Son wallpaper, travertine shower rooms with White Company oils. Rooms at the back get noise from nearby bars at weekends, so ask for a room at the front if that matters. Bristol waits: the water, the Downs, Brunel's spectacular suspension bridge. *Minimum stay: 2 nights at weekends.*

Rooms	17 doubles, 4 twins: £79–£99. 2 triples: £99–£129. 4 airstreams for 2: £90–£160. Singles from £69.
Meals	Restaurants on your doorstep.
Closed	24-27 December.
Directions	Hotel entrance on St Nicholas Court, an alleyway marking the western flank of the covered market; it runs between St Nicholas St & Corn St.

Carla & Andrew Brooks
Brooks Guesthouse Bristol,
St Nicholas Court,
Exchange Avenue, Bristol BS1 1UB

Tel	+44 (0)117 930 0066
Email	info@brooksguesthousebristol.com
Web	www.brooksguesthousebristol.com

SACO Bristol – Broad Quay

SACO and their wonderful serviced apartments are going from strength to strength and here's the evidence: a fantastic new property down by the water in the middle of Bristol. So what do you get? Think cool hotel suites with sparkly kitchens thrown in for good measure. Walls of glass bring in the view, those at the front overlook the water, several have balconies that make the most of good weather. Prices are attractive too – good for business in the week (WiFi and parking) and great for weekends away (you breakfast whenever you want). You're in one of Britain's loveliest cities: stroll around the floating harbour, spin up the hill to Clifton, check out St Nicholas market, or head off to the posh shops at Cabot Circus. Come back to stylish interiors: smartly tiled bathrooms, fully loaded kitchens, chic sofas in front of flat-screen TVs, comfy beds for a good night's sleep; studios are smaller, but nice and snug, perfect for weekends. There are local shops if you want to cook and restaurants everywhere if you don't. Don't miss Brunel's magnificent suspension bridge. The train from London is fast.

Rooms	45 apartments for 2, 11 apartments for 4, 2 apartments for 6: £101–£231. 12 studios for 2: £86–£107.
Meals	Self-catered. Restaurants on doorstep.
Closed	Never.
Directions	Sent on booking.

Emma Granado
SACO Bristol – Broad Quay
Central Quay South,
Broad Quay, Bristol BS1 4AW

Tel	+44 (0)117 927 6722
Email	bristol@sacoapartments.com
Web	www.sacoapartments.com

The Old Bridge Hotel

This lovely hotel, the best in town, inspired the founders of Hotel du Vin. It mixes old-fashioned hospitality with contemporary flair, a template of excellence for others to follow. A battalion of devoted locals come for the food (delicious), the wines (exceptional) and the stylish interiors. Ladies lunch, businessmen chatter, kind staff weave through the throng. You can eat wherever you want: in the muralled restaurant; from a sofa in the lounge; or sitting in a winged armchair in front of the fire in the bar. You feast on anything from homemade soups to rack of lamb (starters are available all day), while breakfast is served in a panelled morning room with Buddha in the fireplace. Julia's beautiful bedrooms have warm colours, fine fabrics, crisp linen and padded bedheads. One has a mirrored four-poster, several have vast bathrooms, others overlook the river Ouse. All have posh TVs, power showers and bathrobes. John, a Master of Wine, has a wine shop in reception, where you can taste before you buy (you will). The A14 may pass at the back, but it doesn't matter a jot. Cambridge is close.

Rooms	18 doubles, 1 twin, 3 four-posters: £120-£230. 2 singles: £89. Dinner, B&B £90-£130 p.p.
Meals	Lunch & dinner £5-£35.
Closed	Never.
Directions	A1, then A14 into Huntingdon. Hotel on southwest flank of one-way system that circles town.

Nina Rhodes
The Old Bridge Hotel
1 High Street,
Huntingdon PE29 3TQ
Tel   +44 (0)1480 424300
Email   oldbridge@huntsbridge.co.uk
Web   www.huntsbridge.com

Entry 14   Map 3

The Anchor Inn

A 1650 ale house on Chatteris Fen. The New Bedford river streams past outside. It was cut from the soil by the pub's first residents, Scottish prisoners of war brought in by Cromwell to dig the dykes that drain the fens. These days, cosy comforts infuse every corner. Inside, you find low ceilings, timber-framed walls, dark panelling and terracotta-tiled floors. A wood-burner warms the bar, so stop for a pint of cask ale, then feast on fresh local produce served by charming staff, perhaps king scallops with chorizo jam, Denham venison with red cabbage, chocolate fondant with beetroot sorbet and marshmallow sauce. Four rooms above the shop fit the mood nicely – very comfy, not too posh. Expect trim carpets, wicker chairs, crisp white duvets and Indian cotton throws. One room gets a little noise from the restaurant below. The suites have sofabeds, three rooms have river views. Footpaths flank the water; stroll down and you might see mallards or Hooper swans, even a seal (the river is tidal to the Wash). Don't miss Ely (the bishop comes to eat), Cambridge, or the nesting swans at Welney.

Rooms	1 double, 1 twin/double: £80–£99. 2 suites for 2: £115–£155. Singles from £59.50. Extra bed £20.
Meals	Lunch, 2 courses, £13.95. Dinner, 3 courses, £25–£30. Sunday lunch from £12.95.
Closed	Never.
Directions	From Ely A142 west. In Sutton left on B1381 for Earith. Right in southern Sutton, signed Sutton Gault. 1 mile north on left at bridge.

Jeanene Flack & Mike Connolly
The Anchor Inn
Bury Lane, Sutton Gault,
Ely CB6 2BD

Tel	+44 (0)1353 778537
Email	anchorinn@popmail.bta.com
Web	www.anchorsuttongault.co.uk

The Crown Inn

A dreamy inn built of mellow stone that stands on the green in this gorgeous village. Paths lead out into open country, so follow the river up to Fotheringhay, where Mary Queen of Scots lost her head. Back at the pub, warm interiors mix style and tradition to great effect. You can eat wherever you want – in the flagged bar where a fire roars, in the airy snug with views of the green, or in the circular conservatory that opens onto a terrace. Chef/patron Marcus Lamb guarantees you dine deliciously, on classic beef, mushroom and ale pie, or Shetland mussels in white wine; there's a kids' menu, too. In summer life spills outside; on May Day there's a hog roast for the village fête. Six hand pumps (including their own Golden Crown) bring in the locals, as do quiz nights, live music and the odd game of rugby on the telly. Bedrooms are excellent. The two quiet courtyard rooms come with padded bedheads, pretty art, lovely fabrics; one has a magnificent bathroom. Those in the main house overlook the green, the small room has a four-poster, the big room is perfect for families. All are spoiling.

Rooms	8 doubles with extra sofabeds: £102–£172. Singles from £65. Sofabed for 2, £30 per child.
Meals	Lunch & dinner £5–£25 (not Sun night or Mon lunch). Restaurant closed first week January.
Closed	Rarely.
Directions	A1(M), junc. 17, then A605 west for 3 miles. Right on B671 for Elton. In village left, signed Nassington.

Marcus Lamb
The Crown Inn
8 Duck Street, Elton,
Peterborough PE8 6RQ

Tel	+44 (0)1832 280232
Email	inncrown@googlemail.com
Web	www.thecrowninn.org

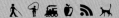

Edgar House

Edgar House, a super-cool bolthole, has a position that's hard to beat, with a garden that runs down to the city's Roman wall and the river Dee pouring past beyond. It's one of those lovely places that mixes the informality of a small B&B with the luxury of a five-star hotel. Downstairs, there's a breakfast room that doubles as a library, a sitting room with a smouldering fire, then doors onto a pretty garden – Chester's equivalent of the royal box – where you tuck into afternoon tea while watching the river pass. Back inside, an honesty bar, a mini-cinema, then a smart staircase that sweeps you up to flawless bedrooms. You get beautiful art, lots of colour, gorgeous beds wrapped in crisp white linen, and sofas and interactive TVs. Two have balconies, all but one have river views and magnificent bathrooms with walk-in showers or a double-ended bath; the suite has a copper bath in the bedroom. Drop down to the river, feed the ducks, then check out the cathedral or the mediaeval quarter for its excellent shopping. Good restaurants wait around the corner, breakfast is a treat. *Children over 14 welcome.*

Rooms	3 doubles, 1 twin/double: £149–£249. 1 suite for 2: £159–£225.
Meals	Lunch from £8. Sunday lunch from £13.95. Afternoon tea £17.75. Dinner (Thur–Sat) about £30.
Closed	Never.
Directions	North into Chester on A483. Over bridge; right with main flow at r'bout; 2nd right onto Lower Bridge Street; 1st left into Duke Road; left into car park after Recorder's Office; keep right and on left.

Tim Mills & Mike Stephen
Edgar House
22 City Walls,
Chester CH1 1SB

Tel	+44 (0)1244 347007
Email	hello@edgarhouse.co.uk
Web	www.edgarhouse.co.uk

Hell Bay

This must be one of the most inaccurately named hotels in Britain – Hell Bay is heaven! It sits on Bryher, one of the smaller islands on the Scillies. You can walk around it in a couple of hours, one sandy beach after another. As for the hotel, it's lovely from top to toe. Bedrooms have a smart beach-house feel with airy colours, wicker sofas and robes in excellent bathrooms, but best of all is your terrace or balcony for fabulous watery views. Elsewhere, there's a heated swimming pool flanked by sun loungers and a treatment room that looks the right way. It's very family friendly, too; children can gather eggs from the coop and have them cooked for breakfast, and there's a playroom with games galore. The hotel lazes on the west coast. There's nothing between you and America, so grab a drink and wander onto the terrace for sunset. Back inside, there's great local food – scallops with chilli and honey, lamb with a rosemary jus, chocolate fondant with pistachio ice-cream. Also, boat trips, babysitters, lovely staff and islands to explore. Honeymooners love it. Dogs are very welcome, too.

Rooms	25 suites for 2: £270-£640. Price includes dinner for 2. Child in parents' room £55 (including high tea). Under 2s free. Dogs £12 a night.
Meals	Lunch from £6.95. Dinner included; non-residents £39.
Closed	November to mid-March.
Directions	Ship from Penzance, or fly to St Mary's from Exeter, Newquay or Land's End; boat transfer to Bryher.

Philip Callan
Hell Bay
Bryher,
Isles of Scilly TR23 0PR

Tel   +44 (0)1720 422947
Email   contactus@hellbay.co.uk
Web   www.hellbay.co.uk

The Seafood Restaurant

In 1975 a young chef called Rick Stein opened a restaurant in Padstow. These days he has four more as well as a deli, a pâtisserie, a seafood cookery school and 40 beautiful bedrooms. Despite this success, his homespun philosophy has never wavered: buy the freshest seafood from fisherman on the quay, then cook it simply and eat it with friends. It is a viewpoint half the country seems to share – the Seafood Restaurant is now a place of pilgrimage – so come to discover the Cornish coast, walk on the cliffs, paddle in the estuary, then drop into this lively restaurant for a fabulous meal, perhaps hot shellfish with garlic and lemon juice, Dover sole with sea salt and lime, apple and quince tartlet with vanilla ice-cream. Book in for the night and a table in the restaurant is yours, though flawless bedrooms are so seductive you may find them hard to leave. They are scattered about town, some above the restaurant, others at the bistro or just around the corner. All are immaculate. Expect the best fabrics, stunning bathrooms, the odd terrace with estuary views. *Minimum stay: 2 nights at weekends.*

Rooms	32 doubles, 8 twin/doubles: £110–£330.
Meals	Lunch £38.50. Dinner £58.50.
Closed	25-26 December.
Directions	A39, then A389 to Padstow. Follow signs to centre; restaurant on left opposite harbour car park.

Jill & Rick Stein
The Seafood Restaurant
Riverside,
Padstow PL28 8BY

Tel	+44 (0)1841 532700
Email	reservations@rickstein.com
Web	www.rickstein.com

Woodlands Country House

A big house in the country, half a mile west of Padstow, with long views across the fields down to the sea. Pippa and Hugo came west to renovate and have done a fine job. You get an honesty bar in the sitting room, a croquet lawn by the fountain and stripped floors in the airy breakfast room, where a legendary feast is served each morning. Spotless bedrooms are smart and homely, some big, some smaller, all with a price to match, but it's worth splashing out on the bigger ones, which are away from the road and have watery views. Expect lots of colour, pretty beds, floral curtains, Frette linen. One room has a four-poster, another comes with a claw-foot bath, there are robes in adequate bathrooms. All have flat-screen TVs and DVD players, with a library of films downstairs. WiFi runs throughout, there's a computer guests can use, taxis can be ordered – but make sure you book restaurants in advance, especially Rick Stein's or Jamie Oliver's Fifteen. Hire bikes in town and follow the Camel trail, take the ferry over to Rock, head down to the beach, walk on the cliffs. Dogs are very welcome.

Rooms	4 doubles, 1 four-poster, 3 twin/doubles: £98–£138. Singles from £74.
Meals	Picnics £18. Restaurants in Padstow, 0.5 miles. Breakfast for non-residents £15.
Closed	20 December to 1 February.
Directions	On A389, just before Padstow, left for Newquay, then west on B3276. House signed on right in village.

Hugo & Pippa Woolley
Woodlands Country House
Treator,
Padstow PL28 8RU

Tel	+44 (0)1841 532426
Email	info@woodlands-padstow.co.uk
Web	www.woodlands-padstow.co.uk

Bedruthan Hotel & Spa

A family friendly hotel that delights adults and children alike. It has beautiful interiors, delicious food, sea views and an inexhaustible supply of distractions. There's a football pitch, a surf school, a zip wire, then a cool spa with a couple of pools. If you can think of it, it's probably here, and younger children can be supervised by lovely, qualified staff. There's lots for adults, too, who get the run of the place during school time: a sitting room that hogs the view, a wood-burner to keep things cosy, a terrace in good weather for sea views. There are three restaurants (one for children's parties). Younger children have early suppers, adults return later for a slap-up meal, perhaps hand-picked crab, chargrilled steak, hazelnut tart with pistachio ice-cream. There's a beach below, but you may spurn it for the indoor pool or a game of tennis. Lovely bedrooms have warm retro colours, blond wood, sparkling bathrooms, then separate rooms for children. Some open onto private terraces, lots have sea views, a few overlook the car park. Impeccable eco credentials and fantastic staff, too.

Rooms	38 twin/doubles: £135-£270.
	27 suites for 4: £205-£490.
	30 family rooms for 4: £175-£305.
	6 singles: £75-£125.
	Dinner, B&B from £95 p.p.
Meals	Lunch from £7. Dinner £30-£35.
	Sunday lunch from £15.
Closed	Christmas & 3 weeks in January.
Directions	On B3276 in Mawgan Porth.

Janie White
Bedruthan Hotel & Spa
Mawgan Porth,
Newquay TR8 4BU

Tel	+44 (0)1637 860860
Email	stay@bedruthan.com
Web	www.bedruthan.com

The Scarlet

A super-cool design hotel which overlooks the sea; a vast wall of glass in reception frames the view perfectly. The Scarlet does nothing by halves – this is a serious contender for Britain's funkiest bolthole – but it also offers a guilt-free destination as it's green to its core. Cutting-edge technology includes a biomass boiler, solar panels and state-of-the-art insulation. You'll find a couple of indoor swimming pools to insure against the weather, then hot tubs in a garden from which you can stargaze at night. There's a cool bar, a pool table in the library, a restaurant that opens onto a decked terrace, where you eat fabulous Cornish food while gazing out to sea. Exceptional bedrooms come with huge views: all have balconies or terraces, private gardens or viewing pods. Expect oak floors from sustainable forests, organic cotton, perhaps a free-standing bath in your room. Some are enormous, one has a dual-aspect balcony, another comes with a rooftop lounge. If that's not enough, there's an ayurvedic-inspired spa, where tented treatment rooms are lit by lanterns. Amazing. *Minimum stay: 2 nights at weekends. Dogs welcome.*

Rooms	21 doubles, 8 twin/doubles: £195–£405. 8 suites for 2: £270–£460. Dinner, B&B from £127.50 p.p.
Meals	Lunch, 3 courses, £22.50. Dinner, 3 courses, £42.50.
Closed	4 January to 12 February.
Directions	North from Newquay on B3276 to Mawgan Porth. Signed left in village halfway up hill.

	Nikki Broom
	The Scarlet
	Tredragon Road,
	Mawgan Porth TR8 4DQ
Tel	+44 (0)1637 861800
Email	stay@scarlethotel.co.uk
Web	www.scarlethotel.co.uk

Watergate Bay Hotel

Watergate Bay is one of those lovely Cornish landscapes where nature rules the roost, a world of sand, sea and sky and nothing but. The few buildings that have taken root here don't qualify as a village and have no name, they're just chattels of the beach, a sandy beach that runs for a mile and is one of the best in Cornwall. The hotel sits directly above it, making the most of the view, with walls of glass in the café/bar, a smart terrace strewn with sun loungers, a swimming pool that looks out to sea. Outside, the hotel's surf school will kit you out to ride the waves and you can kite surf and paddle board, too, while beach polo and music festivals come in summer. As for the hotel, it mixes cool design with an informal vibe. Coastal light floods the café, there's a cute sitting room with an open fire, then a small spa with a cool pool and treatment rooms. Airy bedrooms – some with sea views, others with balconies – have seaside colours and fancy bathrooms. As for the food, you can eat in the café or the grill; walk 50 paces to the Beach Hut for a burger, or head for Jamie Oliver's Fifteen.

Rooms	47 twin/doubles: £135-£335. 2 suites for 2, 20 family suites for 4 (1 double with bunk beds for 2 children): £215-£395. Dinner, B&B from £90 p.p. Extra bed/sofabed available at no charge.
Meals	Lunch from £5.75. Dinner, 3 courses, about £35.
Closed	Never.
Directions	Leave A30 at Indian Queens and follow signs past Newquay Airport. Right at the T-junction and hotel in village.

Mark Williams
Watergate Bay Hotel
On the Beach,
Watergate Bay TR8 4AA

Tel   +44 (0)1637 860543
Email reservations@watergatebay.co.uk
Web   www.watergatebay.co.uk

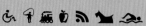

Hotel

Blue Hayes Private Hotel

The view from the terrace is hard to beat, a clean sweep across the bay to St Ives. You breakfast here in good weather in the shade of a Monterey pine, as if transported back to the French Riviera of the fifties. As for the rest of the hotel, it's an unadulterated treat, mostly due to Malcolm, whose infectious generosity is stamped over every square inch. Few hoteliers close for four months to redecorate over winter, but that's the way things are done here and the house shines as a result. It comes in ivory white, with the occasional dash of colour from carpet and curtain. The bar has a vaulted ceiling and a wall of glass that runs along the front to weatherproof the view. Big bedrooms are gorgeous, two with balconies, one with a terrace, all with sparkling bathrooms. Light suppers are on hand, though a short stroll into town leads to dozens of restaurants; Alfresco on the harbour is excellent, torches are provided for the journey back. Penzance, Zennor, the New Tate and a host of beaches are all close. There's folk and jazz for the September festival, a great time to visit. *Children over 10 welcome.*

Rooms	4 doubles: £170–£200. 1 suite for 2: £230–£250. 1 triple: £180–£210. Singles £100–£120.
Meals	Packed lunch by arrangement. Light suppers from £12. Restaurants within walking distance.
Closed	November–February.
Directions	A30, then A3074 to St Ives. Through Lelant & Carbis Bay, over mini-r'bout (Tesco on left) and down hill. On right immed. after garage on right.

Malcolm Herring
Blue Hayes Private Hotel
Trelyon Avenue,
St Ives TR26 2AD

Tel	+44 (0)1736 797129
Email	info@bluehayes.co.uk
Web	www.bluehayes.co.uk

The Tide House

Suzy's eye for beautiful design has turned this medieval building into one of the loveliest small hotels you are ever likely to bump into. It sits on what was the main road into town, a tiny lane that weaves gently downhill towards the harbour. Step inside – the walls are three-foot thick – to discover a small-scale pleasure dome: golden stone walls, padded window seats, an honesty bar in the snug drawing room, fabulous art on the walls. Beautiful simplicity abounds, there isn't an ounce of clutter to be seen. Instead, you find a mirrored sitting room with a wood-burner and the daily papers; a shiny white breakfast room with a wall of glass that opens onto a courtyard; then a kids' room with a PlayStation. Bedrooms are divine: chalk whites, driftwood lamps, beautifully dressed beds, fabulous bathrooms. The big room at the top has views over rooftops to the harbour. Outside: engaging St Ives, the special coastal light, the higgledy-piggledy lanes, the arty vibe. There's a treatment room, too, and great restaurants waiting on your doorstep. Take the whole place and bring your friends.
Minimum stay: 2 nights at weekends, 3 nights on bank holidays.

Rooms	3 doubles: £140-£255.
	1 suite for 2: £240-£295.
	2 family rooms for 4: £185-£235.
	Child in parents' room £30.
Meals	Restaurants nearby.
Closed	2 January to 10 February,
	23-26 December.
Directions	A30 west, then A3074 for St Ives. Pass beach, into town, then right at church. On right after 200m.

David & Suzy Fairfield
The Tide House
Skidden Hill,
St Ives TR26 2DU

Tel	+44 (0)1736 791803
Email	enquiries@thetidehouse.co.uk
Web	www.thetidehouse.co.uk

Primrose Valley Hotel

Roll out of bed, drop down for breakfast, spin off to the beach, stroll into town. If you want St Ives bang on your doorstep, this is the hotel for you; the sands are a 30-second stroll. Half the rooms have views across the bay, two have balconies for lazy afternoons. Inside, open-plan interiors revel in an earthy contemporary chic, with leather sofas, varnished floors, fresh flowers and glossy magazines. Bedrooms aren't huge, but have lots of style, so come for Hypnos beds, bespoke furniture and good bathrooms; the suite comes with a red leather sofa, hi-tech gadgetry and a fancy bathroom. Andrew and Sue are environmentally aware, committed to sustainable tourism and community projects. Their popular breakfast is mostly sourced within the county, and food provenance is listed on the menu. There's a bar that's stocked with potions from far and wide, but St Ives waits at the front door – the old town and beach, the Tate and Barbara Hepworth's sculpture garden, Alba and Alfresco, a couple of lovely restaurants overlooking the harbour. Penzance, a cool little town, is a short drive. *Minimum stay: 2 nights at weekends.*

Rooms	7 doubles, 2 twins: £75-£170. 1 suite for 2: £175-£240. Singles from £65.
Meals	Platters £8. Restaurant 200m.
Closed	Christmas. 3 weeks in January. Open for New Year.
Directions	From A3074 Trelyon Avenue; before hospital sign slow down, indicate right & turn down Primrose Valley; under bridge, left, then back under bridge; signs for hotel parking.

Andrew & Sue Biss
Primrose Valley Hotel
Primrose Valley,
St Ives TR26 2ED

Tel   +44 (0)1736 794939
Email   info@primroseonline.co.uk
Web   www.primroseonline.co.uk

Boskerris Hotel

A lovely little hotel with big views of ocean and headland. In summer, sofas appear on the decked terrace so you can gaze out on the water in comfort. Godrevy lighthouse twinkles to the right, St Ives slips into the sea on the left, the wide sands of Carbis Bay and Lelant shimmer between. Back inside, white walls and big mirrors soak up the light. You get painted floorboards and smart sofas in the sitting room, fresh flowers and big views with your bacon and eggs in the dining room. Airy bedrooms are nicely uncluttered, with silky throws, padded headboards, seaside colours and crisp linen. Eleven rooms have the view, all have fancy bathrooms, some with deep baths and deluge showers. You'll find White Company lotions, Designers Guild fabrics; in one room you can soak in the bath whilst gazing out to sea. Staff are kind, nothing is too much trouble, breakfasts are exceptional. A coastal path leads down to St Ives (20 mins), mazy streets snake up to the Tate. There's good food on your return, perhaps Newlyn crab salad, Trevaskis Farm steak, pear and almond tarte tatin with vanilla ice-cream. *Children over 7 welcome.*

Rooms	10 doubles, 3 twins: £125–£255. 1 family room for 4: £190–£240. 1 triple: £165–£200. Singles from £93.50.
Meals	Dinner, 3 courses, about £30.
Closed	Mid–November to late February.
Directions	A30 past Hayle, then A3074 for St Ives. After 3 miles pass sign for Carbis Bay, then third right into Boskerris Road. Down hill, on left.

Jonathan & Marianne Bassett
Boskerris Hotel
Boskerris Road, Carbis Bay,
St Ives TR26 2NQ

Tel	+44 (0)1736 795295
Email	reservations@boskerrishotel.co.uk
Web	www.boskerrishotel.co.uk

Headland House

A super-cool B&B hotel that stands above Carbris Bay with big views across the water to St Ives. Mark and Fenella refurbished from top to toe, turning their home into a small-scale pleasure dome. Outside, you find sunloungers and a hammock in the lawned garden; inside, there's a snug bar with leather sofas, then a gorgeous breakfast room that floods with light. Here you feast on lavender-scented yogurt, freshly pressed smoothies, perhaps smoked salmon and scrambled eggs or the full Cornish works. In summer, doors open onto a deck for breakfast in the sun. Back inside, seven gorgeous rooms wait. All have the same seaside chic: white walls to soak up the light, pretty fabrics, lovely beds, fabulous bathrooms. Most have sea views, a couple have claw-foot baths, one has its own small garden. There's tea and cake 'on the house' in the afternoon, then a glass of sherry before heading out to St Ives for dinner overlooking the harbour. You can walk down to the beach (glorious), follow the coastal path, or call for a taxi. Leave your car at home and take the sleeper from Paddington. Brilliant.

Rooms	7 doubles: £95–£150.
Meals	Pubs/restaurants 5-minute walk.
Closed	November–March.
Directions	Sent on booking.

Mark & Fenella Thomas
Headland House
Headland Road, Carbis Bay,
St Ives TR26 2NS

Tel	+44 (0)1736 796647
Email	info@headlandhousehotel.co.uk
Web	www.headlandhousehotel.co.uk

The Gurnard's Head

The coastline here is utterly magical and the walk to St Ives hard to beat. Secret beaches appear at low tide, cliffs tumble down to the water and wild flowers streak the land pink in summer. As for this inn, you couldn't hope for a better base. It's earthy, warm, stylish and friendly, with airy interiors, colour-washed walls, stripped wooden floors and fires at both ends of the bar. Logs are piled up in an alcove, maps and art hang on the walls, books fill every shelf; if you pick one up and don't finish it, take it home and post it back. Rooms are warm, cosy and spotless, with Vi-Spring mattresses, crisp white linen, throws over armchairs, Roberts radios. Downstairs, super food, all homemade, can be eaten wherever you want: in the bar, in the restaurant or out in the garden in good weather. Snack on rustic delights — pork pies, crab claws, half a pint of Atlantic prawns — or tuck into more substantial treats, maybe salt and pepper squid, braised shoulder of lamb, pineapple tarte tatin. Picnics are easily arranged, there's bluegrass folk music in the bar most weeks. Dogs are very welcome.

Rooms	4 doubles, 3 twin/doubles: £105–£170. Dinner, B&B £78 p.p.
Meals	Lunch from £12. Dinner, 3 courses, from £25–£35. Sunday lunch from £13.
Closed	24–25 December & 4 days in mid-January.
Directions	On B3306 between St Ives & St Just, 2 miles west of Zennor, at head of village of Treen.

Charles & Edmund Inkin
The Gurnard's Head
Zennor,
St Ives TR26 3DE

Tel	+44 (0)1736 796928
Email	enquiries@gurnardshead.co.uk
Web	www.gurnardshead.co.uk

The Old Coastguard

The Old Coastguard stands bang on the water in one of Cornwall's loveliest coastal villages. It's a super spot and rather peaceful – little has happened here since 1595, when the Spanish sacked the place. Recently, the hotel fell into the benign hands of Edmund and Charles, past masters at reinvigorating lovely small hotels; warm colours, attractive prices, great food and a happy vibe are their hallmarks. Downstairs, the airy bar and the dining room come together as one, the informality of open plan creating a great space to hang out. There are smart rustic tables, earthy colours, local ales and local art, then a crackling fire in the restaurant. Drop down a few steps to find a bank of sofas and a wall of glass framing sea views; in summer, doors open onto a decked terrace, a lush lawn, then the coastal path weaving down to the small harbour. Bedrooms are lovely: sand-coloured walls, excellent beds, robes in fine bathrooms, books everywhere. Most have the view, eight have balconies. Don't miss dinner: crab rarebit, fish stew, chocolate fondant and marmalade ice-cream. Dogs are very welcome.

Rooms	9 doubles, 3 twin/doubles: £120-£185. 1 suite for 2: £200. 1 family room for 4: £170-£200. Dinner, B&B from £75 p.p.
Meals	Lunch from £6. Dinner, 3 courses, about £30. Sunday lunch from £12.50.
Closed	1 week in early Jan.
Directions	Take A30 to Penzance then Land's End. Signs to Newlyn & Mousehole. Hotel on left immed. as you enter Mousehole. Limited parking or public car park next door; £2 on departure.

Charles & Edmund Inkin
The Old Coastguard
The Parade, Mousehole,
Penzance TR19 6PR

Tel   +44 (0)1736 731222
Email bookings@oldcoastguardhotel.co.uk
Web   www.oldcoastguardhotel.co.uk

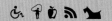

The Abbey Hotel & Restaurant

Jean Shrimpton's Penzance bolthole sits in the old town above the harbour with views from the front across to St Michael's Mount. Outside, a tangle of lanes lead down to the water. Inside, beautiful interiors come in country-house style – a bust of Lafayette in the drawing room, an open fire in the panelled breakfast room, beautiful art everywhere you go. In summer, you decant into a peaceful walled garden for afternoon tea, a perfect spot to escape the crowds. Bedrooms are grand, quirky and laden with comfort. There are chandeliers, quilted bedspreads, French armoires and plump-cushioned armchairs. Those at the front have the view (in one you open a cupboard to find an en suite shower), the suite is perfect for families. As for the food, nip next door to the hotel's restaurant for exciting cooking. Street food waits at lunch – Thai pad noodles, Moroccan couscous, even a mini rump steak burger; then at night it gets fancier, perhaps cucumber soup with curried scallops, wild sea bream with Bombay potatoes, Earl Grey panna cotta with orange jelly. St Ives and the coastal path wait.

Rooms	4 doubles, 1 twin: £105–£200. 1 suite for 2; 1 family room for 4: £150–£210. Singles from £75. 1 apartment for 4 (self-catering): £115–£170 per night.
Meals	Lunch from £3.50. Dinner, 3 courses, about £30.
Closed	Rarely.
Directions	Follow signs to town centre. Up hill (Market Jew St). Left at top, then fork left & 3rd on the left.

Thaddeus Cox
The Abbey Hotel & Restaurant
Abbey Street,
 Penzance TR18 4AR

Tel	+44 (0)1736 366906
Email	hotel@theabbeyonline.co.uk
Web	www.theabbeyonline.co.uk

Artist Residence Penzance

Distinctly hip, deliciously quirky and overflowing with colour, this groovy little bolthole is hard to resist. The house dates to 1600 and stands on the ley line that connects St Michael's Mount to Stonehenge. You're in the old quarter of town, a stone's throw from the harbour. Inside, Charlie and her lovely staff potter about informally, stopping to chat. Inside, you find a cute dining room that doubles variously as a sitting room, a café, an art gallery and bar – a very sociable spot. Each bedroom was designed by a different artist, many with brightly coloured murals. One has exposed rafters, another is pretty in pink, yet another shows a cartoon version of the street outside your window; in short, expect art everywhere. Most have compact shower rooms, one has a claw-foot bath. All have smart beds, white linen and toppers for a good night's sleep; family rooms have fridges, too. Lovely breakfasts offer American pancakes, local eggs, homemade granola – you can scoff it in a pretty courtyard in summer. There's a cute little map for the best of Penzance and some excellent eateries nearby.

Rooms	8 doubles, 2 twin/doubles: £70–£150.
	1 family room for 4: £155–£190.
	2 triples: £125–£150.
	Singles from £60.
Meals	Pub/restaurant across the road.
Closed	Never.
Directions	A30 into Penzance. Follow signs to town centre; up main street; left at top; keep left and on right after 200m.

Charlie Newey & Justin Salisbury
Artist Residence Penzance
20 Chapel Street,
Penzance TR18 4AW

Tel	+44 (0)1736 365664
Email	penzance@artistresidence.co.uk
Web	www.arthotelcornwall.co.uk

The Summer House

A glittering find, a small enclave of Mediterranean goodness a hundred yards up from the sea. It's stylish and informal, colourful and welcoming; what's more, it's super value for money. Linda and Ciro, English and Italian respectively, run the place with great affection. Linda, bubbling away out front, is the designer, her breezy interiors warm and elegant with stripped floors, Ciro's art, panelled windows and murals in the dining room (the breakfast chef is a sculptress). Ciro worked in some of London's best restaurants before heading west to go it alone and will whisk up culinary delights for dinner. In good weather you can eat his ambrosial food in a small, lush courtyard garden, perhaps langoustine with mango and chives, rack of lamb with herbes de Provence, warm apple tart with armagnac sorbet. Breakfast – also served in the courtyard when the sun shines – is a feast. Stylish rooms are the final delight: seaside colours, well-dressed beds, freshly cut flowers, flat-screen TVs, super little bathrooms. *Possible minimum 2 nights at weekends & bank holidays.*

Rooms	4 doubles, 1 twin/double: £95-£150. Singles from £100.
Meals	Simple suppers £20 (Mon-Fri). Dinner, 4 courses, £35 (Sat & Sun).
Closed	November-March.
Directions	With sea on left, along harbourside, past open-air pool, then immediate right after Queens Hotel. House 30 yds up on left. Private car park.

Linda & Ciro Zaino
The Summer House
Cornwall Terrace,
Penzance TR18 4HL

Tel	+44 (0)1736 363744
Email	reception@summerhouse-cornwall.com
Web	www.summerhouse-cornwall.com

Bay Hotel

The Bay Hotel sits beneath a vast Cornish sky with views to the front of nothing but sea – unless you count the beach at low tide, where buckets and spades are mandatory. Outside, the lawn rolls down to the water, sprinkled with deckchairs and loungers in summer, so grab a book, snooze in the sun or listen to the sounds of the English seaside. Stylish interiors are just the ticket, but you can't escape the view: dining room, conservatory and sitting room all look the right way, with big windows to keep your eyes glued to the horizon. Warm colours fit the mood, there are flowers everywhere, cavernous sofas, a small bar for pre-dinner drinks. Bedrooms vary in size, some smaller, suites bigger; one has its own balcony, all have sea views (some from the side). Expect a Cape Cod feel – tongue-and-groove, airy colours, super bathrooms. As for Ric's delicious food, fish comes straight from the sea, though his steak and kidney pie is every bit as good. Try potted brown shrimps, salmon en croute, poached pears with vanilla ice-cream. The coastal path passes directly outside. Don't miss afternoon tea.

Rooms	5 doubles, 5 twin/doubles: £118–£240. 4 suites for 2: £230–£290. Singles £80–£195. Dinner, B&B £75–£145 p.p.
Meals	Lunch from £6. Dinner, 3 courses with coffee, included; non-residents, £34.95.
Closed	New Year.
Directions	A3083 south from Helston, then left onto B3293 for St Keverne. Right for Coverack after 8 miles. Down hill, right at sea, second on right.

Ric, Gina & Zoe House
Bay Hotel
North Corner, Coverack,
Helston TR12 6TF

Tel	+44 (0)1326 280464
Email	enquiries@thebayhotel.co.uk
Web	www.thebayhotel.co.uk

Idle Rocks Hotel

A stunning hotel, bang on the water, in Cornwall's prettiest seaside town. The terrace is hard to beat, a place to linger in the sun, with waves lapping directly below and sail boats cruising beyond. Fisherman land their lobsters at the quay, water taxis whizz you off to sandy beaches, you can hire kayaks and explore the bay. As for Idle Rocks, a recent renovation has turned it into Cornwall's coolest bolthole. Chic interiors flood with light, pristine rooms have flawless bathrooms, delicious food comes from the hills and the water around you. Seaside elegance abounds: sofas in front of the sitting room fire, lamps that hang above the bar, walls of glass in the restaurant that open onto the terrace. Uncluttered bedrooms, most with sea views, have whitewashed walls, fine local art, padded window seats, then the best beds and crisp white linen. Bathrooms are just as good, some with claw-foot baths, others with walk-in power showers, all with robes and aromatherapy oils. Don't miss dinner, perhaps Cornish crab with mango, black bream with chorizo, chocolate and ale ganache. Magical. *Cots £10. Extra beds from £35.*

Rooms	10 doubles, 5 twin/doubles, 1 twin: £150–£335. 3 suites for 2: £280–£350. 1 family room for 4 (1 double, 1 bunk-bedded room): £325–£475.
Meals	Lunch from £7. Dinner: set menu £21–£25; à la carte £35–£45.
Closed	5 January to 5 February.
Directions	Leave A390 between St Austell and Truro for St Mawes on A3078. Drop into village and on left on water.

Tim House
Idle Rocks Hotel
Harbourside, 1 Tredenham Road,
St Mawes TR2 5AN

Tel	+44 (0)1326 270270
Email	info@idlerocks.com
Web	www.idlerocks.com

The Rosevine

A perfect family bolthole on the Roseland Peninsula with views that tumble across trim lawns and splash into the sea. Tim and Hazel welcome children with open arms and have created a small oasis where guests of all ages can have great fun. There's a playroom for kids (Xbox, plasma screen, DVDs, toys), an indoor pool, and a beach at the bottom of the hill. High teas are on hand, there are cots and highchairs, babysitters can be arranged. Parents don't fare badly either: an elegant sitting room with sofas in front of the wood-burner; sea views and Lloyd Loom furniture in a light-filled restaurant; sun loungers scattered about a semi-tropical garden. Family rooms and apartments come with small kitchens (fridge, sink, dishwasher, microwave/oven); you can self-cater, eat in the restaurant or mix and match (there's a deli menu for posh takeaways). Some rooms are open-plan while others have separate bedrooms. Expect airy, uncluttered interiors, flat-screen TVs, top-notch bed linen and robes in good bathrooms. Eight have a balcony or terrace. St Mawes is close.

Rooms	4 family rooms for 2-4: £195-£395. 4 apartments for 2-5: £175-£395. 4 studios for 2: £155-£215. All have kitchenettes.
Meals	Breakfast £3-£12. Lunch from £8. Dinner, 3 courses, about £30.
Closed	January.
Directions	From A390 south for St Mawes on A3078. Signed left after 8 miles. Right at bottom of road; just above beach.

Hazel & Tim Brocklebank
The Rosevine
Rosevine, Portscatho,
Truro TR2 5EW

Tel	+44 (0)1872 580206
Email	info@rosevine.co.uk
Web	www.rosevine.co.uk

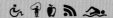

Driftwood Hotel

A faultless position, one of the best. Six acres of gardens drop down to a private beach, coastal paths lead off for cliff-top walks. At Driftwood, Cape Cod meets Cape Cornwall with smart, airy interiors at every turn. The sitting room is stuffed with beautiful things – fat armchairs, deep sofas, driftwood lamps, a smouldering fire. Best of all are walls of glass that pull in the view. In summer doors open onto a decked terrace for breakfast and lunch in the sun. Bedrooms are gorgeous (all but one has a sea view), some big, others smaller, one in a cabin halfway down the cliff with its own terrace. All have the same clipped elegance: warm colours, big beds, white linen, wicker chairs. There are Roberts radios on bedside tables, cotton robes in excellent bathrooms. Drop down to the dining room for your Michelin-starred dinner: cuttlefish consommé, loin of fallow venison, spiced pineapple with coconut meringue. There are high teas for children, hampers for beach picnics and rucksacks for walkers. On clear nights the sky is full of stars. Brilliant. *Minimum stay: 2 nights at weekends.*

Rooms	13 doubles, 1 twin: £180-£270. 1 cabin for 4: £225-£255. Dinner, B&B from £122.50 p.p.
Meals	Dinner £50 (or included in room price in low season). Tasting menu £80.
Closed	Early December to early February.
Directions	From St Austell, A390 west. Left on B3287 for St Mawes; left at Tregony on A3078 for approx. 7 miles. Signed left down lane.

Paul & Fiona Robinson
Driftwood Hotel
Rosevine, Portscatho,
Truro TR2 5EW

Tel	+44 (0)1872 580644
Email	info@driftwoodhotel.co.uk
Web	www.driftwoodhotel.co.uk

Hotel Cornwall

Trevalsa Court Hotel

Trevalsa stands at the top of the cliff with rather good sea views. In summer, the sitting room decants into the garden, with deckchairs and sun loungers sprinkled about. You can nip down to a sandy beach or pick up Cornwall's coastal path, which passes at the end of the garden; turn left for cliff walks or right for Mevagissey, a cute old fishing village. Don't dally too long. Trevalsa is a seaside treat: friendly, stylish, gently spoiling. Inside, the view is weatherproofed by an enormous mullioned window in the beautiful sitting room, a great place to watch the weather spin by. Elsewhere, you'll find a small bar with colourful art, then a panelled dining room for tasty food, perhaps mussels steamed in Cornish cider, lamb cutlets with root vegetables, chocolate fondant with basil ice-cream. Lovely bedrooms have warm colours, pretty fabrics, padded headboards and the odd wall of paper. Most have sea views, bigger rooms have sofas, the family suite is getting a terrace, all have excellent bathrooms. Breakfast is served on the terrace in summer, the Lost Gardens of Heligan are close. *Minimum stay: 2 nights in high season.*

Rooms	7 doubles, 3 twin/doubles, 2 twins: £110-£250. 1 suite for 4: £190-£255. 2 singles: £75-£105.
Meals	Dinner £30.
Closed	December/January.
Directions	B3273 from St Austell signed Mevagissey, through Pentewan to top of the hill, left at the x-roads, over mini r'bout. Hotel on left, signed.

Susan & John Gladwin
Trevalsa Court Hotel
School Hill, Mevagissey,
St Austell PL26 6TH

Tel	+44 (0)1726 842468
Email	stay@trevalsa-hotel.co.uk
Web	www.trevalsa-hotel.co.uk

The Old Quay House Hotel

You drop down the hill, weave through narrow lanes, then pull up at this boutique hotel which started life as a seaman's mission. It's a perfect spot, with the estuary lapping behind the house and a waterside terrace for summer dining, a good spot to watch the boats zip past. Inside, stylish bedrooms have goose down duvets, beautiful fabrics and smart wicker furniture, then spoiling bathrooms that come replete with bathrobes, the odd claw-foot tub, perhaps a separate shower. Most rooms look the right way, eight have balconies (some tiny), the view from the penthouse suite is hard to beat. Downstairs great food waits, so slink onto the terrace for a cocktail, then dig into excellent food prepared from a wealth of local ingredients, perhaps crab ravioli with shellfish bisque, roast bream with a clam broth, passion fruit parfait with mango curd. Fowey is enchanting, bustles with life and fills with sailors for the August Regatta. If you want to escape, take the ferry across to Polruan where Daphne du Maurier lived or potter over to spectacular Lantic Bay for a picnic lunch on the beach. *Minimum stay: 2 nights at weekends in high season.*

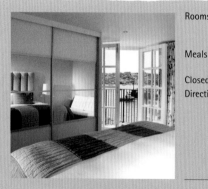

Rooms	5 doubles, 5 twin/doubles: £190-£285. 1 suite for 2: £335. Singles from £130.
Meals	Lunch (April-September) about £15. Dinner £30-£37.50.
Closed	Rarely.
Directions	Entering Fowey, follow one-way system past church. Hotel on right where road at narrowest point, next to Lloyds Bank. Nearest car park 800 yds.

Jane Carson
The Old Quay House Hotel
28 Fore Street,
Fowey PL23 1AQ

Tel	+44 (0)1726 833302
Email	info@theoldquayhouse.com
Web	www.theoldquayhouse.com

Talland Bay Hotel

The position here is magical. First you plunge down rollercoaster lanes, then you arrive at this lovely hotel. Directly in front, the sea sparkles through pine trees, an old church crowns the hill and two acres of lawns end in a ha-ha, then the land drops down to the bay. In summer, sun loungers and croquet hoops appear on lawn and you can nip down to a beach café for lunch by the water. Back at the hotel there's a conservatory brasserie, a sitting room bar, and a roaring fire in the half-panelled dining room. Masses of art hangs on the walls, there are vast sofas, polished flagstones, a terrace for afternoon tea. Follow the coastal path over the hill, then return for a good dinner, perhaps John Dory and squid, Bodmin lamb with black olives, carrot cake with candied walnuts and cinnamon ice-cream. As for the bedrooms, they've been nicely refurbished and pamper you rotten. Expect rich colours, vast beds, beautiful linen, the odd panelled wall. One has a balcony, a couple open onto terraces, all have lovely bathrooms. Gardens, beaches, pretty villages and the coastal path all wait.

Rooms	15 twin/doubles: £125-£225. 4 suites for 2: £200-£245. 3 cottages for 2: £150-£210. Dinner, B&B £95-£155 p.p.
Meals	Lunch from £5.95. Dinner, 3 courses, £32-£38.
Closed	Never.
Directions	From Looe A387 for Polperro. Ignore 1st sign to Talland. After 2 miles, left at x-roads; follow signs.

Vanessa Rees
Talland Bay Hotel
Porthallow,
Looe PL13 2JB
Tel   +44 (0)1503 272667
Email   info@tallandbayhotel.co.uk
Web   www.tallandbayhotel.co.uk

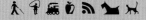

Entry 40   Map 1

Augill Castle

Simon and Wendy's folly castle may look rather grand, but inside is a wonderfully informal world – no uniforms, no rules, just a place to kick off your shoes and relax. Follow your nose and find sofas in front of the fire in the hall, a grand piano in the music room, an honesty bar that opens onto a terrace. Fancy getting married in a castle? They'll do that too… Breakfast is served communally in a vast dining room under a wildly ornate ceiling – local bacon, eggs from resident hens, homemade breads and jams. Elsewhere, panelled walls, roaring fires, art, books and antiques. Bedrooms are deliciously different. Some are enormous, one has a wardrobe in the turret, you'll find big bathrooms, bold colours and vintage luggage. Cottage suites have extra space for families. If you decide to bring the children along there's lots for them to do too – dressing up boxes, five acres of gardens with a treehouse and a playground, even a cinema in the old potting shed. The Dales and the Lakes are close for spectacular walking and cycling, but sybarites may just want to stay put. *Minimum stay: 2 nights at weekends.*

Rooms	8 doubles, 2 four-posters: £130-£180. 1 suite for 2: £240. 6 family rooms for 4: £200-£280. Singles from £100.
Meals	Dinner, 3 courses, £30 (booking essential). Supper platter £15. Afternoon tea £18. Children's high tea £10.
Closed	Never.
Directions	M6 junc. 38; A685 thro' Kirkby Stephen. Before Brough right for South Stainmore; signed on left in 1 mile. Kirkby Stephen station 3 miles.

Simon & Wendy Bennett
Augill Castle
South Stainmore,
Kirkby Stephen CA17 4DE

Tel	+44 (0)17683 41937
Email	enquiries@stayinacastle.com
Web	www.stayinacastle.com

The Black Swan

A lovely small hotel in the middle of a pretty village that's surrounded by blistering country. It's all things to all men: a smart restaurant, a lively bar, a village shop; they even hold a music festival here in September. A stream runs through the big garden, where you can eat in good weather; free-range hens live in one corner. Inside, chic country interiors fit the mood perfectly. You get fresh flowers, tartan carpets, games and books galore. There's a bar for local ales, a sitting-room bar with an open fire, but the hub of the hotel is the bar in the middle, where village life gathers. You can eat wherever you want – there's an airy restaurant, too – so dig into delicious country fare, with meat from the hills around you, perhaps a tasty home-made soup, Galloway beef and root vegetable stew, sticky toffee pudding with vanilla ice-cream. Pretty bedrooms are fantastic for the money. Expect warm colours, beautiful linen, smart furniture, super bathrooms; one suite has a wood-burner. Stunning walking waits, the Lakes and Dales are close, children and dogs are welcome. A very happy place.

Rooms	10 twin/doubles: £80-£100.
	5 suites for 2: £115-£130.
	Singles from £65.
Meals	Lunch from £4.50.
	Dinner, 3 courses, £25-£30.
Closed	Never.
Directions	Off A685 between M6 junc. 38 & A66 at Brough.

Alan & Louise Dinnes
The Black Swan
Ravenstonedale,
Kirkby Stephen CA17 4NG
Tel   +44 (0)15396 23204
Email   enquiries@blackswanhotel.com
Web   www.blackswanhotel.com

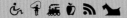

The Sun Inn

This lovely old inn sits between the Dales and the Lakes in an ancient market town, one of the prettiest in the north. It backs onto St Mary's churchyard, where wild flowers flourish, and on the far side you'll find 'the fairest view in England,' to quote John Ruskin. Herons fish the river Lune, lambs graze the fells, a vast sky hangs above. Turner came to paint it in 1825 and benches wait for those who want to gaze upon it. As for the Sun, it does what good inns do – looks after you in style. There's lots of pretty old stuff – stone walls, rosewood panelling, wood-burners working overtime – and it's all kept spic and span, with warm colours, fresh flowers and the daily papers on hand. You find leather banquettes, local art and chairs in the dining room from Cunard's Mauretania, so eat in style, perhaps mussels with cider, saddle of venison, Yorkshire rhubarb and ginger sponge trifle. Bedrooms upstairs are stylishly uncluttered with Cumbrian wool carpets, robes in smart bathrooms and earplugs to ward off the church bells. Car-park permits come with your room and can be used far and wide. Brilliant. *Min. stay: 2 nights at weekends. Free parking permits for town and beyond.*

Rooms	8 doubles, 2 twin/doubles: £108-£178. 1 family room for 4: £148-£178. Singles £78-£158. Dinner, B&B £79-£117 p.p. Extra bed/sofabed available £20 p.p. per night.
Meals	Lunch from £7.95. Dinner, 3 courses, £29.95. Sunday lunch from £13.95. Not Monday lunch.
Closed	Never.
Directions	M6 junc. 36, then A65 for 5 miles following signs for Kirkby Lonsdale. In town centre.

Mark & Lucy Fuller
The Sun Inn
6 Market Street, Kirkby Lonsdale,
Carnforth LA6 2AU

Tel	+44 (0)15242 71965
Email	email@sun-inn.info
Web	www.sun-inn.info

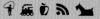

Aynsome Manor Hotel

A small country house with a big heart. It may not be the grandest place in the book but the welcome is genuine, the peace is intoxicating and the value unmistakable. From the front, a long sweep across open meadows leads south to Cartmel and its priory, a view that has changed little in 800 years. The house, a mere pup by comparison, dates to 1512. Step in to find red armchairs, a grandfather clock and a coal fire in the hall. There's a small bar for a dram at the front and a cantilever staircase with cupola dome that sweeps you up to a first-floor drawing room, where panelled windows frame the view. Downstairs, you eat under a wildly ornate ceiling with Georgian colours and old portraits on the walls. You get lovely country cooking, too: French onion soup, roast leg of Cumbrian lamb, rich chocolate mousse served with white chocolate sauce. Bedrooms are simple, spotless, cosy and colourful. Some have views over the fields, one may be haunted, all have good bathrooms. Staff are lovely, nothing is too much trouble, kippers with lemon at breakfast are a treat. Windermere and Coniston are close.

Rooms	5 doubles, 4 twins, 1 four-poster: £90–£125. 2 family rooms for 4: £90–£150. Dinner, B&B £75 p.p.
Meals	Packed lunches by arrangement £9.50. Dinner, 4 courses, £33.
Closed	Christmas.
Directions	From M6 junc. 36 A590 for Barrow. At top of Lindale Hill follow signs left to Cartmel. Hotel on right 3 miles from A590.

Christopher & Andrea Varley
Aynsome Manor Hotel
Aynsome Lane, Cartmel,
Grange-over-Sands LA11 6HH

Tel	+44 (0)15395 36653
Email	aynsomemanor@btconnect.com
Web	www.aynsomemanorhotel.co.uk

Masons Arms

A perfect Lakeland inn tucked away two miles inland from Windermere. You're on the side of a hill with huge views across ancient fields to Scout Scar in the distance. In summer, all pub life decants onto a spectacular terrace – a sitting room in the sun – where window boxes and flowerbeds tumble with colour. The inn dates from the 16th century and is impossibly pretty. The bar is wonderfully traditional with roaring fires, flagged floors, wavy beams and some good local ales to quench your thirst. Rustic elegance upstairs comes courtesy of stripped floors, country rugs and red walls in the first-floor dining room – so grab a window seat for fabulous views and dig into devilled crab cakes, Cartmel lamb shank, warm fudge sundae with Lakes ice-cream. Apartments (in the pub, nicely cosy) and cottages (off the courtyard, great for families) are a steal. All come with good kitchens to cook your own breakfast (hampers can be arranged). You get cool colours and comfy beds; several have private terraces. There's jazz on Sundays in summer and Cartmel Priory is close. *Minimum stay: 2 nights at weekends.*

Rooms	5 apartments for 2: £75-£140. 1 cottage for 2-4 (self-catering), 1 cottage for 2-6 (self-catering): £110-£165.
Meals	Breakfast hampers £15-£25. Lunch from £4.95. Bar meals from £9.95. Dinner, 3 courses, £25-£30.
Closed	Never.
Directions	M6 junc. 36; A590 west, then A592 north. 1st right after Fell Foot Park. Straight ahead for 2.5 miles. On left after sharp right-hand turn.

John & Diane Taylor
Masons Arms
Cartmel Fell,
Grange-over-Sands LA11 6NW

Tel	+44 (0)15395 68486
Email	info@masonsarmsstrawberrybank.co.uk
Web	www.masonsarmsstrawberrybank.co.uk

The Swan Hotel & Spa

This lovely hotel, originally a 17th-century monastic farmhouse, stands on the river Leven, a wide sweep of water that pours out of Windermere on its way to Morecambe Bay. It's a fabulous spot and the Swan makes the most of it, with a terrace that runs along to an ancient packhorse bridge. Interiors are just as good – this is a happy hotel with a relaxed vibe and lots of style. Pretty sitting rooms come dressed in Designer Guild fabrics, there's a lively bar for a pint of local ale, then a stylish brasserie for good food. Potter about and find cool colours, beautiful wallpapers, then sofas in front of open fires. There's also a spa – hard to miss as the swimming pool shimmers behind a wall of glass in reception. Treatment rooms, a sauna, steam room and gym all wait. Pretty bedrooms have the same crisp style: comfy beds, smart white linen, a wall of paper, a sofa if there's room. Those at the front have river views, family suites have doll's houses and PlayStations. Back downstairs, dig into tasty food in the bar or brasserie, perhaps crispy squid, Carmel venison, damson Bakewell tart.

Rooms	13 doubles, 30 twin/doubles: £99-£234. 8 family suites for 4: £189-£329.
Meals	Lunch from £5.95. Bar meals from £9.95. Dinner, 3 courses, £25-£35. Sunday lunch from £13.95.
Closed	Never.
Directions	M6 junc. 36, then A590 west. Into Newby Bridge; over roundabout, then 1st right for hotel.

Sarah Gibbs
The Swan Hotel & Spa
Newby Bridge LA12 8NB
Tel   +44 (0)15395 31681
Email   reservations@swanhotel.com
Web   www.swanhotel.com

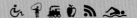

Entry 46   Map 5

The Punch Bowl Inn

You're in the hills above Windermere in a pretty village encircled by lanes that defeat most tourists. It's a lovely spot, deeply rural, with ten-mile views down the valley and a church that stands next door; bell ringers practise on Friday mornings, the occasional bride glides out in summer. Yet while the Punch Bowl sits lost to the world, it is actually a deliciously funky inn. Rescued from neglect and renovated in great style, it now sparkles with a stylish mix of old and new. Outside, honeysuckle and roses ramble on stone walls. Inside, a clipped elegance runs throughout, with Farrow & Ball colours, rugs on wood floors and sofas in front of the wood-burner. Scott Fairweather's ambrosial food is a big draw, perhaps Lancashire cheese soufflé, loin of rabbit with crayfish mousse, pear soufflé and pecan ice-cream. Chic bedrooms are lovely, too, all with beautiful linen, pretty fabrics and Roberts radios, while fabulous bathrooms have double-ended baths, separate showers and white robes. Four have the view, the suite is enormous, weekday prices are tempting. There's a terrace for lunch in the sun, too.

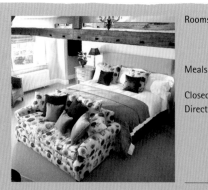

Rooms	5 doubles, 1 twin/double, 2 four-posters: £105-£235. 1 suite for 2: £180-£305. Dinner, B&B from £87.50 p.p.
Meals	Lunch from £5. Dinner, 3 courses, £30-£35.
Closed	Never.
Directions	M6 junc. 36, then A590 for Newby Bridge. Right onto A5074, then right for Crosthwaite after 3 miles. Pub on southern flank of village, next to church.

Lorraine Stanton
The Punch Bowl Inn
Crosthwaite,
Kendal LA8 8HR
Tel   +44 (0)15395 68237
Email   info@the-punchbowl.co.uk
Web   www.the-punchbowl.co.uk

Gilpin Hotel

Gilpin is one of the loveliest places to stay in the country, simple as that. Run by two generations of the same family, it delivers at every turn, its staff delightful, its food divine – a treasure trove of beautiful things. It is a country house that has moved with the times, its sparkling interiors a beautiful fusion of contemporary and traditional styles. Cool elegance flows throughout – smouldering coals, Zoffany wallpaper, gilded mirrors, flowers everywhere. Afternoon tea is served every day, the wine cellar is on display in the bar, there's a beautiful sitting room in golden hues that overflows with art. Doors open onto a pretty terrace, perfect for Pimm's in the sun; magnolia trees, cherry blossom and a copper beech wait in the garden. Bedrooms are divine: crisp white linen, exquisite fabrics, delicious art, fabulous bathrooms; garden suites have contemporary flair and hot tubs on private terraces. As for the food, it's marvellous stuff, perhaps poached pear with blue cheese mousse, Cartmel venison with liquorice and brambles, chocolate tart with orange sherbet and fennel ice. Unbeatable. *Min. stay: 2 nights at weekends. Special rates for 3 or more nights.*

Rooms	8 doubles, 12 twin/doubles: £335-£385. 6 suites for 2: £385-£485. Price includes dinner for 2.
Meals	Lunch £10-£35. Dinner included; non-residents £58.
Closed	Never.
Directions	M6 junc 36, A591 north, then B5284 west for Bowness. On right after 5 miles.

John, Christine, Barnaby
& Zoe Cunliffe
Gilpin Hotel
Crook Road, Windermere LA23 3NE

Tel	+44 (0)15394 88818
Email	hotel@thegilpin.co.uk
Web	www.thegilpin.co.uk

Gilpin Lake House & Spa

Every now and then you bump into a hotel that knocks your socks off, and Gilpin Lake House does just that. This is an extraordinary little place – a tiny spa hotel with only six rooms, luxury and intimacy entwined. It sits away from the crowds, lost in the hills, surrounded by acres of peaceful woodland, with a private lake in front and a hot tub on the terrace. Sun loungers are sprinkled about, there are beautiful gardens, sun-dappled trees, and a rowing boat for fun on the water. Best of all is the cabin above the lake that's a treatment room – pure heaven. There's an indoor pool and sauna, too, while the house itself is coolly elegant at every turn. You'll find sofas, a wood-burner and lake views in the sitting room, books galore and beautiful art. Bedrooms above are luxurious – sofas and armchairs, fabulous beds and fabrics, bathrooms that don't hold back. Breakfast is served wherever you want: in your room, on the terrace, in the conservatory. There's a chauffeur to take you to dinner, too. Come with friends and take the whole place. Out of this world.
Minimum stay: 2 nights at weekends, 3 nights on bank holidays & Easter. Children over 7 welcome.

Rooms	6 twin/doubles: £495–£605. Price includes dinner for 2 at Gilpin Hotel and a chauffeured car to and fro.
Meals	Dinner included.
Closed	Never.
Directions	B5284 west for Bowness. Left at Wild Boar pub, right through village and straight ahead for 2 miles. Keep right at fork and on left.

John, Christine, Barnaby
& Zoe Cunliffe
Gilpin Lake House & Spa
Crook, Windermere LA8 8LN
Tel   +44 (0)15394 88818
Email   hotel@thegilpin.co.uk
Web   www.thegilpin.co.uk/lake-house

Linthwaite House Hotel & Restaurant

It's not just the view that makes Linthwaite so special, though Windermere sparkling half a mile below with a chain of peaks rising beyond does grab your attention. There's loads to enjoy here – 15 acres of gardens and grounds, a fantastic terrace for sunny days and interiors that go out of their way to pamper your pleasure receptors. The house itself is beautiful, one of those grand Lakeland Arts & Crafts wonders, with original woodwork and windows in all the right places. Logs are piled high by the front door, fires smoulder, sofas wait in the conservatory sitting room, where big views loom. Gorgeous country-house bedrooms are coolly uncluttered with warm colours, chic fabrics, hi-tech gadgetry, fabulous bathrooms. Those at the front have lake views, a couple have hot tubs, you can stargaze from one of the suites. Downstairs, ambrosial food waits in the dining rooms (one is decorated with nothing but mirrors), perhaps seared tuna with pickled ginger, chargrilled pigeon with beetroot purée, caramelised banana tart with peanut butter. Sunbeds wait on the terrace. Fabulous. *Minimum stay: 2 nights at weekends.*

Rooms	22 doubles, 5 twin/doubles: £202-£490. 3 suites for 2: £410-£630. Singles £136-£195. Dinner, B&B £135-£315 p.p.
Meals	Lunch from £6.95. Dinner for non-residents £52.
Closed	Rarely.
Directions	M6 junc. 36. A590 north, then A591 for Windermere. Left at roundabout onto B5284. Past golf course and hotel signed left after 1 mile.

Mike Bevans
Linthwaite House Hotel & Restaurant
Crook Road, Bowness-on-Windermere,
Windermere LA23 3JA
Tel   +44 (0)15394 88600
Email   stay@linthwaite.com
Web   www.linthwaite.com

AWARD WINNER

Fabulous food

Cedar Manor Hotel

A small country house on the edge of Windermere with good prices, pretty interiors and delicious food. Jonathan and Caroline love their world and can't stop spending money on it. Their most recent extravagance is the coach-house suite, a hedonist's dream; the bathroom is out of this world, the sitting room has a vast sofa, gadgets are sprinkled about (iPod dock, PlayStation, Nespresso coffee machine). The main house, originally a 17th-century cottage, was once home to a retired vicar, hence the ecclesiastic windows. Outside, an ancient cedar of Lebanon shades the lawn. Inside, cool colours and an easy style flourish. There's a beautiful sitting room in brown and cream with clumps of sofas and local art, then a sparkling dining room that overlooks the garden, where you dig into excellent food, perhaps crab cakes, rack of lamb, pear Charlotte with caramel mousse. Bedrooms – some warmly traditional, others nicely contemporary – have Zoffany fabrics, Lloyd Loom wicker and flat-screen TVs; most have fancy bathrooms, some have big views. All things Windermere wait. *Minimum stay: 2 nights at weekends.*

Rooms	7 doubles, 1 twin: £125–£175. 2 suites for 2: £225–£385. Singles £100–£385. Dinner, B&B £102–£232 p.p. Extra bed/sofabed available £40–£70 p.p. per night.
Meals	Dinner £32.95–£39.95.
Closed	Rarely.
Directions	From Windermere A591 east out of town for Kendal; hotel on right, next to church, before railway station.

Jonathan & Caroline Kaye
Cedar Manor Hotel
Ambleside Road,
Windermere LA23 1AX

Tel	+44 (0)15394 43192
Email	info@cedarmanor.co.uk
Web	www.cedarmanor.co.uk

Jerichos

A friendly B&B hotel with attractive prices in the middle of Windermere. Chris and Jo had a small restaurant in town, wanted something bigger, found this house, then spent a king's ransom doing it up. Step inside to find airy interiors with stripped wooden floors, Victorian windows and a splash of colour on the walls. There's a residents' sitting room with a couple of baby chesterfields, then a pretty restaurant where you breakfast on homemade bread, local bacon and eggs, perhaps a grilled kipper. Spotless bedrooms are nicely priced. Those on the first floor have high ceilings, you get leather bedheads, comfy armchairs, fat white duvets and excellent bathrooms. Most have fancy showers, all come with iPod docks, a wall of paper, Lakeland art. There are good restaurants in town – Hooked for fish, Francine's for tasty bistro fare – but Chris cooks on Saturday and his food is exceptional, perhaps cauliflower, apple and blue cheese soup, silver hake with braised leeks, vanilla panna cotta with raspberry sorbet. The Lake is a short stroll, a good way to round off breakfast. *Minimum stay: 2 nights at weekends, 3 nights on bank holiday weekends.*

Rooms	8 doubles: £85-£130. 2 singles: £50-£60.
Meals	Dinner, 3 courses, about £35 (Saturday only).
Closed	Last 3 weeks in January.
Directions	A591 from Kendal to Windermere. Pass train station, don't turn left into town, rather next left after 200 yards. First right and on right after 500m.

	Chris & Jo Blaydes Jerichos College Road, Windermere LA23 1BX
Tel	+44 (0)15394 42522
Email	info@jerichos.co.uk
Web	www.jerichos.co.uk

Miller Howe Hotel & Restaurant

The view is breathtaking, a clean sweep over Windermere to the majestic Langdale Pikes. As for Miller Howe, this Edwardian country house was made famous by TV chef John Tovey in the 1970s. These days the atmosphere is nicely relaxed. Interiors flood with light, contemporary art mixes with period features, and you can grab the daily papers, then sink into a sofa and roast away in front of the fire. You'll find vintage wallpapers, the odd bust, beautiful fabrics, original wood floors. There's a cute little bar, a conservatory for afternoon tea, then a terrace for drinks in summer, with five acres of beautiful gardens rolling down towards the lake. Back inside, spin into the dining room, where walls of glass frame the view. Menus offer local delights, perhaps Cartmel venison, Cumbrian pork with a cider jus, ginger panna cotta with roast pineapple. Bedrooms vary in size, but all are individually designed with smart fabrics, period furniture and posh TVs. Some have balconies with big lake views, cottage suites in the garden offer sublime peace. Don't miss sunset. *Minimum stay: 2 nights at weekends. Pets are allowed in 2 rooms.*

Rooms	5 doubles, 7 twin/doubles: £170–£240. 3 suites for 2: £170–£270. Dinner, B&B extra £20 p.p.
Meals	Lunch from £6.50. Sunday lunch £27.50. Dinner £45.
Closed	Rarely.
Directions	From Kendal A591 to Windermere. Left at mini-r'bout onto A592 for Bowness; 0.25 miles on right.

Helen & Martin Ainscough
Miller Howe Hotel & Restaurant
Rayrigg Road,
Windermere LA23 1EY

Tel	+44 (0)15394 42536
Email	info@millerhowe.com
Web	www.millerhowe.com

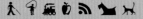

Nanny Brow

A beautiful Lakeland Arts & Crafts house which dates to 1903. It sits peacefully on the hill with views sweeping up the valley with the river Brathay pottering off towards Wrynose Pass. Interiors are no less beautiful. Sue and Peter rescued Nanny Brow from neglect, spent a small fortune doing it up and now it shines, a country house reborn. All the lovely old stuff has been restored, but the feel is fresh with airy rooms that bask in the light and an easy elegance flowing throughout. The half-panelled drawing room is gorgeous: smart sofas, original windows, an open fire, ornate ceiling friezes, vases of beautiful flowers. Bedrooms are lovely, too. Some have arched windows that frame the view, all have super-comfy beds, crisp colours, the odd wall of designer paper; gorgeous bathrooms have double-ended baths or walk-in power showers or both. Cumbrian breakfasts set you up for the day, paths through ancient woodlands lead onto the fells. There's a sitting-room bar, a drying room for walkers, secure storage for bikes and excellent restaurants in Ambleside, a mile up the road. *Minimum stay: 2 nights at weekends.*

Rooms	7 doubles: £130–£200.
	6 suites for 2: £190–£300.
	Singles £115–£265.
Meals	Restaurants 1 mile.
Closed	Never.
Directions	West from Ambleside on A593.
	On right after a mile.

Peter & Susan Robinson
Nanny Brow
Clappersgate,
Ambleside LA22 9NF

Tel	+44 (0)15394 33232
Email	unwind@nannybrow.co.uk
Web	www.nannybrow.co.uk

The Eltermere Inn

This gorgeous Lakeland inn seems lost to the world, yet it's only a couple of miles from Grasmere. In summer you sit in the garden with local sheep for company and dig into afternoon tea; in winter you order a pint at the bar, then roast away in front of the fire. You're in an unblemished village that stands back from the water in the shade of forested hills. Inside, beautifully refurbished interiors are part country house, part village pub. There's a grand piano in the dining room, ancient slate floors in the bar, then big sofas and lovely art in the airy sitting rooms. Upstairs, stylish rooms have warm colours, local wool carpets, big beds and Mulberry fabrics. Some have padded window seats, others are open to the eaves, all have excellent bathrooms, those at the front have views of lake and mountain. Downstairs, you find the sort of food you crave after a day in the hills, perhaps mussels with white wine and garlic, rack of Cumbrian lamb, banana gingerbread with toffee sauce. Walks start from the front door, there's croquet on the lawn, they even grow their own vegetables. *Minimum stay: 2 nights at weekends.*

Rooms	12 twin/doubles: £140–£225. Singles from £125.
Meals	Lunch from £6.95. Dinner, 3 courses, £30–£35.
Closed	Christmas.
Directions	West from Ambleside for 3 miles on A593, then right for Eltermere. On right in village.

Mark & Ruth Jones
The Eltermere Inn
Elterwater,
Ambleside LA22 9HY

Tel	+44 (0)15394 37207
Email	info@eltermere.co.uk
Web	www.eltermere.co.uk

Borrowdale Gates

This super hotel sits peacefully in Borrowdale, 'the loveliest square mile in Lakeland' to quote Alfred Wainwright. High peaks encircle you, sheep grace the fields, the river Derwent potters past. The view from the top of High Seat is one of the best in the Lakes with Derwent Water sparkling under a vast sky, but the lowland walking is equally impressive: long or short, high or low, Borrowdale always delivers. At the end of the day, roll back to this deeply comfy hotel and recover in style. Downstairs, big windows follow you around and there are sofas and armchairs scattered about to make the most of the view. You get binoculars, the daily papers, afternoon tea in front of roaring fires. Bedrooms are immaculately traditional. Expect warm colours, super beds, smart bathrooms, armchairs or sofas if there's room. Some open onto terraces, several have small balconies, most have the view. As for the restaurant, a wall of glass looks out over the village and beyond, a perfect spot for a tasty meal, perhaps sweet potato soup, fell-bred lamb, sticky toffee pudding. *Minimum stay: 2 nights at weekends. Pets by arrangement.*

Rooms	18 twin/doubles: £186–£216. 3 suites for 2: £220–£310. 4 singles: £93–£108. Price includes dinner.
Meals	Light lunches from £8. Dinner included; non-residents, 2–3 courses, £30–£41.
Closed	Rarely.
Directions	M6 to Penrith, A66 to Keswick, then B5289 south for 4 miles. Right at humpback bridge, through Grange, hotel on right.

Colin Harrison
Borrowdale Gates
Grange-in-Borrowdale,
Keswick CA12 5UQ

Tel	+44 (0)17687 77204
Email	hotel@borrowdale-gates.com
Web	www.borrowdale-gates.com

Swinside Lodge Hotel

This small, intimate country house sits in silence at the foot of Cat Bells. Pheasants strut across the lawn, fells rise all around, Derwent Water, Queen of the Lakes, is a short stroll through the woods. Kath and Mike – the real stars of the show – came back from France to take up the reins of this ever-popular hotel and have given their home a lovely makeover: warm colours, new sash windows, smart bedrooms and fancy new bathrooms. Downstairs, you'll find fresh flowers and comfy sofas in the yellow drawing room, shelves of books and a jukebox in the sitting room, red walls and gilt-framed mirrors in the dining room, where windows frame views of Skiddaw. There's super food here, too, just what you want after a day on the fells, perhaps smoked salmon with a beetroot dressing, carrot and ginger soup, roast duck with a red wine jus, a warm apple sponge with a calvados syrup. Lovely bedrooms have a cool country elegance with crisp linen, golden throws and super comfy beds. Outside, a host of characters visit the garden: a woodpecker, red squirrels, roe deer. Wonderful. *Children over 12 welcome.*

Rooms	5 doubles, 2 twins: £184–£304. Price includes dinner for 2. Singles from £122.
Meals	Dinner, 4 courses, included; non-residents £38. Packed lunches £9.
Closed	December/January.
Directions	M6 junc. 40. A66 west past Keswick, over r'bout, then 2nd left for Portinscale & Grange. Follow signs to Grange for 2 miles (not right hand turns). House signed on right.

Mike & Kathy Bilton
Swinside Lodge Hotel
Newlands,
Keswick CA12 5UE

Tel	+44 (0)17687 72948
Email	info@swinsidelodge-hotel.co.uk
Web	www.swinsidelodge-hotel.co.uk

The Cottage in the Wood

A great little base for the northern Lakes with lots of style, super food and owners who go the extra mile. You're on the side of Whinlatter Pass with big views east to a chain of Lakeland peaks. Outside, the terrace looks the right way, a great spot for a drink in summer. Inside, chic interiors are just the ticket: an airy sitting room, a fire that burns on both sides, books and games to keep you amused, windows galore in the restaurant. Nicely priced bedrooms have white walls to soak up the light and sparkling bathrooms for a good wallow. One in the eaves has a claw-foot bath, four have mountains views, one has a fabulous bathroom and opens onto its own terrace. There's lots to do — lakes to visit, hills to climb, cycle trails to follow. Whatever you do, come home to some lovely local food, perhaps Curthwaite goat curd with beetroot and rocket, Herdwick hoggart with garlic dumplings, passion fruit soufflé with mango ice-cream. There's a drying room for walkers, secure storage for bikes, a burn that tumbles down the hill. Starry skies on clear nights will amaze you. Brilliant. *Minimum stay: 2 nights at weekends.*

Rooms	6 doubles, 2 twin/doubles: £110–£175. 1 suite for 2: £190–£215. Singles £88–£96.
Meals	Lunch from £14.95. Sunday lunch £25. Dinner £36–£55. Not Sunday night or Monday.
Closed	January. Mondays.
Directions	M6 junc. 40, A66 west to Braithwaite, then B5292 for Lorton. On right after 2.5 miles (before visitor centre).

Kath & Liam Berney
The Cottage in the Wood
Braithwaite,
Keswick CA12 5TW

Tel	+44 (0)17687 78409
Email	relax@thecottageinthewood.co.uk
Web	www.thecottageinthewood.co.uk

Askham Hall

Despite its grandeur – this is a Grade I-listed manor house with a 12th-century peel tower – Charlie runs Askham with huge informality and you're encouraged to kick off your shoes and treat the place as home. Part-hotel, part-restaurant with fancy rooms, there's lots to keep you amused: contemporary art and open fires, a beautiful drawing room with an honesty bar, a small spa with an outdoor pool, then gardens that open to the public and a café for pizza at lunch. The hall sits in 40 acres of prime Cumbrian grazing land between Ullswater and the Eden Valley with paths that follow the river below into glorious parkland. It's all part of the Lowther estate, where Charlie rears his own meat for Richard Swale's kitchen. And the restaurant lies at the heart of Askham, its seasonal food a big draw, perhaps slow-cooked duck with fig and walnut, Lowther venison with parmesan gnocchi, buttermilk panna cotta with sorrel sorbet. Chic bedrooms have a contemporary country-house style: some vast, one with a tented bathroom, others have views to Knipe Scar. Home-laid duck eggs wait at breakfast, too. *Pets by arrangement.*

Rooms	9 twin/doubles: £150–£260. 4 suites for 2: £250–£320. Singles from £130.
Meals	Lunch from £8. Dinner, 3 courses, £45. 5-course tasting menu £60.
Closed	Sundays & Mondays. January & early February.
Directions	M6, junc. 39, then A6 north. Askham signed left after 7 miles. In village.

Charlie Lowther
Askham Hall
Askham CA10 2PF

Tel   +44 (0)1931 712350
Email   enquiries@askhamhall.co.uk
Web   www.askhamhall.co.uk

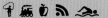

Howtown Hotel

Welcome to Howtown, a world lost in time on a lane that goes nowhere on the quiet side of Ullswater. The position here is heavenly – water, mountain, field and sky – one of the best in the Lakes. The house sits in its own hamlet, dates to 1640, and has been welcoming guests for 114 years, a licensed farmhouse that has passed though five generations of the same family, who still run sheep and cattle on 400 acres of Lakeland fell. Inside, the past lives on: a panelled bar, William Morris wallpaper, smouldering coal fires, wall clocks and lots of brass. Homely bedrooms upstairs have simple pleasures: good beds, sheets and blankets, toile throws, fabulous views. Most are en suite, three have bathrooms one step across the landing. Dinner is old-school – you're summonsed by a gong – then served at oak tables with a beautiful dresser at one end of the dining room. There's a set menu, perhaps vegetable soup, roast lamb, then Howtown's famous sherry trifle; delicious sandwiches are available at lunch. David has an amphibious car for the odd lake cruise. Walking starts from the front door. Matchless. *No email – phone enquiries only.*

Rooms	8 doubles (en suite); 3 twin/doubles each with separate bathroom: £178. 1 single sharing shower room: £89. Dinner included. 2 cottages for 5, 2 cottages for 7, (self-catering): £450-£700 per week.
Meals	Lunch (cold table) £14. Dinner included; non-residents £25. Sunday lunch £16.
Closed	1st Sunday in November to mid-March.
Directions	South from Pooley Bridge with Ullswater on right. On left after 4 miles.

Jacquie & David Baldry
Howtown Hotel
Ullswater, Penrith CA10 2ND

Tel	+44 (0)17684 86514
Web	www.howtown-hotel.co.uk

The Peacock at Rowsley

You rise leisurely, breakfast indulgently, then follow the river three miles north to Chatsworth House, not a bad way to arrive at one of Britain's most beautiful stately homes. As for the Peacock, it dates to 1653 and was once the dower house to Haddon Hall. It stands by the bridge in the middle of the village and opened as a coaching inn 200 years ago. Its lawns run down to the river, where you may spot the odd fisherman trying his luck. Inside, old and new mix harmoniously: mullioned windows, hessian rugs, aristocratic art, then striking colours that give a contemporary feel. French windows in the restaurant open onto the terrace in summer, a fire smoulders in the bar all year. Stylish rooms have crisp linen, good beds, Farrow & Ball colours, the odd antique. One has a bed from Belvoir Castle, the new suite is open to the eaves. As for the food, it's serious stuff, perhaps squab pigeon with fruit and nuts, monkfish with a coconut sauce, chocolate marquise with barley ice-cream. Circular walks start from the front door, so you can walk off any excess in beautiful hills.

Rooms	10 doubles, 2 four-posters: £160-£260. 1 suite for 2: £275-£450. 2 singles: £90-£122. Dinner, B&B from £112.50 p.p.
Meals	Lunch from £4.50. Sunday lunch £22.50-£29.50. Dinner, 3 courses, £35-£60.
Closed	Rarely.
Directions	A6 north through Matlock, then to Rowsley. On right in village.

Jenni MacKenzie
The Peacock at Rowsley
Bakewell Road, Rowsley,
Matlock DE4 2EB

Tel	+44 (0)1629 733518
Email	reception@thepeacockatrowsley.com
Web	www.thepeacockatrowsley.com

Cavendish Hotel

Chatsworth House stands a mile or two across the fields from this smart estate hotel. You can rise leisurely, scoff your bacon and eggs, then follow footpaths over, a great way to arrive at one of Britain's loveliest houses with fabulous gardens and a jaw-dropping collection of art. As for the Cavendish, it comes in warm country-house style. Sofas wait in front of a roaring fire in the golden sitting room, art from the 'big house' hangs on the walls, there's afternoon tea on the lawn in summer. Lovely bedrooms come in different shapes and sizes, some with pretty florals, others in period colours. None are small, all but one have country views and some are seriously swanky. You'll find robes in decent bathrooms, lots of colour, a sofa if there's room. Back downstairs, you can eat in the Garden room (more informal, big views) or in the elegant restaurant, perhaps mushroom risotto with truffle foam, Chatsworth beef with blue cheese bon bons, tarte tatin with star anise ice-cream. Outside, the Peak District waits, so bring your walking boots. Fishing can be arranged, too.

Rooms	20 doubles, 2 twins: £189–£219. 1 suite for 2: £300. 1 family room for 4: £169–£219. Singles from £133.
Meals	Continental breakfast £9.70, full English £18.90. Lunch from £6. Dinner £30–£45.
Closed	Never.
Directions	M1 junc. 29, A617 to Chesterfield, A619 to Baslow. On left in village.

Philip Joseph
Cavendish Hotel
Church Lane, Baslow,
Bakewell DE45 1SP
Tel   +44 (0)1246 582311
Email info@cavendish-hotel.net
Web   www.cavendish-hotel.net

The George

Charlotte Brontë set part of *Jane Eyre* here. She called the village Morton, referred to this hotel as The Feathers and stole the name of an old landlord for her heroine. A copy of her famous novel sits on the shelves of 'the smallest library in the world', which occupies a turret in the sitting room. The bigger turret, equally well employed, is now the bar. The George, a 500-year-old ale house, has grown in stature over time and a smart refurbishment recently propelled it into the 21st century. As a result, wood floors, stone walls and heavy beams mix with purple sofas, fancy wallpaper and Lloyd Loom furniture. It's an unexpected marriage that works rather well, making this small hotel quite a find in the northern Peak District. Airy bedrooms are good value for money, full of colour with spotless bathrooms. Excellent beds are dressed in crisp linen; those at the back are quietest. As for the food, a good meal waits in the dining room, so scale Arbor Low, then return to smoked salmon, chestnut and venison pudding, chocolate pavé with hazelnut macaroons.

Rooms	17 doubles, 4 twin/doubles: £95-£198. 3 singles: £70.
Meals	Lunch from £4.75. Dinner, 3 courses, £36.50.
Closed	Never.
Directions	In village at junction of A6187 and B6001, 10 miles west of M1 at Sheffield.

James Fair
The George
Main Road, Hathersage,
Hope Valley S32 1BB

Tel	+44 (0)1433 650436
Email	info@george-hotel.net
Web	www.george-hotel.net

Loyton Lodge

You get the impression the tiny lanes that wrap around this small estate act as a sort of fortification, one designed to confuse invaders and protect this patch of heaven. And heaven it is – 280 acres of rolling hills and ancient woodland, with wild flowers, pristine rivers, strutting pheasants and the odd red deer commuting across the fields. It's England circa 1964 with nothing but birdsong to break the peace and glorious walks that start at the front door. As for Loyton, it's a great little base for a night or two deep in the hills. It mixes contemporary interiors with an old-school feel – roaring fires, comfy sofas, wonderful art, even a snooker room. Bedrooms have warm colours and smart fabrics, perhaps a sleigh bed or a claw-foot bath, then books and robes and crisp white linen. Breakfast is a treat – bacon and sausages from home-reared pigs, eggs from estate hens – and there's dinner by arrangement, perhaps local asparagus, lemon sole, walnut and fruit crumble. Take the whole house and bring the family or come for the odd night of live jazz. Exmoor waits, as do good local restaurants.

Rooms	7 doubles, 2 twin/doubles, 1 twin: £95-£130. Singles from £80. Extra beds £20 (under 12s free).
Meals	Dinner, 3 courses, about £30 by arrangement.
Closed	Rarely.
Directions	A396 north from Tiverton to Bampton, then right onto B3227. After 1 mile, left for Loyton. Over x-roads, left at hill. Lodge on right after 0.5 mile.

Isobel, Sally & Angus Barnes
Loyton Lodge
Morebath,
Tiverton EX16 9AS

Tel	+44 (0)1398 331051
Email	thelodge@loyton.com
Web	www.loyton.com

Heasley House

Welcome to the rural idyll. This is a beautiful house in a sleepy village lost in a stunning Exmoor valley. A river runs below, tree-clad hills rise above, swifts and swallows play in the air. As for this 19th-century mine captain's house, it stands in the middle of the village with a sun-trapping terrace at the front and big views from the garden behind. Miles and Mandy bought it recently, closed for six weeks, then spent lots of money making it even lovelier. Inside: stripped boards, timber frames, period colours and Georgian windows. There's an open fire in the sitting room, golden walls in the bar, maps for walkers, lovely art, fresh flowers in the hall. Airy bedrooms have big beds, crisp linen, pretty colours, lovely bathrooms. Those at the front have the view, those in the eaves have beams. All have bathrobes, armchairs and flat-screen TVs. Spin back down for a good dinner, perhaps duck with honey and ginger, rack of Devon lamb, chocolate mousse with clotted cream. Paths lead into the hills, the coasts waits a few miles north. House parties are welcome, as are dogs. A great escape.

Rooms	1 double, 5 twin/doubles: £150. 1 suite for 2: £170. Singles from £110. Dinner, B&B from £100 p.p. (2-night minimum).
Meals	Dinner £26-£32.
Closed	Christmas, New Year & February.
Directions	M5 junc. 27, A361 for Barnstaple. After South Molton right for North Molton, then left for Heasley Mill.

Miles & Mandy Platt
Heasley House
Heasley Mill,
South Molton EX36 3LE

Tel	+44 (0)1598 740213
Email	enquiries@exmoor-hotel.co.uk
Web	www.exmoor-hotel.co.uk

The Old Rectory Hotel Exmoor

A gorgeous small hotel in the hills above the Exmoor coast. The road from Lynton is a great way in, through woods that cling to a hill with the sea below. As for the Old Rectory, it's a mini Gidleigh Park, charming from top to toe. Three acres of spectacular gardens wrap around you, only birdsong disturbs you, though Exmoor deer occasionally come to drink from the pond. Inside, Huw and Sam continue to lavish love and money in all the right places. Their most recent addition is a beautiful orangery with smart sofas and warm colours then doors onto the garden for afternoon tea in the sun. Interiors are lovely: Farrow & Ball colours, the odd stone wall, a cute little sitting room, fresh flowers and books everywhere. Bedrooms are just as good with big beds, crisp linen, cool colours and beautiful bathrooms. You'll find digital radios, flat-screen TVs and the odd leather sofa, too. Spin into the restaurant for an excellent meal, perhaps Ilfracombe crab, Exmoor duck, champagne strawberry trifle. Afternoon tea 'on the house' is served in the garden in good weather.

Rooms	3 doubles, 4 twin/doubles: £185-£230. 4 suites for 2: £245-£270. Price includes dinner for 2.
Meals	4-course dinner included in price; non-residents £35.
Closed	November-March.
Directions	M5 junc. 27, A361 to South Molton, then A399 north. Right at Blackmore Gate onto A39 for Lynton. Left after 3 miles, signed Martinhoe. In village, next to church.

Huw Rees & Sam Prosser
The Old Rectory Hotel Exmoor
Martinhoe, Parracombe,
Barnstable EX31 4QT

Tel	+44 (0)1598 763368
Email	info@oldrectoryhotel.co.uk
Web	www.oldrectoryhotel.co.uk

Northcote Manor

A small country-house hotel built on the site of a 15th-century monastery. Those who want peace in deep country will find it here. You wind up a one-mile drive, through a wood that bursts with colour in spring, then emerge onto a plateau of lush rolling hills; the view from the croquet lawn drifts east for ten miles. As for the house, wisteria wanders along old stone walls outside, while the odd open fire smoulders within. There's an airy hall that doubles as the bar, a country-house drawing room that floods with light, and a sitting room where you gather for pre-dinner drinks. Super food waits in a lovely dining room, steps lead down to a pretty conservatory, doors lead onto a gravelled terrace for summer breakfasts with lovely views. Bedrooms are no less appealing – more traditional in the main house, more contemporary in the garden rooms. Expect padded bedheads, mahogany dressers, flat-screen TVs, silky throws. You can walk your socks off, then come home for a good meal, perhaps white Cornish crab, local lamb, strawberry soufflé with vanilla ice-cream. Exmoor and North Devon's coasts are close. *Pets by arrangement.*

Rooms	9 twin/doubles: £170–£225.
	7 suites for 2: £280. Singles from £120.
	Dinner, B&B from £130 p.p.
Meals	Lunch from £6.50.
	Dinner, 3 courses, £45.
	Tasting menu £80.
	Sunday lunch from £25.50.
Closed	Never.
Directions	M5 junc. 27, A361 to S. Molton. Fork left onto B3227; left on A377 for Exeter. Entrance 4.1 miles on right, signed.

Richie Herkes
Northcote Manor
Burrington,
Umberleigh EX37 9LZ

Tel	+44 (0)1769 560501
Email	rest@northcotemanor.co.uk
Web	www.northcotemanor.co.uk

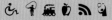

Lewtrenchard Manor

A magnificent Jacobean mansion, a wormhole back to the 16th century. Sue and James have returned to this fine country house, which they established 20 years ago as one of the loveliest hotels in the land. Inside, the full aristocratic monty: a spectacular hall with a cavernous fireplace, a dazzling ballroom with staggering plasterwork. There are priest holes, oak panelling, oils by the score. Best of all is the 1602 gallery with its majestic ceiling and grand piano; *Onward Christian Soldiers* could have been written in the library. Bedrooms are large. Most tend to be warmly traditional (the four-poster belonged to Queen Henrietta Maria, wife of Charles I), but some are contemporary with chic fabrics and fancy bathrooms. All have jugs of iced water, garden flowers and bathrobes. Delicious food waits — perhaps lemon sole, loin of venison, peanut parfait with banana sorbet — and there's a chef's table where you can watch the kitchen at work on a bank of TVs. Outside, a Gertrude Jekyll garden and an avenue of beech trees that make you feel you're in a Hardy novel. *Minimum stay: 2 nights at weekends.*

Rooms	4 doubles, 6 twin/doubles: £165–£220. 4 suites for 2: £220–£235. Singles £120–£200. Dinner, B&B £165–£245 p.p.
Meals	Lunch: bar meals from £5.25; restaurant from £19.50. Dinner, 3 courses, £49.50. Children over 7 welcome in restaurant.
Closed	Rarely.
Directions	From Exeter, exit A30 for A386. At T-junc., right, then 1st left for Lewdown. After 6 miles, left for Lewtrenchard. Keep left and house on left after 0.5 miles.

Sue, James, Duncan & Joan Murray
Lewtrenchard Manor
Lewdown,
Okehampton EX20 4PN

Tel	+44 (0)1566 783222
Email	info@lewtrenchard.co.uk
Web	www.lewtrenchard.co.uk

Tor Cottage

A rural idyll at the end of a track in a pretty valley lost to the world. It's a fabulous hideaway wrapped up in 28 acres of majestic country and those who seek peace and a place to unwind will love it here. Hills rise, cows sleep, streams run, birds sing. Bridle paths lead onto the hill, wild flowers carpet the hay meadow. Big rooms in converted outbuildings are the lap of old-school, rustic luxury. Each comes with a wood-burner and private terrace, one is straight out of *House and Garden*, another has ceilings open to the rafters. Most romantic of all is the cabin in its own valley – a wonderland in the woods – with a hammock in the trees, a stream passing below, the odd deer pottering past. Maureen's magnificent breakfasts are served in the conservatory or on the terrace in good weather: homemade muesli, local sausages, farm-fresh eggs. You can have smoked salmon sandwiches by the pool for lunch or spark up the barbecue and cook your own dinner; all rooms have fridges and microwaves, so you don't have to go out. Maureen is the star of the show, her staff couldn't be nicer. Wonderful. *Minimum stay: 2 nights.*

Rooms	2 doubles, 1 twin/double; 1 suite for 2: £150. 1 cabin for 2: £155. Singles from £98.
Meals	Picnic platters £16. Pubs/restaurants 3 miles.
Closed	Mid-December to end of January.
Directions	In Chillaton keep pub & Post Office on left, up hill towards Tavistock. After 300 yards right down bridleway (ignore 'No Access' signs).

Maureen Rowlatt
Tor Cottage
Chillaton, Lifton PL16 0JE
Tel   +44 (0)1822 860248
Email   info@torcottage.co.uk
Web   www.torcottage.co.uk

The Horn of Plenty

The Horn of Plenty is one of those lovely hotels that has survived the test of time by constantly improving itself. This year's contribution is six new rooms, four of which have terraces or balconies that give 40-mile views over the Tamar Valley. Potter about outside and find eight acres of gardens, then paths that lead down through bluebell woods to the river. Inside, the essence of beautiful simplicity: stripped floors, gilt mirrors, exquisite art, fresh flowers everywhere. Bedrooms in the main house come in country-house style, those in the garden have a contemporary feel. All have cool colours, big comfy beds, perhaps a claw-foot bath or a ceiling open to the rafters; ten have a terrace or a balcony. Despite all this, the food remains the big draw, so come to eat well, perhaps beetroot mousse with goat's cheese parfait, grilled duck with chicory and orange, chocolate cannelloni with banana sorbet; views of the Tamar snaking through the hills are included in the price! Afternoon tea is served in the shade of a magnolia tree in summer. Tavistock, Dartmoor and The Eden Project are close.

Rooms	16 twin/doubles: £95-£225. Singles from £85. Dinner, B&B from £82.50 p.p.
Meals	Lunch from £19.50. Dinner, 3 courses, £49.50. Tasting menu £65.
Closed	Never.
Directions	West from Tavistock on A390 following signs to Callington. Right after 3 miles at Gulworthy Cross. Signed left after 0.75 miles.

Julie Leivers & Damien Pease
The Horn of Plenty
Gulworthy, Tavistock PL19 8JD

Tel	+44 (0)1822 832528
Email	enquiries@thehornofplenty.co.uk
Web	www.thehornofplenty.co.uk

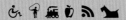

The Henley Hotel

A small house above the sea with fabulous views, super bedrooms and some of the loveliest food in Devon. Despite these credentials, it's Martyn and Petra who shine most brightly, their kind, generous approach making this a memorable place to stay. Warm interiors have wooden floors, Lloyd Loom furniture, the odd potted palm, then big windows to frame the view. Below, the Avon estuary slips gracefully out to sea. At high tide surfers ride the waves, at low tide you can walk on the sands. There's a pretty garden with a path tumbling down to the beach, binoculars in each room, a wood-burner in the snug and good books everywhere. Bedrooms are a steal (one is huge). Expect warm colours, crisp linen, tongue-and-groove panelling and robes in super little bathrooms. As for Martyn's table d'hôte dinners, expect to eat very well. Fish comes daily from Kingsbridge market, you might find grilled figs with goat's cheese and Parma ham, roast monkfish with a lobster sauce, then hot chocolate soufflé with fresh raspberries. Gorgeous Devon is all around. Better than the Ritz! *Minimum stay: 2 nights at weekends.*

Rooms	2 doubles, 2 twin/doubles: £120-£137. 1 suite for 2: £150. Singles from £85. Dinner, B&B £87-£97 p.p. (2-night minimum).
Meals	Dinner £36.
Closed	November-March.
Directions	From A38, A3121 to Modbury, then B3392 to Bigbury-on-Sea. Hotel on left as road slopes down to sea.

Martyn Scarterfield & Petra Lampe
The Henley Hotel
Folly Hill, Bigbury-on-Sea,
Kingsbridge TQ7 4AR

Tel	+44 (0)1548 810240
Email	thehenleyhotel@btconnect.com
Web	www.thehenleyhotel.co.uk

Burgh Island Hotel

Burgh is unique – grand English Art Deco trapped in aspic. Noël Coward loved it, Agatha Christie wrote here. It's much more than a hotel – you come to join a cast of players – so bring your pearls and come for cocktails under a stained-glass dome. By day you lie on steamers in the garden, watch gulls wheeling above, dip your toes into Mermaid's pool or try your hand at a game of croquet. At night you dress for dinner, sip vermouth in a palm-fringed bar, then shuffle off to the ballroom and dine on delicious organic food while the sounds of swing and jazz fill the air. Follow your nose and find flowers in vases four-feet high, bronze ladies thrusting globes into the sky, walls clad in vitrolite, a 14th-century smugglers inn. Art Deco bedrooms are the real thing: Bakelite telephones, ancient radios, bowls of fruit, panelled walls. Some have claw-foot baths, others have balconies, the Beach House suite juts out over rocks. There's snooker, tennis, massage, a sauna. You're on an island, so sweep across the sands at low tide or hitch a ride on the sea tractor. *Minimum stay: 2 nights at weekends.*

Rooms	10 doubles, 3 twin/doubles: £400–£430. 12 suites for 2: £485–£640. Price includes dinner for 2.
Meals	Lunch from £13.50. Sunday lunch £48. Dinner included; non-residents £60. 24-hour residents' menu from £10.50.
Closed	Rarely.
Directions	Drive to Bigbury-on-Sea. At high tide you are transported by sea tractor, at low tide by Landrover. Walking over the beach takes 3 minutes. Eco-taxis can be arranged.

Deborah Clark & Tony Orchard
Burgh Island Hotel
Burgh Island, Bigbury-on-Sea,
Kingsbridge TQ7 4BG

Tel	+44 (0)1548 810514
Email	reception@burghisland.com
Web	www.burghisland.com

Seabreeze

A 16th-century teahouse with rooms on Slapton Sands: only in England. The sea laps ten paces from the front door, the hills of Devon soar behind, three miles of beach shoot off before your eyes. Seabreeze is a treat: cute, relaxed, a slice of old-world magic. Inside, you find Carol and Bonni baking the old-fashioned way, and it's all delicious: hot scones, Victoria sponge, banana and chocolate chip brownies. The tearoom itself — white walls, pretty art, tables topped with maps — is warmed by a wood-burner in winter. In summer you decamp onto the terrace, where sea and sky fuse. Bedrooms are lovely with seaside colours, jars of driftwood and a warm, cosy feel; you can lie in bed and look out to sea from those at the front. Outside, there's lots to do: buckets and spades on the beach, cliff-top walks to local pubs, a huge lake for migratory birds, kayaks for intrepid adventures. Breakfast sets you up for the day (the bacon sandwich is a thing of rare beauty). Local restaurants wait at night: Start Bay in the village, Church House Inn up the road. *Minimum stay: 2 nights at weekends in high season.*

Rooms	2 doubles, 1 twin/double: £80–£140. Singles from £70.
Meals	Lunch from £5. Dinner by arrangement. Restaurants in local villages.
Closed	Never.
Directions	A379 south from Dartmouth to Torcross. House on seafront in village.

Carol Simmons & Bonni Lincoln
Seabreeze
Torcross, Kingsbridge TQ7 2TQ
Tel   +44 (0)1548 580697
Email   info@seabreezebreaks.com
Web   www.seabreezebreaks.com

South Sands Hotel

Two coves west from the bustle of town, this super-smart hotel stands above the beach with views of water, hill and sky. Interiors have a New England feel – seaside colours, softly painted wood, walls of glass for views you can't escape. Doors in the restaurant open onto a decked terrace, where at high tide the beach disappears and the sea laps against the wall below. Pull yourself away to walk in the hills, sail on the water, hire a kayak or try your hand at paddle boarding. Alternatively, just drop down to the beach for family fun. Children are very welcome and you'll find beach towels, buckets and spades, even crabbing nets for excursions to rock pools. Back at the hotel, lovely food waits, perhaps duck liver brûlée, seafood spaghetti, chocolate sundae drenched in chocolate sauce. As for the rooms, those at the front have sublime views, a couple get terraces, all have fabulous bathrooms, cool colours and super-comfy beds. One has 'his and hers' claw-foot baths that look out to sea; the family suites have kitchens, dining tables and separate bedrooms for kids. Brilliant. *Minimum stay: 2 nights at weekends.*

Rooms	16 doubles, 6 twin/doubles: £150–£375. 5 suites for 4: £320–£435. Extra beds £35. Cots £12.50 per stay. Dogs £12.50 per night.
Meals	Lunch from £17.95. Dinner £15.95–£40.
Closed	Rarely.
Directions	A381 to Salcombe, then signed right to South Sands. Follow road down hill, then along water. On left.

Stephen Ball
South Sands Hotel
Bolt Head, Salcombe TQ8 8LL

Tel	+44 (0)1548 859000
Email	enquiries@southsands.com
Web	www.southsands.com

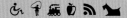

Plantation House

Plantation House is a small hotel where great food and cool interiors go hand in hand. To some this makes it a restaurant with rooms, but whatever it is, all who stay agree on one thing – it's an irresistible little place that shines from top to toe. Downstairs, a fire smoulders in the sitting room bar; upstairs, fine Georgian windows frame views of hill and forest; everywhere, vases of wild flowers. Bedrooms pamper you rotten: two are huge, the rest are merely big. They come with stunning bathrooms, lovely beds, crisp linen and warm colours. You get padded bedheads, sound systems, bowls of fruit. As for Richard's food, it bursts with flavour, perhaps turbot with crab and chardonnay bisque, crispy Devon duckling, cider and bramley apple jus, chocolate espresso tart and hazelnut ice cream. Soft fruits, vegetables and potatoes come from the garden in summer, as do home-laid eggs at breakfast. The river Erme passes across the road, so follow it down to the sea and discover Wonwell Beach. Further afield you'll find Dartmoor and Dartmouth, Salcombe and Slapton Sands. Wonderful.

Rooms	5 doubles, 1 twin: £125–£180.
	1 suite for 2: £240.
	1 single: £70.
Meals	Dinner, 5 courses, from £36.
Closed	Never.
Directions	A38, then A3121 for Ermington.
	In village on western fringe.

Richard Hendey
Plantation House
Totnes Road, Ermington,
Ivybridge PL21 9NS

Tel	+44 (0)1548 831100
Email	info@plantationhousehotel.co.uk
Web	www.plantationhousehotel.co.uk

Browns Hotel

Browns is all things to all men, a cool little wine bar bang in the middle of town. You can pop in for coffee, stay for lunch, come for a glass of excellent wine or book in for a good dinner. It's smart but informal with chic interiors: leather banquettes in the restaurant, Philippe Starck chairs in the bar, comfy sofas scattered about. An open-plan feel runs throughout with big seaside oils on the walls and flames leaping from a pebbled fire. The bar buzzes at weekends, and there's some lovely food, too, perhaps tasty tapas with grilled chorizo and hummus focaccia or sharing plates of artisan cheeses and charcuterie. As for the rooms, the stunning new suite has a huge bed and a magnificent bathroom (walk-in glass shower, contemporary double-ended bath). Other rooms are stylish too, with warm colours, padded bedheads and small leather armchairs. Those at the back are quieter, all have radios, good bathrooms and a book that spills local secrets (the best walks and beaches, which ferries to use). If you like the wine, you can buy a bottle to take home. The Seahorse restaurant is close, too. *Minimum stay: 2 nights at weekends.*

Rooms	7 doubles: £90–£185.
	1 suite for 2: £130–£225.
Meals	Lunch from £6.95 (Tue–Sat).
	Dinner from £10.50 (Wed–Sat).
Closed	First 2 weeks in January.
Directions	Into Dartmouth on A3122. Left at 1st r'bout, straight over 2nd r'bout, then 3rd right (Townstal Road). Down into town. On right.

James & Clare Brown
Browns Hotel
27-29 Victoria Road,
Dartmouth TQ6 9RT
Tel   +44 (0)1803 832572
Email   enquiries@brownshoteldartmouth.co.uk
Web   www.brownshoteldartmouth.co.uk

Bayards Cove Inn

In 1620 the Mayflower stopped in Bayards Cove before sailing for America. It docked just outside this gorgeous little inn, one of the oldest buildings in Dartmouth. But if its timber frames are ancient, then its jaunty interiors are the polar opposite with a warm contemporary feel that spreads itself far and wide. Once inside you realise you're really in a café/tapas bar that does a good line in world wines and local ales. You also realise you've landed in heaven and soon you're trying to muscle your way onto one of the sofas in the bay windows, from which you can survey life inside and out. Interiors have warm colours, low beams, white stone walls and ancient wood everywhere; there are fairy lights, too, a bar weighted down by freshly baked cakes, and cool tunes afloat in the air. Upstairs, lovely rooms have timber frames, padded bedheads, pretty fabrics, comfy beds. Most have compact shower rooms, but you won't mind for a minute; others have views of the water or wildly wonky floors. There's great food, too, and live flamenco on Sunday nights. Dartmouth waits at the front door. *Minimum stay: 2 nights at weekends.*

Rooms	4 doubles, 1 twin/double: £90–£155. 1 suite for 2: £130–£180. 1 family room for 4: £110–£160. Singles £95–£150.
Meals	Lunch from £5.95. Dinner from £9.95 (not Mon–Wed off season).
Closed	Never.
Directions	In Dartmouth south along sea front for lower ferry. Follow road right for 200m and on left at T-junction.

Charlie & Zuzana Deuchar
Bayards Cove Inn
Lower Street, Dartmouth TQ6 9AN

Tel	+44 (0)1803 839278
Email	bayardscove@gmail.com
Web	www.bayardscoveinn.co.uk

The Cary Arms at Babbacombe Bay

The Cary Arms hovers above Babbacombe Bay with huge views of water and sky that shoot off to Dorset's Jurassic coast. It's a cool little place – half seaside pub, half dreamy hotel – and it makes the most of its spectacular position: five beautiful terraces drop downhill towards a small jetty, where locals fish. The pub has six moorings in the bay, you can charter a boat and explore the coast. Back on dry land the bar comes with stone walls, wooden floors and a fire that burns every day. In good weather you eat on the terraces, perhaps a pint of prawns, fillet of sea bass, lavender panna cotta; groups of friends can hold their own barbecues, too. Dazzling bedrooms come in New England style. All but one opens onto a private terrace or balcony, you get decanters of sloe gin, flat-screen TVs, fabulous beds, super bathrooms (one has a claw-foot bath that looks out to sea). Back outside, you can snorkel on mackerel reefs or hug the coastline in a kayak. If that sounds too energetic, either head to the treatment room or sink into a deck chair on the residents' sun terrace. *Minimum stay: 2 nights at weekends.*

Rooms	6 doubles, 1 twin/double: £155–£375. 1 family room for 4: £295–£375. 4 cottages for 2-8 (self-catering): £750–£2,950 per week. Extra bed/sofabed available £25 p.p. per night. Dogs £20 per night.
Meals	Lunch from £7.95. Dinner £25–£35.
Closed	Never.
Directions	From Teignmouth south on A379; 5 miles to St Mary Church, thro' lights, left into Babbacombe Downs Rd. Follow road right; left downhill.

Felicia Crosby
The Cary Arms at Babbacombe Bay
Beach Road, Babbacombe,
Torquay TQ1 3LX

Tel	+44 (0)1803 327110
Email	enquiries@caryarms.co.uk
Web	www.caryarms.co.uk

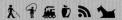

Lydgate House Hotel

You're in 36 acres of heaven, so come for the wonder of Dartmoor: deer and badger, fox and pheasant, kingfisher and woodpecker all live here. A 30-minute circular walk takes you over the East Dart river, up to a wild hay meadow where rare orchids flourish, then back down to a 12th-century clapper bridge. Herons dive in the river, you may spot them from the conservatory as you dig into your locally cured bacon and eggs. The house is a nourishing stream of homely comforts: a drying room for walkers, deep white sofas, walls of books, a wood-burner in the sitting room. Karen cooks the sort of food you'd hope for after a day on the moors, perhaps mushroom and ricotta ravioli, roast partridge with a port and damson jus, plum and almond tart with clotted cream. Homely bedrooms are warm and cosseting with crisp florals and comfy beds. Two are big and have claw-foot baths, all have a nice price. There's breakfast on the terrace in good weather and a stone cottage for six if you want to look after yourselves. Fabulous walks start from the front door, while Castle Drogo and Buckland Abbey are close. *Discounts for stays of 3 or more nights.*

Rooms	4 doubles, 1 twin/double: £85–£120. 2 singles: £45–£55.
Meals	Dinner, 2–3 courses, £21.95–£27.50.
Closed	January.
Directions	From Exeter A30 west to Whiddon Down, A382 south to Moretonhampstead, B3212 west to Postbridge. In village, left at pub. House signed straight ahead.

Stephen & Karen Horn
Lydgate House Hotel
Postbridge,
Yelverton PL20 6TJ

Tel	+44 (0)1822 880209
Email	info@lydgatehouse.co.uk
Web	www.lydgatehouse.co.uk

Prince Hall Hotel

A small country house lost to the world on beautiful Dartmoor. You spin down an avenue of beech trees, note the majestic view, then decant into this warm and friendly bolthole. It's one of those places that brilliantly blends informality with good service: lovely staff look after you during your stay. Potter about and find a sitting room bar where you can sink into sofas in front of a wood-burner; binoculars in the drawing room where long views are framed by shuttered windows; then a smart white restaurant where you gather for delicious local food, perhaps pea soup with poached asparagus, rack of Dartmoor lamb, vanilla panna cotta with rhubarb soup. Bedrooms are all different, but it's worth splashing out on the big ones at the back which have the view. They're altogether grander and come with smart beds, warm colours, excellent bathrooms, perhaps a sofa, too. Those at the side are simpler, but earthy walkers will find much rest here. Outside, lawns run down to fields, the river passes beyond, then moor and sky. Dogs are very welcome. *Minimum stay: 2 nights at weekends.*

Rooms	4 doubles, 4 twin/doubles: £135–£190. Singles from £95. Dinner, B&B from £85 p.p.
Meals	Lunch from £6.25. Dinner from £36.50.
Closed	Never.
Directions	A38 to Ashburton, then follow signs through Poundsgate & Dartmeet. Hotel signed on left 1 mile before Two Bridges.

Fi & Chris Daly
Prince Hall Hotel
Two Bridges, Princetown,
Yelverton PL20 6SA

Tel   +44 (0)1822 890403
Email info@princehall.co.uk
Web   www.princehall.co.uk

Mill End

A smart, dog-friendly hotel with fabulous walking from the front door. Mill End is flanked by the Two Moors Way, which leads along the river Teign, then up to Castle Drogo – not a bad way to follow your bacon and eggs. As for the hotel, you'll find an elegant country retreat with timber frames, nooks and crannies, bowls of fruit and pretty art. Vases of flowers sit on plinths in the sitting room, sofas wait in front of a smouldering fire, there's an airy restaurant for lovely food. Well-priced bedrooms come in country-house style: white linen, big beds, moor views, the odd antique. Most look the right way, a couple have padded window seats, one has a large balcony. Back in the restaurant, where the old mill wheel looms in the window, excellent local food flies from the kitchen, perhaps river Exe mussels with chorizo and cider, Chagford lamb with dauphinoise potatoes, toffee apple crumble tart. Children have high tea at 6pm, there's porridge with cream and brown sugar for breakfast, then afternoon tea in the sitting room after a day in the hills. There are treats for your pooch, too.

Rooms	10 doubles, 2 twins: £90–£160. 2 suites for 2: £120–£210. 1 family room for 4: £110–£160. Singles from £75.
Meals	Lunch from £5.50. Sunday lunch from £15.95. Dinner £21–£35.
Closed	2 weeks in January.
Directions	M5, then A30 to Whiddon Down. South on A382, through Sandy Park, over small bridge and on right.

	Peter & Sue Davies Mill End Chagford, Dartmoor TQ13 8JN
Tel	+44 (0)1647 432282
Email	info@millendhotel.com
Web	www.millendhotel.com

Magdalen Chapter

Where on earth do we start? It might be simpler to confine ourselves to a bald statement of facts to describe this contemporary wonderland. An open fire, terrazzo floors, big warm colours and the odd sofa greet you in the entrance hall. Contemporary art hangs on every wall. There's a curated library, where you can sit and flick through glossy pages; a sitting room bar with a funky fireplace and a Hugo Dalton mural; an interior courtyard with walls of glass that looks onto a gorgeous garden. The brasserie is magnificent, open to the rafters with white pods of light hanging on high and an open kitchen on display. In summer, glass doors fly open and you eat on the terrace, perhaps seafood spaghetti or a good steak. There are deckchairs on the lawn, a small kitchen garden, treatment rooms for stressed-out guests; there's even a small swimming pool that comes with a wood-burner. Bedrooms have an uncluttered, contemporary feel: iPads, flat-screen TVs, black-and-white photography, handmade furniture. Bathrooms are excellent; expect power showers, big vats of REN lotions and white bathrobes.

Rooms	52 doubles, 2 twin/doubles: £120–£250. 5 singles: £105.
Meals	Lunch from £8. Dinner from £12.95; à la carte about £30.
Closed	Never.
Directions	Sent on booking.

Fiona Moores
Magdalen Chapter
Magdalen Street,
Exeter EX2 4HY

Tel	+44 (0)1392 281000
Email	magdalen_ge@chapterhotels.com
Web	www.themagdalenchapter.com

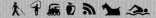

Southernhay House

A gorgeous small hotel on the loveliest square in town, a short stroll from the cathedral. The house dates to 1805 and was built for a major returning from the Raj. These days interiors sparkle, all the result of a wonderful refurbishment. It's proved hugely popular with locals – the restaurant was brimming the day we visited – and those clever enough to check in for the night find some deeply spoiling bedrooms. Downstairs, French windows at the back of the house draw you out to a small terrace. You can eat here when the sun shines, though the house is weatherproofed with a smart restaurant and a cool little bar should the rain dare to fall. Potter about and find electric blue sofas, 50s starlets framed on the wall, old style radiators and beautiful art. Delicious bedrooms wait upstairs – some are bigger, all are lovely. Expect grand colours, sumptuous fabrics, Indian art and hi-tech gadgetry. Fancy bathrooms come as standard, though bigger rooms have free-standing baths. Don't miss the food – Brown Windsor soup, Dover sole, damson gin jelly and cream. Exeter, Dartmoor and the south coast wait.

Rooms	10 doubles: £150–£240.
Meals	Dinner, 3 courses, about £30.
Closed	Never.
Directions	Sent on booking.

Deborah Clark & Tony Orchard
Southernhay House
36 Southernhay East,
Exeter EX1 1NX

Tel	+44 (0)1392 435324
Email	home@southernhayhouse.com
Web	www.southernhayhouse.com

The Lazy Toad Inn

This lovely little inn is humble and gracious and not like those fancy places that always want to blow their own trumpets. It's a way of life. Clive rears sheep and grows masses of food on their land behind, then Mo helps to cook it to keep the locals smiling. You're in a tiny Devon village, close to the church, where you'll find a river you can walk alongside. Back at the pub there's a cobbled courtyard, then a small lawn behind; in good weather both make a lovely spot for lunch. Inside, a warm cottage style runs throughout: painted settles, a wood-burner, the odd sofa, good art. Bedrooms above have irresistible prices and come in various shapes and sizes. You get pretty furniture, colourful throws, painted beams and Farrow & Ball colours; one has a funky bathroom. Back in the bar, find local ales, Devon wines, even homemade cordials. As for the food, some of which is foraged, well, we've left the best for last, perhaps goat's cheese soufflé, shoulder of Devon lamb, home-grown rhubarb mousse. Exeter is five miles away, but it feels like a hundred. Fabulous. *All ages welcome to dine. Children over 12 welcome to stay.*

Rooms	5 doubles: £85–£105. Singles £58–£78. Dinner, B&B £73–£88 p.p. Extra bed/sofabed available £15–£25 p.p. per night.
Meals	Lunch from £5.35. Bar meals from £11.50. Sunday lunch from £12.50. Dinner, 3 courses, £25–£35. Not Sunday eves & Monday.
Closed	Last 3 weeks in January.
Directions	North from Exeter on A377 for Crediton. At roundabout at Cowley, take A377 for Brampford Speke. Right again after 1 mile & in village.

Mo & Clive Walker
The Lazy Toad Inn
Brampford Speke,
Exeter EX5 5DP

Tel   +44 (0)1392 841591
Email   thelazytoadinn@btinternet.com
Web   www.thelazytoadinn.co.uk

The Lamb Inn

This 16th-century inn is nothing short of perfect, a proper local in the old tradition with gorgeous rooms and the odd touch of quirkiness to add authenticity to earthy bones. It stands on a cobbled walkway in a village lost down Devon's tiny lanes, and those lucky enough to chance upon it leave reluctantly. Outside, all manner of greenery covers its stone walls; inside there are beams, but they are not sandblasted, red carpets with a little swirl, sofas in front of an open fire and rough-hewn oak panels painted black. Boarded menus trumpet award-winning food – carrot and orange soup, whole baked trout with almond butter, an irresistible tarte tatin. There's a cobbled terrace, a walled garden, an occasional cinema, an open mic night, and a back bar where four ales are hand-pumped. Upstairs, seven marvellous bedrooms elate. One is large with a bath and a wood-burner in the room, but all are lovely with super-smart power showers, sash windows that give village views, hi-fis, flat-screen TVs, good linen and comfy beds. Dartmoor waits but you may well linger. There's Tiny the guard dog, too.

Rooms	5 doubles, 1 twin/double: £65-£120. 1 suite for 3: £170-£190.
Meals	Lunch from £9. Dinner, 3 courses, £20-£30. Sunday lunch from £10.
Closed	Rarely.
Directions	A377 north from Exeter. 1st right in Crediton, left, signed Sandford. 1 mile up & in village.

Mark Hildyard & Katharine Lightfoot
The Lamb Inn
Sandford, Crediton EX17 4LW

Tel	+44 (0)1363 773676
Email	thelambinn@gmail.com
Web	www.lambinnsandford.co.uk

Combe House Devon

Combe is matchless, an ancient house on a huge estate, the full aristocratic monty. You spin up a long drive, pass the odd Arabian horse dawdling in the fields, then skip through the front door and enter a place of architectural wonder. A fire smoulders in the vast panelled hall, the muralled dining room gives huge country views, the sitting room bar in racing green opens onto the croquet lawn. Best of all is the way things are done: the feel is more home than hotel, with a battalion of lovely staff on hand to attend to your every whim. Wander around and find medieval flagstones, William Morris wallpaper, Victorian kitchen gardens that provide much for the table; expect home-buzzed honey and fresh eggs from a roving band of exotic chickens. Rooms are stately with wonderful beds, stunning bathrooms and outstanding views, while the vast suite, once the laundry press, is the stuff of fashion shoots. There are 3,500 acres to explore, then ambrosial food waiting on your return, but it's Ruth and Ken who win the prize; they just know how to do it. Dogs are very welcome with well-behaved owners! *Minimum stay: 2 nights at weekends.*

Rooms	9 twin/doubles, 2 four-posters: £220–£380. 4 suites for 2: £460. Combe Thatch House for 8: £460 for 2; £65 each extra person.
Meals	Lunch from £9. Cream tea from £10. Dinner £54. Sunday lunch £39.
Closed	Rarely.
Directions	M5 junc. 29, then A30 to Honiton. Follow signs to Heathpark, then Gittisham. Hotel signed in village.

	Ruth & Ken Hunt
	Combe House Devon
	Gittisham, Honiton EX14 3AD
Tel	+44 (0)1404 540400
Email	stay@combehousedevon.com
Web	www.combehousedevon.com

Old favourite

Alexandra Hotel & Restaurant

Everything here is lovely, but the view is hard to beat, a clean sweep up the Jurassic coast towards Portland Bill. The hotel overlooks Lyme Bay; the only thing between you and it is the lawn. Below, the Cobb curls into the sea, the very spot where Meryl Streep withstood the crashing waves in *The French Lieutenant's Woman*. In summer, steamer chairs pepper the garden and guests fall asleep, book in hand, under an English sun. As for the hotel, it's just as good. Kathryn, ex-Firmdale, bought it from her mother and has refurbished brilliantly. You get stripped wood floors, windows everywhere, an airy bar for pre-dinner drinks, an attractive sitting room with plenty of books. The dining room could double as a ballroom, the conservatory brasserie opens onto a terrace; both provide excellent sustenance, perhaps Lyme Bay scallops, roast rump of Devon lamb, gingerbread pudding with vanilla ice-cream. Beautiful rooms hit the spot, most have the view. Expect super beds, padded headboards, robes in lovely bathrooms. Lyme, the beach and the fossil-ridden coast all wait. *Minimum stay: 2 nights at weekends.*

Rooms	19 twin/doubles:
	3 family rooms for 4: £177–£225.
	2 singles: £85.
	1 apartment for 6: £320.
	Dinner, B&B £120–£147.50 p.p.
Meals	Lunch from £9.90.
	Afternoon tea from £6.50.
	Dinner, 3 courses, about £35.
	Sunday lunch from £19.50.
Closed	Rarely.
Directions	In Lyme Regis up hill on high street; keep left at bend; on left after 200m.

Kathryn Haskins
Alexandra Hotel & Restaurant
Pound Street,
Lyme Regis DT7 3HZ

Tel	+44 (0)1297 442010
Email	enquiries@hotelalexandra.co.uk
Web	www.hotelalexandra.co.uk

Entry 87   Map 2

The Bull Hotel

Urban-chic meets rural simplicity at Richard and Nikki's Regency-style coaching inn. Funky and fun sums up this vibrant place; you feel good the moment you step through the door. Escape Bridport's bustle, kick off your shoes, plonk yourself down on a squashy sofa with a pint of Otter Ale. The bar is open all day, for hearty English breakfasts, cappuccino and cake, for lunchtime sandwiches and high tea. For seriously good food, there's a candlelit restaurant; for summer lunches, a Victorian courtyard. Enjoy live music in the Hayloft, take a turn in the ballroom, order a cocktail in the sumptuous lounge. Daily menus are contemporary and work with the seasons while organic ingredients are locally sourced: fish is a speciality, mostly caught in Lyme Bay, and there's stone-baked pizza, vanilla rice pudding, handmade cheeses... As for the bedrooms... classic period features mix with modern pieces and antiques, there are Designer Guild fabrics, Milo sofas, big beds, Tivoli radios, waffle robes, roll top tubs and Neal's Yard delights. A boon for arty Bridport – and the fantastic Jurassic coast is a mile away. *Minimum stay: 2 nights at weekends.*

Rooms	10 doubles, 1 twin, 3 four-posters: £100–£210. 1 suite for 2: £235–£265. 4 family rooms for 4: £190–£220. 1 single: £90–£115.
Meals	Lunch, 2 courses, from £12. Dinner, 3 courses, around £35. Sunday lunch £19.
Closed	Never.
Directions	On main street in town. Car park at rear.

Nikki & Richard Cooper
The Bull Hotel
34 East Street,
Bridport DT6 3LF

Tel	+44 (0)1308 422878
Email	info@thebullhotel.co.uk
Web	www.thebullhotel.co.uk

BridgeHouse Hotel

Beaminster – Emminster in Thomas Hardy's *Tess* – sits in a lush Dorset valley. From the hills above, rural England goes on show: quilted fields lead to a country town, the church tower soars towards heaven. At BridgeHouse stone flags, mullioned windows, old beams and huge inglenooks sweep you back to a graceful past. This is a comfortable hotel in a country town – intimate, friendly, quietly smart. There are rugs on parquet floors, a beamed bar in a turreted alcove, a sparkling dining room with Georgian panelling. Breakfast is served in the brasserie, where huge windows look onto the lawns, so watch the gardener potter about as you scoff your bacon and eggs. Delicious food – local and organic – is a big draw, perhaps seared scallops, Gressingham duck, champagne sorbet. And so to bed. Rooms in the main house are bigger and smarter, those in the coach house are simpler and less expensive; all are pretty with chic fabrics, crisp linen, flat-screen TVs and stylish bathrooms. There are river walks, antique shops and Dorset's Jurassic coast. *Minimum stay: 2 nights at weekends.*

Rooms	6 twin/doubles, 2 four-posters: £125-£220. 3 doubles, 1 family room for 4 (Coach House): £125-£165. 1 single: £95-£165.
Meals	Lunch from £12.50. Dinner à la carte £15-£40.
Closed	Never.
Directions	From Yeovil A30 west; A3066 for Bridport to Beaminster. Hotel at far end of town as road bends to right.

Mark & Jo Donovan
BridgeHouse Hotel
3 Prout Bridge,
Beaminster DT8 3AY
Tel   +44 (0)1308 862200
Email   enquiries@bridge-house.co.uk
Web   www.bridge-house.co.uk

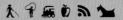

Plumber Manor

A grand old country house that sits in a couple of acres of green and pleasant land with the river Divelish running through. It dates from 1650, with mullioned windows, huge stone flags and a fine terrace for afternoon tea. An avenue of horse chestnuts takes you to the front door. Inside, a pair of labradors rule the roost. Expect no designer trends – Plumber is old-school, defiantly so. Take the first-floor landing with its enormous sofa, gallery of family oils and grand piano thrown in for good measure. Bedrooms are split between the main house and converted barns. The latter tend to be bigger and are good for those with dogs. Décor is dated – 1980s florals – as are most bathrooms, though a couple now sparkle in travertine splendour. The family triumvirate of Brian (in the kitchen), Richard (behind the bar) and Alison (simply everywhere) excel in the art of old-fashioned hospitality. Delicious country food waits in the restaurant, try seared scallops with pea purée, rack of lamb with rosemary and garlic, lemon meringue pie. Bulbarrow Hill is close.

Rooms	2 doubles, 14 twin/doubles; 1 twin/double with separate bath: £150-£230. Singles from £115.
Meals	Sunday lunch £29.50. Dinner, 2-3 courses, £29-£36.
Closed	February.
Directions	West from Sturminster Newton on A357. Across traffic lights, up hill & left for Hazelbury Bryan. Follow brown tourism signs. Hotel signed left after 2 miles.

Richard, Alison & Brian Prideaux-Brune
Plumber Manor
Plumber,
Sturminster Newton DT10 2AF
Tel   +44 (0)1258 472507
Email   book@plumbermanor.com
Web   www.plumbermanor.com

Entry 90   Map 2

Stapleton Arms

A perfect village inn: loads of style, lovely staff, super food, excellent prices. The Stapleton started life as a Georgian home, becoming an inn after the war. These days its warm, hip interiors carry a streak of country glamour. Downstairs, amid the happy vibe, find sofas in front of the fire, a piano for live music, a restaurant with shuttered windows and candles in the fireplace. You can eat whatever you want wherever you want; delicious pork pies wait at the bar, but it's hard to resist a three-course feast, perhaps Welsh rarebit with sautéed field mushrooms, Beef Wellington with horseradish mash, Mississippi mud pie. There's a beer menu to beat all others (ale matters here) and on Sundays groups can order their own joint of meat; there's always a menu for kids, too. Super rooms are soundproofed to ensure a good night's sleep. All have beautiful linen, fresh flowers, happy colours, fantastic showers. Also: maps and wellies if you want to walk, a DVD library for all ages, and a playground for kids in the garden. Wincanton is close for the races. One of the best.

Rooms	4 doubles: £80–£120. Extra bed/sofabed available £15 p.p. per night.
Meals	Lunch & bar meals from £7. Dinner, 3 courses, about £30.
Closed	Rarely.
Directions	A303 to Wincanton. Into town right after fire station, signed Buckhorn Weston. Left at T-junction after 3 miles. In village, pub on right.

Rupert & Victoria Reeves
Stapleton Arms
Church Hill, Buckhorn Weston,
Gillingham SP8 5HS

Tel	+44 (0)1963 370396
Email	relax@thestapletonarms.com
Web	www.thestapletonarms.com

Castleman Hotel & Restaurant

It's a little like stepping into the pages of a Hardy novel: an untouched corner of idyllic Dorset, a 400-year-old bailiff's house, sheep grazing in lush fields and a rich cast of characters. The Castleman – part country house, part restaurant with rooms – is a true one-off: quirky, intimate, defiantly English. It pays no heed to prevailing fashions, not least because the locals would revolt if it did. Barbara runs the place with relaxed informality, though touches of grandeur are hard to miss: a panelled hall, art from Chettle House, a magnificent Jacobean ceiling in one of the sitting rooms. Potter about and find a cosy bar, fresh flowers everywhere and good books galore. The restaurant has garden views though your eyes will attend only to Barbara's deliciously old-fashioned English food, perhaps potted shrimp terrine, haunch of local venison, meringues with chocolate mousse and toasted almonds. Smart homely bedrooms fit the bill: eminently comfortable, delightfully priced, a couple with claw-foot baths. Magical Dorset will fill your days with splendour. Don't miss it.

Rooms	4 doubles, 1 four-poster, 1 twin/double, 1 twin, 1 family room for 4: £95–£110. Singles from £70.
Meals	Sunday lunch £25. Dinner, 3 courses, about £27.
Closed	February.
Directions	A354 north from Blandford Forum. 3rd left (about 4 miles up) and on left in village.

Barbara Garnsworthy
Castleman Hotel & Restaurant
Chettle,
Blanford Forum DT11 8DB

Tel	+44 (0)1258 830096
Email	enquiry@castlemanhotel.co.uk
Web	www.castlemanhotel.co.uk

La Fosse at Cranborne

This is a lovely restaurant with rooms in a pretty Dorset village – small and friendly, nicely homespun, owner-run and owner-cooked. Emmanuelle and Mark love their world, it's a way of life and they share it with guests happily and generously. Downstairs, there's a smart sitting room with stripped floors and maps for walkers. Upstairs, a clutch of pretty bedrooms wait with warm colours, attractive fabrics, comfy beds and spotless bathrooms. They're very well priced, so splash out on the bigger rooms and find a sofa or a separate sitting room. Not that you'll linger long. Mark's food is the big draw, much of it sourced within 20 miles. You eat in a pretty dining room with an open fire roaring beyond a couple of sofas. It's delicious stuff, perhaps game terrine with ale chutney, slow-cooked lamb with village vegetables, then pears poached in sloe gin with chocolate ice-cream. Best of all is the cheese board, a tasting menu of ten local cheeses – utterly irresistible. You can walk it all off a few miles west at Hambledon Hill (a prehistoric hill fort) with big country views. Brilliant. *Minimum stay: 2 nights at weekends.*

Rooms	3 doubles, 2 twin/doubles: £85–£115. 1 suite for 2: £115.
Meals	Dinner, 3 courses, £27.50. Not Sunday.
Closed	Never.
Directions	A338 to Fordingbridge, then B3078 into Cranborne. Right at village shop and on right.

Emmanuelle & Mark Hartstone
La Fosse at Cranborne
The Square, Cranborne,
Wimborne BH21 5PR

Tel	+44 (0)1725 517604
Email	lafossemail@gmail.com
Web	www.la-fosse.com

Bishops Cottage

A homespun restaurant with rooms on the side of a hill above Lulworth Cove. The house was once home to the Bishop of Salisbury, Wordsworth's grandson. Outside: a swimming pool in the garden where you can soak up the sun while watching walkers pour off the hill. Inside: smart interiors have low beamed ceilings, painted wood floors, Farrow & Ball colours and a couple of sofas in front of the fire. Philip, larger than life, studied art at Goldsmiths and his work appears on a wall or two; he also made the bar from a hatch recovered from a military vessel sunk by a U-boat. Three lovely bedrooms wait upstairs: one has the view, the others have sofas in sitting rooms, then big comfy beds and lovely bathrooms. You get toppers, bathrobes, duck down duvets – Liesl's determination to pamper you rotten is unstinting. Outside, the coastal path weaves past one sandy cove after another, a rollercoaster ride through this magnificent World Heritage landscape. Come back for lovely food, perhaps seared scallops, wild sea bass, chocolate tart with vanilla ice-cream. *Minimum stay: 2 nights at weekends.*

Rooms	2 doubles, 1 twin/double: £120–£150. Singles from £110.
Meals	Lunch from £6.50. Dinner, 3 courses, £25–£30.
Closed	Christmas.
Directions	West from Wareham on A352, right for Lulworth on B3070. Last house on left before sea.

Liesl & Philip Ashby Rudd
Bishops Cottage
West Lulworth,
Wareham BH20 5RQ

Tel	+44 (0)1929 400552
Email	bishopscottagelulworth@gmail.com
Web	www.bishopscottage.co.uk

The Priory Hotel

The lawns of this 16th-century priory run down to the river Frome. Boats float past, an old church rises behind, a gorgeous garden wraps around you filled with colour. As for this lovely country house, you'll find a grand piano in the drawing room, a first-floor sitting room with garden views, and a stone-vaulted dining room in the old cellar. Best of all is the terrace, where you can sit in the sun and watch the river pass – a perfect spot for lunch in summer. Bedrooms in the main house come in different sizes, some cosy in the eaves, others grandly adorned in reds and golds. You get Zoffany fabrics, padded window seats, bowls of fruit, the odd sofa. Eight have river views, others look onto the garden or church. Chic bathrooms – some dazzlingly contemporary – all come with white robes. Rooms in the boathouse, a 16th-century clay barn, are lavish, with oak panelling, stone walls and sublime views. Outside, climbing roses, a duck pond, then banks of daffs and snowdrops. Corfe Castle and Studland Bay are close. A slice of old England with delicious food to boot.
Minimum stay: 2 nights at weekends. Children over 14 welcome.

Rooms	13 twin/doubles: £215–£315.
	5 suites for 2: £345–£375.
Meals	Lunch from £14.95.
	Dinner, 3 courses, £45.
Closed	Never.
Directions	West from Poole on A35, then A351 for Wareham and B3075 into town. Through lights, 1st left, right out of square, then keep left. Entrance on left beyond church.

	Jeremy Merchant
	The Priory Hotel
	Church Green, Wareham BH20 4ND
Tel	+44 (0)1929 551666
Email	reservations@theprioryhotel.co.uk
Web	www.theprioryhotel.co.uk

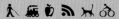

The Green House Hotel

Two streets up from the sea, a handsome Edwardian mansion that harks back to Bournemouth's Belle Epoque. Inside, zippy 21st-century interiors are as green as can be: pure lambswool carpets come from the Isle of Bute, eco beds were specially commissioned from Hypnos, solar panels provide all the hot water. Follow your nose and find cubist seats, a sitting room bar and delicate Farrow & Ball wallpapers. The restaurant, with its fine Art Deco bay window, serves great food from local farms, forests and waters, perhaps Dorset hedgerow garlic and pea soup, Poole Bay hake with tarragon gnocchi, apple soufflé with iced Granny Smith parfait, all of which you can wash down with English wines. Contemporary bedrooms in grey, plum and chocolate have goose down duvets, iPod docks and luxurious stone shower rooms; five rooms have roll top baths centre stage, and zany lime and charcoal wallpaper. Laid-back staff are non-preachy, the restaurant and bar are open every day, and the location couldn't be better – you're a short stroll from Bournemouth's sandy beach for swimming, sailing, golf and gardens. *Minimum stay: 2 nights at weekends in high season.*

Rooms	32 doubles: £99-£240.
Meals	Lunch from £9.99.
	Dinner, 3 courses, about £30.
	Afternoon tea £18.50.
Closed	Never.
Directions	Sent on booking,

Olivia O'Sullivan
The Green House Hotel
4 Grove Road, Bournemouth BH1 3AX

Tel	+44 (0)1202 498900
Email	reservations@thegreenhousehotel.com
Web	www.thegreenhousehotel.co.uk

Urban Beach Hotel

A quirky little place close to the beach with cool interiors and a happy buzz in the bar. Mark and Fiona have a great way of doing things: they employ a Head of Happy and go out of their way to help their lovely staff flourish. It works brilliantly, if you stay it's hard not to notice a difference. Inside, the bar/restaurant is the hub of the house. Surf movies play silently, a couple of surf boards hang on the walls, you get big circular leather booths, then driftwood lamps and a house guitar. There's a table of cakes, a bar for cocktails, candle lanterns scattered about, the daily papers and a few cool tunes. Bedrooms upstairs are nicely priced, some bigger than others, but even the smaller rooms are lovely with warm colours, crisp linen and excellent bathrooms. A decked terrace outside is popular for summer barbecues, but the beach waits at the end of the road, seven miles of sand with a surf shop on the way down. Urban Reef, their cool sister restaurant, has a balcony and terrace overlooking the sea; they'll book you in for dinner, you can even have your breakfast there. *Minimum stay: 2 nights at weekends, 3 nights on bank holidays.*

Rooms	9 doubles, 1 twin/double: £97–£180. 2 singles: £72.
Meals	Lunch & dinner £5–£25.
Closed	Never.
Directions	South from Ringwood on A338; left for Boscombe (east of centre). Over railway, right onto Centenary Way. Keep with the flow (left, then right) to join Christchurch Rd; 2nd left (St John's Rd); 2nd left.

Mark & Fiona Cribb
Urban Beach Hotel
23 Argyll Road,
Bournemouth BH5 1EB

Tel	+44 (0)1202 301509
Email	reception@urbanbeach.co.uk
Web	www.urbanbeach.co.uk

Captain's Club Hotel and Spa

A sparkling hotel on the banks on the Stour, where a tiny ferry potters along the river dodging swans and ducks. The hotel has its own launch and those who want to skim across to the Isle of Wight can do so in style. Back on dry land, locals love the big bar which hums with happy chatter, and they sink into sofas, sip cocktails or dig into a crab sandwich. There's live music on Sunday nights, newspapers at reception and doors that open onto a pretty terrace, perfect in good weather. Bedrooms all have river views and come in an uncluttered contemporary style, with low-slung beds, crisp white linen, neutral colours and excellent bathrooms. None are small, some are huge with separate sitting rooms, while apartments have more than one bedroom, thus perfect for families and friends. Residents have free access to the spa (hydrotherapy pool, sauna, four treatment rooms). Dinner is in an ultra-airy restaurant, where you dig into tasty brasserie-style food, perhaps goat cheese soufflé, Gressingham duck, pear mousse with Kir royale sorbet. Christchurch is a short walk upstream. *Minimum stay: 2 nights at weekends.*

Rooms	17 doubles: £199–£259.
	12 apartments for 2-6: £289–£649.
Meals	Bar meals all day from £6.
	Lunch from £15. Dinner £30–£35.
Closed	Never.
Directions	M27/A31 west, then A338/B3073 south into Christchurch. At A35 (lights at big r'bout) follow one-way system left. Double back after 100m. Cross r'bout heading west and 1st left into Sopers Lane. Signed left.

Timothy Lloyd & Robert Wilson
Captain's Club Hotel and Spa
Wick Ferry, Wick Lane,
Christchurch BH23 1HU

Tel	+44 (0)1202 475111
Email	reservations@captainsclubhotel.com
Web	www.captainsclubhotel.com

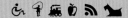

The Kings

This is one of those lovely places that delivers what many of us want: lots of style, delicious food, happy staff, attractive prices. The setting is just as good, a slice of Georgian England, with the river Stour to the left, the ruined castle to the right and the old bowling green in between. A riverside path leads down to Christchurch Quay, and another to the gardens at the priory – blissful stuff. As for the hotel, you'll find a cool bar in greens and browns for gin cocktails, an airy sitting room (that doubles as a meeting room) with local art on the walls, then comfy bedrooms with lots of style: smart colours, fine beds, good bathrooms, perhaps a sofa if there's room. Three overlook the front, those in the eaves have a cute, cosy feel. Back downstairs, excellent food waits in the candlelit restaurant, perhaps Poole Bay scallops, duck shepherd's pie, white chocolate crème brûlée. It's all local with well-priced menus from an amazing £15. Supper clubs and lobster nights are a big hit with locals, while the Christchurch Food Festival comes in May with stalls on the bowling green. Brilliant.
Minimum stay: 2 nights at weekends.

Rooms	14 doubles, 6 twins: £99-£199.
Meals	Lunch from £6.50.
	Sunday lunch from £15.
	Dinner, 3 courses: table d'hôte £18.50; à la carte about £30.
Closed	Never.
Directions	West into Christchurch on A35. 2nd left onto High Street, then left at roundabout into Castle Street. On left after 200m. Parking on right in lay-by.

Lukasz Dwornik
The Kings
18 Castle Street,
Christchurch BH23 1DT

Tel	+44 (0)1202 588933
Email	kings@harbourhotels.co.uk
Web	www.thekings-christchurch.co.uk

Rose & Crown

A charming northern refuge, beautiful inside and out. It stands in an idyllic village of mellow stone where little has changed in 200 years. The inn sits on the green next to a Saxon church and dates to 1733. Roses ramble above the door in summer, so pick up a pint, head for the terrace and watch life pass by. Inside, you can roast away in front of the fire in the bar while reading the *Teesdale Mercury*. Bedrooms are split between the converted barn (large and colourful, but less character), the main house (smarter altogether with the odd beam or wonky floor) and the cottage next door (warmly contemporary with a communal sitting room). All have Bose radios, good bathrooms, DVD players and free WiFi. Downstairs, the same menu runs in the colourful bar and the panelled restaurant, so grab a table wherever you like for some very tasty food, perhaps whitebait with courgette fritters, slow-roasted pork belly with bubble and squeak, tarte tatin with calvados ice-cream. High Force waterfall, the Yorkshire Dales and the Bowes Museum all wait. There's a drying room for walkers, too.

Rooms	8 doubles, 3 twins: £115–£160. 3 suites for 2: £180–£200.' Singles £95. Dinner, B&B from £79 p.p.
Meals	Lunch from £6.50. Dinner in bistro from £12; 4 courses in restaurant £35. Sunday lunch £19.50.
Closed	23-27 December and 1 week in January.
Directions	From Barnard Castle B6277 north for 6 miles. Right in village towards green. Inn on left.

Thomas & Cheryl Robinson
Rose & Crown
Romaldkirk,
Barnard Castle DL12 9EB

Tel	+44 (0)1833 650213
Email	hotel@rose-and-crown.co.uk
Web	www.rose-and-crown.co.uk

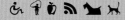

The Sun Inn

An idyllic village made rich by mills in the 16th century. These days you can hire boats on the river, so order a picnic at the inn, float down the glorious Stour, then tie up on the bank for lunch al fresco. You're in the epicentre of Constable country; the artist attended school in the village and often returned to paint St Mary's with its soaring tower; it stands directly opposite. As for The Sun, you couldn't hope to wash up in a better place. Step in to find open fires, boarded floors, timber frames and an easy elegance. A panelled lounge comes with sofas and armchairs, the bar is made from a slab of local elm and the dining room is beamed and airy, so come for fabulous food inspired by Italy: Calabrian salami, pheasant ravioli, spaghetti with chilli and lemon, venison stew with red wine and shallots. Rooms are gorgeous: creaking floorboards, timber-framed walls, a panelled four-poster. Those at the back (a recent addition) are bigger and come in grand style, but all are lovely with crisp linen and power showers in excellent bathrooms. There's afternoon tea on arrival if you book in advance. *Minimum stay: 2 nights if booking Saturday night.*

Rooms	5 doubles, 1 twin/double, 1 four-poster: £85–£155. Singles £85–£130. Dinner, B&B £86–£110 p.p. Extra bed/sofabed available £15 p.p. per night.
Meals	Lunch from £10.95. Dinner from £16.95. Not Monday lunch.
Closed	Christmas.
Directions	A12 north past Colchester. 2nd exit, signed Dedham. In village opposite church.

Piers Baker
The Sun Inn
High Street, Dedham,
Colchester CO7 6DF

Tel	+44 (0)1206 323351
Email	office@thesuninndedham.com
Web	www.thesuninndedham.com

Maison Talbooth

An outdoor swimming pool that's heated to 29°C every day, a chauffeur on hand to whisk you down to the hotel's riverside restaurant, a grand piano in the golden sitting room where those in the know gather for a legendary afternoon tea. They don't do things by halves at Maison Talbooth, a small-scale pleasure dome with long views across Constable country. The house, an old rectory, stands in three acres of manicured grounds, the fabulous pool house a huge draw with its open fire, honesty bar, beautiful art and treatment rooms. Interiors are equally alluring. There are no rooms, only suites, each divine. Some on the ground floor have doors onto terraces where hot tubs wait, but all pamper you rotten with flawless bathrooms, fabulous beds, vintage wallpapers, hi-tech excess. At dinner you're chauffeured to the family's restaurants (both within half a mile): Milsoms for bistro food served informally, Le Talbooth for more serious fare, perhaps roasted scallops with a Sauternes velouté, fillet of halibut with walnuts and apple, banoffee soufflé with caramelised banana crumble. A great escape.

Rooms	12 suites for 4: £210–£420. Singles from £170.
Meals	Dinner, 3 courses, at Milsoms £25; at Le Talbooth £35–£50.
Closed	Never.
Directions	North on A12 past Colchester. Left to Dedham, right after S-bend. Maison Talbooth is on right; follow brown signs.

Paul & Geraldine Milsom
Maison Talbooth
Stratford Road, Dedham,
Colchester CO7 6HN

Tel	+44 (0)1206 322367
Email	maison@milsomhotels.com
Web	www.milsomhotels.com

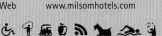

The Mistley Thorn

This Georgian pub stands on the high street and dates back to 1746, but inside you find a fresh contemporary feel that will tickle your pleasure receptors. The mood is laid-back with a great little bar, an excellent restaurant and bedrooms that pack an understated punch. Downstairs, an open-plan feel sweeps you through high-ceilinged rooms that flood with light. Expect tongue-and-groove panelling, Farrow & Ball colours, blond wood furniture and smart wicker chairs. Climb up to excellent rooms for smartly dressed beds, flat-screen TVs, DVD players and iPod docks; you get power showers above double-ended baths too. Those at the front have fine views of the Stour estuary, all are exceptional value for money. Back down in the restaurant dig into delicious food; Sherri runs a cookery school next door and has a pizzeria in town. Try smoked haddock chowder, Debden duck with clementine sauce, chocolate mocha tart. Constable country is all around. There's history, too; the Witch-Finder General once lived here. Sunday nights are a steal: £100 for two with dinner included. Brilliant.

Rooms	5 doubles, 3 twin/doubles: £100–£145. Singles from £85. Dinner, B&B, from £72.50 p.p.
Meals	Lunch from £4.95. Dinner, 3 courses, about £30.
Closed	Rarely.
Directions	From A12 Hadleigh/East Bergholt exit north of Colchester. Thro' East Bergholt to A137; signed Manningtree; continue to Mistley High St. 50 yds from station.

David McKay & Sherri Singleton
The Mistley Thorn
High Street, Mistley,
Manningtree CO11 1HE

Tel	+44 (0)1206 392821
Email	info@mistleythorn.co.uk
Web	www.mistleythorn.co.uk

The Pier at Harwich

You're bang on the water, overlooking the historic Ha'penny Pier, with vast skies and watery views that shoot across to Felixstowe. The hotel was built in 1862 in the style of a Venetian palazzo and has remained in continuous service ever since. Inside are boarded floors, big arched windows, a granite bar and travel posters framed on the walls. Eat informally in the bistro downstairs (fish pie, grilled bream, beef stew and dumplings) or grab a window seat in the first-floor dining room and tuck into lobster bisque while huge ferries glide past outside. The owners took over the adjoining pub several years ago and have carved out a pretty lounge with port-hole windows, leather sofas, coir matting, timber frames, even a piano. Bedrooms are scattered about, some above the sitting room, others in the main house. All are pretty, with padded bedheads, seaside colours, crisp white linen, super bathrooms; if you want the best view in town, splash out on the Mayflower suite. Don't miss the blue flag beach at Dovercourt for exhilarating walks, or the Electric Palace, the second oldest cinema in Britain.

Rooms	1 suite for 2: £200-£230.
	13 annexes for 2: £120-£230.
	Singles from £92.
Meals	Lunch, 2 courses, from £20.
	Sunday lunch £29.
	Dinner à la carte £25-£40.
Closed	Never.
Directions	M25 junc. 28, A12 to Colchester
	bypass, then A120 to Harwich. Head
	for quay. Hotel opposite pier.

Paul & Geraldine Milsom
The Pier at Harwich
The Quay,
Harwich CO12 3HH

Tel	+44 (0)1255 241212
Email	pier@milsomhotels.com
Web	www.milsomhotels.com

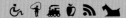

Tudor Farmhouse Hotel

This gorgeous small hotel sits on the edge of the Forest of Dean, a magical world of woodland walks, medieval castles, meandering rivers and bleating sheep. You're in the middle of a tiny village with lush views from a pretty garden – stone walls, postage-stamp lawn, a couple of cottages forming a courtyard. Inside, an airy elegance mixes with exposed stone walls and original timber frames, the house bearing testament to its Tudor roots. Bedrooms are lovely, some smaller, others huge, but all have smart fabrics, robes in fine bathrooms and super-comfy beds. They are scattered about, a few in the main house, others with exposed stone walls in pretty outbuildings; the loft suite is exceptional and comes with a claw-foot bath and an enormous glass shower. But it's not just style, there's plenty of substance, with fabulous food in the chic little restaurant, perhaps smoked salmon mousse, rare-breed beef, treacle tart with stout ice-cream. There are home-laid eggs for breakfast, too. Don't miss Puzzle Wood or Clearwell Caves. You can kayak on the Wye or join a guide and forage in the forest.

Rooms	14 doubles, 3 twins, 2 four-posters: £95-£170. 2 suites for 2: £190-£210. Singles from £85.
Meals	Lunch from £6.95. Sunday lunch from £14.50. Dinner, 3 courses, £30-£40.
Closed	Never.
Directions	South from Monmouth on A466. Clearwell signed left after 3 miles.

Colin & Hari Fell
Tudor Farmhouse Hotel
High Street,
Clearwell GL16 8JS
Tel   +44 (0)1594 833046
Email   info@tudorfarmhousehotel.co.uk
Web   www.tudorfarmhousehotel.co.uk

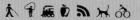

Three Choirs Vineyards

England's answer to the Napa Valley. After 15 years of tilling the soil (very sandy, good drainage), Thomas's 75 acres of Gloucestershire hillside now produce 300,000 bottles a year. There are regular tastings, a shop in which to buy a bottle or two, and paths that weave through the vines – a perfect stroll after a good meal. What's more, three fabulous lodges wait down by the lake, all with decks and walls of glass. You'll find claw-foot baths and comfy beds, so camp out in grand savannah style and listen to the woodpeckers. Rooms up at the restaurant are smart and spacious with terraces that overlook the vineyard. They come with padded bedheads, walls of colour, leather armchairs, flat-screen TVs and good little bathrooms. Finally, the restaurant: claret walls, an open fire, lovely views. Excellent food waits, perhaps goat's cheese soufflé with beetroot crisps, spiced monkfish with mango purée, sticky toffee pudding with cinnamon ice-cream. World wines are on the list, but you'll plump for something from the vines that surround you; there's a microbrewery, too. Wonderful. *Minimum stay: 2 nights at weekends.*

Rooms	6 doubles, 2 twins, 3 vineyard lodges for 2: £135–£195. Singles from £105. Half-board from £105 p.p. (min. 2 nights).
Meals	Lunch from £7.50. Dinner à la carte about £35.
Closed	Christmas & New Year.
Directions	From Newent north on B4215 for about 1.5 miles. Follow brown signs to vineyard.

Thomas Shaw
Three Choirs Vineyards
Castle Tump,
Newent GL18 1LS

Tel   +44 (0)1531 890223
Email info@threechoirs.com
Web   www.three-choirs-vineyards.co.uk

Beaumont House

Fan and Alan have lived all over the world and came back to England to open the sort of hotel they like to stay in themselves. It's a very friendly place, nothing is too much trouble. Throw a few luxuries into the mix – stylish bedrooms, excellent breakfasts, an honesty bar in the airy sitting room – and you have a great base for all things Cheltenham. Spotless bedrooms spread over three floors. Some are simpler, others more extravagant, but all have lovely bathrooms and every budget will be happy. Compact, airy doubles on the lower ground floor are perfect for short stays. Rooms above are bigger, some with striking design. One has an African theme, another has far-eastern wood carvings, there are vast headboards, smart furniture and flat-screen TVs. You breakfast in an elegant dining room, perhaps freshly made porridge, American pancakes, smoked haddock, the full cooked works. Good restaurants wait in town (and there's live jazz at Daffodil's on Monday nights). As for Cheltenham, it has festivals coming out of its ears: folk, jazz, food, science, music, literature and horses. Brilliant. *Sofabed available.*

Rooms	9 doubles, 2 twin/doubles: £89-£190. 2 suites for 4: £165-£249. 1 family room for 4: £125-£180. 2 singles: £69-£79.
Meals	Restaurants within walking distance. Room service Mon-Thur eves.
Closed	Rarely.
Directions	Leave one-way system in centre of town for Stroud (south) on A46. Straight ahead, through lights and right at 1st mini-roundabout. On left after 500m.

Alan & Fan Bishop
Beaumont House
56 Shurdington Road,
Cheltenham GL53 0JE

Tel	+44 (0)1242 223311
Email	reservations@bhhotel.co.uk
Web	www.bhhotel.co.uk

No. 131

This funky new addition to Cheltenham's buzzing scene is a bone fide jaw-dropper – impeccable Georgian architecture outside, 21st-century chic within. Interiors mix all the lovely old stuff: stripped floors, chandeliers, ceiling friezes, period colours, with lots of lovely new stuff: enormous sofas, hanging lampshades, a cool collection of contemporary art. You'll find roaring fires, blue leather bar stools, vintage tiles, old wooden fridges piled high with hams and cheese. Downstairs, the bar has a retractable roof, turning itself into a terrace in summer, with a DJ station for the odd weekend. Upstairs, bedrooms have huge style: piles of art books, big beds, the best linen, perhaps a fancy bath in your room; all have robes and walk-in showers in flawless bathrooms. Downstairs, you mingle with happy locals in the bars and restaurants, where great food waits, perhaps grilled sardines with chilli and garlic, half a lobster or a juicy steak, treacle tart with clotted cream. In summer life spills onto the front terrace, overlooking Imperial Gardens. Don't miss the jazz festival in May.

Rooms	11 doubles: £150-£220.
Meals	Lunch from £7.
	Sunday lunch from £12.
	Dinner, 3 courses, about £40.
Closed	Never.
Directions	Pick up one-way system in the middle of town and follow it to its southwestern corner at Imperial Square; left onto the Promenade, signed 'M5, Gloucester, Oxford'. Hotel on right after 400m before lights.

Stephen Wadcock
No. 131
131 The Promenade,
Cheltenham GL50 1NW

Tel	+44 (0)1242 822939
Email	reservations@no131.com
Web	www.no131.com

No. 38

Not content with having one super-cool hotel in town, Sam and Georgina have opened another. The idea here is that you get the same stunning style, but in the peace and privacy of a design B&B. Downstairs, there's an elegant sitting room with deep sofas, fresh flowers and contemporary art, then a breakfast room that could double as an American diner, where you can eat on stools at a bar watching the chef cook your breakfast. You can eat out on the terrace when the sun shines, or in front of a fire in winter. Drinks at the honesty bar are chilled in a wall of antique wooden refrigerators – nothing here is done by halves. Bedrooms are flawless, infinitely better than most hotels. Smaller rooms have beautiful beds, mohair throws, fantastic art and walk-in showers. Bigger rooms have all that and more – perhaps a zinc bath in the room, or enormous wet rooms with showers for two. Pitt Park is opposite, the racecourse up the road, taxis are provided to whisk you up to the other hotel for cocktails and a slap-up dinner. Take the whole place for a house party and a chef will come to cook. Dogs are welcome.

Rooms	13 doubles: £120-£180.
Meals	Breakfast £5-£12. Restaurants within 500m. Taxis to their sister restaurant provided free.
Closed	Never.
Directions	Head north from centre on A435, following signs to racecourse and Pittville Pump Room. On left, at crossroads/traffic lights, after 0.5 mile.

Stephen Wadcock
No. 38
38 Evesham Road,
Cheltenham GL52 2AH

Tel	+44 (0)1242 822929
Email	reservations@no38thepark.com
Web	www.no38thepark.com

The Wheatsheaf

The Wheatsheaf stands at the vanguard of a cool new movement: the village local reborn in country-house style. It's a winning formula with locals and travellers flocking in for a heady mix of laid-back informality and chic English style. The inn stands between pretty hills in this ancient wool village on the Fosse Way. Inside, happy young staff flit about, throwing logs on the fire, ferrying food to diners, or simply stopping for a chat. Downstairs, you find armchairs in front of smouldering fires, noble portraits on panelled walls, cool tunes playing in the background. Outside, a smart courtyard garden draws a crowd in summer, so much so it has its own bar; English ales, jugs of Pimm's and lovely wines all wait. Back inside, beautiful bedrooms come as standard, some bigger than others, all fully loaded with comfort and style. Expect period colours, Hypnos beds, Bang & Olufsen TVs, then spectacular bathrooms with beautiful baths and/or power showers. As for the food, you feast on lovely local fare, perhaps devilled kidneys, coq au vin, pear and almond tart. Don't miss it.

Rooms	14 doubles: £120–£180.
	Extra bed £25 child, £50 adult.
Meals	Continental breakfast included;
	cooked extras £5-£12. Lunch from £9.
	Dinner, 3 courses, about £30.
Closed	Never.
Directions	In village centre, off A429 between
	Stow & Burford.

James Parn
The Wheatsheaf
West End, Northleach,
Cheltenham GL54 3EZ

Tel	+44 (0)1451 860244
Email	reservations@cotswoldswheatsheaf.com
Web	www.cotswoldswheatsheaf.com

Wesley House Restaurant

A 15th-century timber-framed house on Winchcombe's ancient high street; John Wesley stayed in 1755, hence the name. Not satisfied with one excellent restaurant, Matthew has opened another next door. The elder statesman comes in traditional style with sofas in front of a roaring fire, candles flickering on smartly dressed tables and a conservatory for delicious breakfasts with views of town and country. Next door, the young upstart is unashamedly contemporary with a smoked-glass bar, faux zebra-skinned stools and hidden alcoves. Both buildings have lots of original architecture: timber frames, beamed ceilings, stone flags and stripped boards. Bedrooms up in the eaves are decidedly cosy, but fine for a night or two. One has a balcony with views over rooftops field and hill. All come in traditional style with good beds, floral fabrics, small showers and wonky floors. Back downstairs, dig into food as simple or as rich as you want, anything from fishcakes or a good burger to a three-course feast. The Cotswolds Way skirts the town, so bring your walking boots.

Rooms	3 doubles, 1 twin/double, 1 twin: £90–£100. Singles from £65. Dinner, B&B (for 1-night stays on Sat) £185 per room.
Meals	Bar & grill: lunch & dinner from £9.50 (not Sun or Mon). Restaurant: lunch from £14.50, dinner £20–£25 or £39.50 on Sat. Not Sun nights (except B&B).
Closed	Boxing Day.
Directions	From Cheltenham B4632 to Winchcombe. Restaurant on right. Drop off luggage, parking nearby.

Matthew Brown
Wesley House Restaurant
High Street, Winchcombe,
Cheltenham GL54 5LJ

Tel	+44 (0)1242 602366
Email	enquiries@wesleyhouse.co.uk
Web	www.wesleyhouse.co.uk

Horse & Groom

A happy pub informally run with lovely food, stylish interiors and wines and beers for all. It stands at the top of the hill with views on one side that pour over the Cotswolds. Inside, stripped floors, open fires and the odd stone wall give a smart rustic feel. Outside you can sit under the shade of damson trees and watch chefs gather eggs from the coop or carrots from the kitchen garden. Uncluttered bedrooms are nicely plush and come in contemporary country-house style with beautiful linen, pretty art, a padded window seat or two. One room is huge, the garden room opens onto the terrace, and those at the front are soundproofed to minimise noise from the road. This is a hive of youthful endeavour with two brothers at the helm. Will cooks, Tom pours the ales (or Cotswold vodka), and a cheery conviviality flows. Delicious food waits. Most is sourced within 30 miles and it's much prized by canny locals, so come for fish soup, pork and chorizo meatballs, Granny G's unmissable toffee meringue. Breakfast is a feast with homemade croissants, local milk in bottles and blocks of patted butter. *Minimum stay: 2 nights at weekends.*

Rooms	5 doubles: £120–£170. Singles from £80.
Meals	Lunch from £4.75. Dinner, 3 courses, £25–£30. Not Sunday night.
Closed	Christmas Day & New Year's Eve.
Directions	West from Moreton-in-Marsh on A44. Climb hill in Bourton-on-the-Hill; pub at top on left. Moreton-in-Marsh railway station 2 miles away.

Tom & Will Greenstock
Horse & Groom
Bourton-on-the-Hill,
Moreton-in-Marsh GL56 9AQ
Tel   +44 (0)1386 700413
Email   greenstocks@horseandgroom.info
Web   www.horseandgroom.info

Entry 112   Map 3

The Malt House

A 300-year-old malt house built of golden stone in a peaceful Cotswold village. Outside, the garden rolls down to a stream with a small orchard rising beyond; in summer you can have breakfast on the terrace with colour all around. Inside, total refurbishment. There's lots of old world charm: parquet flooring, mullioned windows, original beams and a mantelpiece that almost touches the ceiling. Sofas wait in front of the fire, Arts & Crafts furniture abounds, you'll find the daily papers and an honesty bar. Bedrooms come with beautiful wallpapers, colourful fabrics and delicious white linen on comfy beds. There are old-style radiators and sparkling bathrooms, while garden rooms tend to be a little bigger: one has ceilings open to the rafters, another a tiny balcony. Breakfast is a treat: fruit from the orchard in season, bacon and eggs cooked on the Aga, croissants and muffins, figs and rhubarb compote. There's croquet on the lawn, a productive kitchen garden and champagne cocktails on the terrace before dinner, maybe pan-fried scallops, Cotswold lamb, sticky toffee pudding. *Minimum stay: 2 nights at weekends May-August.*

Rooms	1 double, 4 twin/doubles, 1 four-poster: £120-£150. 1 suite for 2: £165. Extra bed/sofabed available £20-£60 p.p. per night.
Meals	Pub 200 yards. Dinner by arrangement (min. 12 guests). Seagrave Arms 3 miles.
Closed	One week over Christmas.
Directions	From Oxford A44 through Moreton-in-Marsh; right on B4081 for Chipping Campden. Entering village 1st right for Broad Campden. Hotel 1 mile on left.

June Denton
The Malt House
Broad Campden,
Chipping Campden GL55 6UU

Tel	+44 (0)1386 840295
Email	stay@thecotswoldmalthouse.com
Web	www.thecotswoldmalthouse.com

The Cotswold House Hotel & Spa

A deeply cool hotel – fabulous gardens, wonderful art, bedrooms that pack a beautiful punch. It stands on the high street in one of the Cotswolds prettiest villages, an ornament in golden stone with a wool-packers hall that dates to 1340. As for the hotel, it stretches back through stunning gardens to a smart spa with treatment rooms, a hammam, even a hydrotherapy pool. There's a croquet lawn, a beautiful terrace, deep borders packed with colour, deckchairs and sun loungers scattered about. Inside, a clipped elegance runs throughout: a pillared entrance hall, a restaurant filled with contemporary art, an airy brasserie that's open all day. Bedrooms spoil you rotten. Huge beds have shimmering throws, you get Bang & Olufsen TVs, armchairs or sofas, then seriously fancy bathrooms. A couple have Italian stone baths, another a shower for two. As for the suites, some have open fires or hot tubs on private terraces. Lovely food waits downstairs, perhaps salmon fishcakes, a good steak, a plate of local cheeses. Don't miss Broadway Tower for extraordinary views. *Minimum stay: 2 nights at weekends.*

Rooms	14 doubles, 10 twin/doubles: £120–£500. 6 suites for 2: £270–£450.
Meals	Lunch from £6. Dinner: brasserie from £12.50; dining room, 5 courses, £55.
Closed	Never.
Directions	From Oxford, A44 north for Evesham. 5 miles after Moreton-in-Marsh, right on B4081 to Chipping Campden. Hotel in square by town hall.

Michael Obray
The Cotswold House Hotel & Spa
The Square,
Chipping Campden GL55 6AN

Tel	+44 (0)1386 840330
Email	reservations@cotswoldhouse.com
Web	www.cotswoldhouse.com

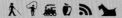

Entry 114   Map 3

Seagrave Arms

An elegant Georgian inn at the foot of Dover's Hill – climb up for huge views over the Vale of Evesham. Inside, it's almost Dickensian, a warren of small rooms with low ceilings, period colours, good art and crackling fires. Ancient flagstones lead to the bar, where locals gather to chew the cud over a pint of Hook Norton. Paul, once an advisor to the government of Botswana, swapped the city for the country and hasn't stopped since. You'll find padded window seats, half-panelled walls, candles flicking at night, then lots of colour and a happy vibe. Bedrooms are scattered about, some in the main house, others in converted stables (dog-friendly). They may differ in size (a couple are small), but all have the same cool style with Farrow & Ball colours, the crispest linen and excellent bathrooms with REN oils; the suite, with its super-cool bathroom, is worth splashing out on. Good food waits downstairs, perhaps smoked salmon mousse, venison bourguignon, apple and cinnamon crumble. In summer you decant onto a gravelled terrace or a small lawned garden. The Cotswold Way is close.

Rooms	7 doubles: £95–£125. 1 suite for 3: £125–£150.
Meals	Lunch from £5.95. Dinner, 3 courses, about £30. Not Monday.
Closed	Never.
Directions	Leave A44 at Broadway for B4632 towards Stratford-upon-Avon. In village.

Paul Denton
Seagrave Arms
Friday Street, Weston Subedge,
Chipping Campden GL55 6QH
Tel   +44 (0)1386 840192
Email   info@seagravearms.co.uk
Web   www.seagravearms.co.uk

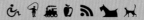

The Anchor Inn

This smart country dining pub has a lovely style. The house is Edwardian with 14th-century roots and its treasure-trove interiors are full of beautiful things: timber frames, wavy beams, oils by the score, trumpets and a piano in the bar. Old photographs of Charterhouse School cover the walls, there are sofas by the fire in the panelled bar and busts on plinths in the airy restaurant, where you dine on proper English food: devilled kidneys, lemon sole, treacle tart with clotted cream. Doors open onto a lawned garden with country views, so come in summer for lunch in the sun. Bedrooms upstairs are seriously indulging. Expect beautifully upholstered armchairs, seagrass matting, fine linen on comfy beds, flat-screen TVs. There are power showers, huge towels and bathrobes, too. The suite is open to the rafters and comes with Nelson and friends framed on the wall, then an enormous window that opens onto a private balcony. Don't come looking for a gastropub; do come looking for good ales, sublime food and old-world interiors. A treat.

Rooms	4 doubles, 1 suite for 2: £120.
Meals	Lunch & dinner £6.50–£30.
Closed	Rarely.
Directions	Leave A31 for Bentley, 4 miles west of Farnham. West through village, north for Lower Froyle. Inn on left in village.

Kevin Chandler
The Anchor Inn
Lower Froyle,
Alton GU34 4NA

Tel	+44 (0)1420 23261
Email	info@anchorinnatlowerfroyle.co.uk
Web	www.anchorinnatlowerfroyle.co.uk

The Peat Spade

You're lost in the lanes of the Test Valley, its famous river passing 300 metres from the front door. This is a lovely rural base from which to explore: Danebury hillfort is a short stroll, Winchester, Salisbury and the New Forest are close. The inn stands in the middle of the village in the shadow of a fine old church. Inside, interiors have lots of colour and style – stripped floorboards, an open fire, fishing rods that hang from the ceiling in the rod room. You'll find lovely old photographs on the walls, the odd pith helmet on display, even a local cat that comes to snooze. Attractive bedrooms – some above the shop, others in the old peat house – have wooden beds, pretty fabrics, painted beams and walk-in showers. Back downstairs tasty food waits, maybe Portland crab, Dover sole, spotted dick and custard. In summer, doors open onto a terrace with a fire pit. Don't miss Longstock Park Water Gardens, part of the Leckford estate: it's owned by Waitrose and the farm shop is quite something. As for the Test, its legendary chalk streams wait for fishermen; permits are available at the bar.

Rooms	6 doubles, 2 twin/doubles: £100–£130. Singles from £80.
Meals	Lunch from £6.50. Dinner, 3 courses, about £30. Sunday lunch from £22.
Closed	Rarely.
Directions	A3057 north from Stockbridge, then left after a mile for Longstock. In village.

Ben Mayberry
The Peat Spade
Village Street, Longstock,
Stockbridge SO20 6DR

Tel	+44 (0)1264 810612
Email	info@peatspadeinn.co.uk
Web	www.peatspadeinn.co.uk

Daisybank Cottage Boutique B&B

This cute B&B in the New Forest mixes a warm contemporary style with some fine old-fashioned hospitality – Ciaran and Cheryl go out of their way to make your stay special. As for their Arts & Crafts house, it sits on the southern fringes of Brockenhurst with a pretty garden at the back, where free-range hens strut their stuff. Inside, spoiling bedrooms come with airy colours, plantation shutters, then Vi-Spring mattresses for beautiful beds and robes in striking bathrooms. One has a small courtyard, another a claw-foot bath, and the room at the back opens onto the garden. All have coffee machines, silent fridges in which to chill drinks, iPod docks and flat-screen TVs. Breakfast is a local feast – eggs from the garden, artisan jams and honey, home-baked soda bread and granola, bacon and sausages from a New Forest farm. After which you can walk by the sea, hire bikes and explore the forest or spin across to the Isle of Wight. A shepherd's hut in the garden may soon be available for B&B. Good restaurants wait in town (a ten-minute stroll); posher ones are further afield. *Children over 10 welcome. Extra beds £40.*

Rooms	5 doubles: £100–£140. Singles from £90.
Meals	Local restaurants within half a mile.
Closed	One week over Christmas.
Directions	M27, junc. 1, then A337 south for Lymington. Right onto B3055 as you approach Brockenhurst. Over x-roads and signed left after half a mile.

Cheryl & Ciaran Maher
Daisybank Cottage Boutique B&B
Sway Road,
Brockenhurst SO42 7SG

Tel	+44 (0)1590 622086
Email	info@bedandbreakfast-newforest.co.uk
Web	www.bedandbreakfast-newforest.co.uk

The Master Builder's House Hotel

The position here is hard to beat: lawns roll down to the river, curlews race across the water, a vast sky hangs above. The house, built in 1729, was home to the shipwrights who built Nelson's fleet, with Agamemnon, Euryalus and Swiftsure all going on to fight at Trafalgar. Flags commemorating his victories hang in the hall, bedrooms are named after his ships. As for the hotel, there's a pretty sitting room that opens onto a smart terrace, a yachtsman's bar for a pint of ale, then open fires, warm colours, and good food in the chic restaurant, perhaps smoked salmon and mackerel cannelloni, Gressingham duck with spicy red cabbage, ginger beer jelly with poached rhubarb. There's a barbecue in the garden at weekends that's popular with walkers, and a giant chess board for visiting grand masters. Bedrooms in the main house have lots of colour, bags of character, big views and Indian furniture. Those in the annexe are small, standard hotel rooms, though bathrooms are good. Walk by the river, take a ferry up to the estuary or bring your bike and explore the forest.

Rooms	7 doubles, 18 twin/doubles £110-£205. 1 suite for 2: £130-£205. 2 cottages for 4: £205. Singles from £120. Dinner, B&B from £100 p.p.
Meals	Lunch from £7.50. Dinner, 3 courses, £22-£30.
Closed	Never.
Directions	From Lyndhurst B3056 south past Beaulieu turn-off. 1st left, signed Bucklers Hard. Hotel signed left after 1 mile.

Clive Watts
The Master Builder's House Hotel
Bucklers Hard, Beaulieu,
Brockenhurst SO42 7XB

Tel	+44 (0)1590 616253
Email	enquiries@themasterbuilders.co.uk
Web	www.themasterbuilders.co.uk

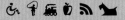

The Montagu Arms Hotel

Beaulieu, an ancient royal hunting ground, was gifted to Cistercian monks by King John in 1204. Their abbey took 40 years to build and you can see its ruins in the nearby grounds of Palace House, seat of the Montagu family since 1538. As for the village, its tiny high street is a hotchpotch of 17th-century timber-framed houses that totter by the tidal estuary drinking in the view. The hotel dates to 1742, but was re-modelled in 1925 and interiors have an Edwardian country-house feel. You'll find roaring fires, parquet flooring, a library bar and a courtyard garden, where you can eat in summer. Traditional bedrooms vary in size, but all come with pretty fabrics, period furniture, good bathrooms, a sofa if there's room. Downstairs, a Michelin star in the dining room brings with it some fabulous food, so try Dover sole with brown shrimps, saddle of roe deer with parsnip purée, praline soufflé with dark chocolate ice-cream. There's a gastropub if you want something lighter: local fish pie, great steaks, ham and chips with poached eggs from resident hens. Beautiful walks start from the front door. *Minimum stay: 2 nights at weekends.*

Rooms	7 doubles, 3 twin/doubles, 4 four-posters: £143-£238. 5 suites for 2: £233-£348. Singles from £129. Dinner, B&B from £121.50 p.p.
Meals	Lunch £6.50-£25. Sunday lunch £29.50. Dinner, 3 courses, £70 (not Monday nights in main restaurant).
Closed	Never.
Directions	South from M27, junc. 1 to Lyndhurst on A337, then B3056 for Beaulieu. Left into village and hotel on right.

Sunil Kanjanghat
The Montagu Arms Hotel
Palace Lane, Beaulieu,
Brockenhurst SO42 7ZL

Tel	+44 (0)1590 612324
Email	reservations@montaguarmshotel.co.uk
Web	www.montaguarmshotel.co.uk

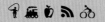

The Mill at Gordleton

Another wormhole back to old England, a 400-year-old mill on Avon Water with mallards, lampreys and Indian runners to watch from the terrace in summer. The house stands in three acres of gardens that are filled with art and beautiful things. Inside, cosy interiors mix old and new delightfully: low ceilings, wonky walls, busts and mirrors, smouldering fires. Colour tumbles from pretty fabrics, there's a panelled bar for pre-dinner drinks, then bedrooms which are full of character. The suite above the wheelhouse has a fabulous bathroom, you'll find lots of colour, sheets and blankets, bowls of fruit. Three rooms have watery views (you can fall asleep to the sound of the river), most have fancy new bathrooms, all have robes and White Company oils; and while a lane passes outside, you are more likely to be woken by birdsong. Downstairs, the beautifully refurbished restaurant continues to draw a happy crowd for its delicious local food, perhaps wild mushroom ravioli, Creedy Carver free-range duck, blackberry soufflé with apple crumble ice-cream. The forest and coast are both on your doorstep. *Minimum stay: 2 nights at weekends April-October.*

Rooms	3 doubles, 3 twin/doubles: £150-£195. 2 suites for 2: £150-£275. Singles from £115.
Meals	Lunch from £6.95. Sunday lunch from £21.50. Dinner £22.50-£27.50; à la carte about £40.
Closed	Christmas Day.
Directions	South from Brockenhurst on A337 for 4 miles. After 2nd roundabout 1st right, signed Hordle. On right after 2 miles.

Liz Cottingham
The Mill at Gordleton
Silver Street, Sway,
Lymington SO41 6DJ

Tel	+44 (0)1590 682219
Email	info@themillatgordleton.co.uk
Web	www.themillatgordleton.co.uk

Chewton Glen

Chewton Glen is one of England's loveliest country-house hotels. It opened in 1964 with eight bedrooms and even though it now has over 50, it remains delightfully intimate. Fifty years of evolution have brought a pillared swimming pool, a hydrotherapy spa, a golf course and a tennis centre. It recently added 12 treehouse suites, which sit peacefully in their own valley with hot tubs on balconies and wood-burners waiting inside. As for the hotel, beauty waits at every turn: stately sitting rooms, roaring fires, busts and oils, a bar that opens onto a sun-trapping terrace. Bedrooms are the best. Some come in country-house style, but most have a contemporary feel. Expect marble bathrooms, private balconies, designer fabrics, faultless housekeeping. Outside, four gardeners tend 130 acres of lawns and woodland, with a kitchen garden that helps the restaurant, so you'll eat well; perhaps Dorset crab, Devon duck, Charentais melon soup. You can atone in style: a walk on the beach, mountain biking in the New Forest, croquet on the lawn in summer. Hard to beat. *Minimum stay: 2 nights at weekends.*

Rooms	5 doubles, 30 twin/doubles: £325–£685. 23 suites for 2: £610–£1,580. 12 treehouses for 2: £700–£1,450.
Meals	Breakfast: £21–£26. Lunch, 3 courses, £25. Sunday lunch £39.50. Dinner, 3 courses, £55–£65. Tasting menu £70. Light meals available throughout the day.
Closed	Never.
Directions	A337 west from Lymington. Through New Milton for Christchurch. Right at r'bout, signed Walkford. Right again; hotel on right.

Andrew Stembridge
Chewton Glen
Christchurch Road,
New Milton BH25 7QT

Tel	+44 (0)1425 275341
Email	reservations@chewtonglen.com
Web	www.chewtonglen.com

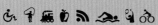

Castle House

Hereford's loveliest hotel stands 200 paces from the city's magnificent 11th-century cathedral, home to the Mappa Mundi. It's English to its core with a beautiful garden that overlooks what remains of the old castle's moat; in summer you can eat out here watching ducks glide by. Inside, the lap of luxury waits: a fine staircase, painted panelling, a delicious restaurant for the best food in town. Big bedrooms are lavish. Those in the main house are more traditional (the top-floor suite runs all the way along the front of the house); those in the townhouse (a 30-second stroll) are distinctly 21st century. All have a smart country-house feel with beautiful fabrics, super-comfy beds, crisp white linen, excellent bathrooms. Seriously good food, much from the owner's nearby farm, waits in the restaurant, perhaps goat's cheese ravioli, pan-fried sea bass, rhubarb mousse with ginger ice-cream. You can atone with a stroll along the river Wye, which runs through the park behind. Pop-up opera, guided walks and Evensong in the cathedral... and don't miss the Three Choirs Festival in July.

Rooms	1 double, 3 doubles: £150–£190. 16 suites for 2: £195–£230. 4 singles: £130.
Meals	Lunch from £5. Sunday lunch from £18.50. Dinner, 3 courses, about £35.
Closed	Never.
Directions	Follow signs to Hereford city centre, then City Centre east. Right off Bath St into Union St, through St Peters Sq to Owen's St, right into St Ethelbert St. Hotel on left as road veers right.

Michelle Marriott-Lodge
Castle House
Castle Street,
Hereford HR1 2NW

Tel	+44 (0)1432 356321
Email	info@castlehse.co.uk
Web	www.castlehse.co.uk

The Verzon

The Verzon, once a Georgian farmhouse, sits on the road between Hereford and Ledbury with long views across open country to the Malvern Hills. It's owned by William and Kate Chase, farmers who turn potatoes and apples into into rather good vodka and gin. They also rear cattle and pigs up the road and have recently added a vineyard in the Luberon to their larder, so come to eat great local food and wash it down with lovely wines. Inside, big rooms mix contemporary touches with original features. Timber frames and Union Jack sofas wait in the bar, so grab a pint of Ledbury Gold – brewed next door – and roast away in front of the fire. Bedrooms upstairs have warm colours, crisp linen and robes in good bathrooms. Two have a bath in the room, the suites are huge, those at the back have the view (and no noise from the road). As for the food, it's the raison d'être of the hotel. Almost everything is sourced within 30 miles, with producers listed on the back of the menu, so try Hereford rarebit, Chase steaks, Evesham rhubarb and almond tart. Walk in Malvern Hills or head to Hereford cathedral for the Mappa Mundi.

Rooms	5 twin/doubles: £120.
	2 suites for 2: £150.
	1 single: £80-£90.
Meals	Lunch, 2 courses, from £16.
	Sandwiches from £5.
	Sunday lunch from £20.
	Dinner, 3 courses, £25-£35.
Closed	Never.
Directions	A438 west from Ledbury for 4 miles. On right, signed.

Imogen Heath
The Verzon
Hereford Road, Trumpet,
Ledbury HR8 2PZ

Tel	+44 (0)1531 670381
Email	info@verzonhouse.com
Web	www.verzonhouse.com

Glewstone Court Country House Hotel & Restaurant

Those in search of the small and friendly will love it here. Bill and Christine run their home with great style, instinctively disregarding the ordinary for a more colourful world. Their realm is this attractive country house filled with an eclectic collection of art and antiques. Eastern rugs cover wood floors, Bill's sporting caps hang on the walls, resident dogs snooze in front of the fire. Guests gather in the drawing-room bar to eat, drink and relax, decanting in summer to a pretty terrace, with croquet on the lawn in the shade of an ancient cedar of Lebanon. Back inside a fine Regency staircase spirals up to a galleried landing, where homely bedrooms wait (two are huge). Those at the front have views across the Wye Valley to the Forest of Dean; those at the back overlook orchards. Back downstairs, you dig into Christine's fabulous food in a beautiful dining room, where a fire burns brightly in winter. It's a big treat, perhaps honey-baked figs and Perl Las cheesecake, roast rump of Marches lamb, a deconstructed banoffee pie. There's roast beef with claret gravy for Sunday lunch, too. *Bargain breaks available. One-night bookings at weekends not always accepted.*

Rooms	6 doubles, 1 four-poster: £135-£160. 1 suite for 2: £160. 1 single: £75.
Meals	Lunch from £16. Sunday lunch £21. Dinner, 3 courses, about £30.
Closed	25-27 December.
Directions	From Ross-on-Wye A40 towards Monmouth. Right 1 mile south of Wilton r'bout for Glewstone. Hotel on left after 0.5 miles.

Christine & Bill Reeve-Tucker
Glewstone Court Country House Hotel
Glewstone,
Ross-on-Wye HR9 6AW

Tel	+44 (0)1989 770367
Email	info@glewstonecourt.com
Web	www.glewstonecourt.com

Wilton Court Restaurant with Rooms

A Grade-II listed house with a Grade-I listed mulberry tree; its berries are turned into sorbets and pies. The house dates to 1510 and looks across the lane to the river Wye: herons dive, otters swim, kingfishers nest. Roses ramble outside, happy guests potter within. This is a small, intimate hotel with pretty rooms, tasty food and owners that care. Bedrooms upstairs come in different shapes and sizes, but all have a nice fresh style. Those at the front have watery views, William Morris wallpaper, lots of space, perhaps a four-poster. A couple of rooms are small (as is their price), but, along with several others, have recently been refurbished. Expect warm colours, a wall of paper, white bathrooms and sofas in the bigger rooms. Back downstairs there's a wood-burner in the panelled bar, so stop for a pre-dinner drink, then hop across to the conservatory restaurant for some tasty food, perhaps seared king prawns, Barbary duck, and a silken cider panna cotta with apple crisp. A small garden across the lane drops down to the river for summer sundowners. Ross is a five-minute stroll. *Minimum stay: 2 nights at weekends.*

Rooms	3 doubles, 1 four-poster, 5 twin/doubles: £125–£175. 1 family suite for 4: £155–£195. Singles from £100.
Meals	Lunch from £12.75. Sunday lunch £16.95–£18.95. Dinner, 3 courses, about £35. 7-course tasting menu £52.50.
Closed	First 2 weeks in January.
Directions	South into Ross at A40/A49 Wilton roundabout. 1st right into Wilton Lane. Hotel on right.

Roger & Helen Wynn
Wilton Court Restaurant with Rooms
Wilton Lane, Wilton,
Ross-on-Wye HR9 6AQ

Tel	+44 (0)1989 562569
Email	info@wiltoncourthotel.com
Web	www.wiltoncourthotel.com

The Bridge House

The exterior of this Georgian house gives little idea of the lovely things that wait inside. It stands a few paces from Wilton Bridge, with gardens that run down towards the river Wye and St Mary's church looming beyond. Inside, a beautiful renovation comes in an uncluttered contemporary style, though Georgian bones have been allowed to shine, too. You'll find stripped floors, fresh flowers and an antique wall clock in the hall, then a chandelier and painted beams in the airy breakfast room. There's a fancy sitting room – charcoal walls and a wood-burner by the sofa – where Darren and Elena serve homemade cakes and tea on arrival, an extremely popular touch. Then it's upstairs to six lovely bedrooms that come with style and comfort in spades. Two have four-posters, a couple have claw-foot baths, most have river views. You'll find Farrow & Ball colours, luxurious linen atop fine mattresses, perhaps a sofa or a piece of antique furniture. The quietest rooms are at the back, a couple have views of the ruined castle. Also, period prints, excellent bathrooms and the full works at breakfast. *Minimum stay: 2 nights at weekends, Friday / Saturday.*

Rooms	6 doubles: £95–£115. Singles from £85.
Meals	Pubs/restaurants opposite.
Closed	Rarely.
Directions	A40 to Ross, then B4260 south for Ross-on-Wye. On left after 200m.

Darren & Elena Isiorho
The Bridge House
Wilton,
Ross-on-Wye HR9 6AA

Tel	+44 (0)1989 562655
Email	info@bridgehouserossonwye.co.uk
Web	www.bridgehouserossonwye.co.uk

The George Hotel

The George is a kingly retreat: Charles II stayed in 1671 and you can sleep in his room with its panelling and high ceilings. The house – a grand mansion in the middle of tiny Yarmouth – has stupendous views of the Solent; Admiral Sir Robert Holmes took full advantage when in residence, nipping off to sack passing ships. These days traditional interiors mix with contemporary design. Ancient panelling and stone flags come as standard in the old house, but push on past the crackling fire in the bar and find Isla's Conservatory, where big windows pull in the view. Doors opens onto the terrace and you can eat here in summer, next to the castle walls, with sailboats zipping past – a good spot for bouillabaisse, steak frites or a goat's cheese salad. Bedrooms come in country-house style, some with crowns above the bed, others with fabulous views. Two rooms have balconies that overlook the water, but smaller rooms at the back have the same homely style. Head off to Osborne House, Cowes for the regatta or The Needles for magical coastal walks. A great escape.
Minimum stay: 2 nights at weekends.

Rooms	17 twin/doubles: £190-£287.
	2 singles: £99.
Meals	Lunch from £15.
	Dinner, 3 courses, about £40.
Closed	Rarely.
Directions	Lymington ferry to Yarmouth, then follow signs to town centre.

Dianne Thompson
The George Hotel
Quay Street,
Yarmouth PO41 0PE

Tel	+44 (0)1983 760331
Email	res@thegeorge.co.uk
Web	www.thegeorge.co.uk

Hillside

A lovely small hotel with a cool Scandinavian feel that stands at the foot of forested hills with fine views over Ventnor and out to sea. Outside, five and a half acres of lawn, field and woodland with beehives, Hebridean sheep, red squirrels and white doves; there's an extensive kitchen garden, too, that provides much for the table. Inside, a pristine wonderland in white. There's a cosy bar with books, newspapers and a wood-burner, a sitting room/gallery with Danish leather sofas, a conservatory that opens onto a manicured terrace, and an airy restaurant with great art on the walls. Spotless bedrooms upstairs have a smart, uncluttered feel with comfy beds, vintage throws, more good art and lovely bathrooms. Those at the front look out to sea. Back downstairs, tasty food flies from the kitchen. The hotel has a share in a local fishing boat and lands its own fish, then rears its own cattle in nearby fields and harvests fresh vegetables from the kitchen garden. It also has a bistro with an open kitchen in town, so you can make the most of two culinary worlds. Beaches, gardens and the coastal path wait. *Minimum stay: 2 nights at weekends.*

Rooms	6 doubles, 2 twin/doubles, 1 twin: £140–£160.
	3 singles: £65–£80.
	2 apartments for 4: £190–£250.
	Dinner, B&B £99 p.p.
Meals	Lunch from £5.
	Dinner, 3 courses, £28.
Closed	Never.
Directions	South to Ventnor on A3055, then right (on approach to town) onto B3277. Past tennis courts, up hill, on right.

Gert Bach
Hillside
151 Mitchell Avenue,
Ventnor PO38 1DR

Tel	+44 (0)1983 852271
Email	mail@hillsideventnor.co.uk
Web	www.hillsideventnor.co.uk

Priory Bay Hotel

This lovely old house stands one field up from the sea with woodland paths leading down to the hotel's sandy beach. Medieval monks, Tudor farmers and Georgian gentry have all lived here. The house dates from the 14th century and stands in 60 acres of sprawling grounds. Inside, high ceilings, huge windows and a baby grand wait in the drawing room, but it's all very relaxed with a sitting-room bar and a playroom for children. The odd bag of golf clubs waits for the six-hole course, sunloungers flank the pool in summer, croquet hoops stand on the lawn. Bedrooms have an uncluttered feel: warm colours, tongue-and-groove bathrooms, a sofa if there's room. Some are enormous with timber frames, while luxurious yurts on the estate have claw-foot baths and terraces that look out to sea. As for the food, it's serious stuff, mostly local, some foraged, the fish from the waters around you, the meat from the hills behind. You eat in a stylish brasserie with walls of glass to bring in the view; try Bembridge crab, a tasty steak, Eton Mess with Isle of Wight strawberries and cream. *Minimum stay: 2 nights at weekends.*

Rooms	16 twin/doubles: £160-£300.
	2 family rooms for 4: £240-£330.
	2 barns for 6: £300-£455.
	Singles from £90.
Meals	Lunch from £8. Afternoon tea £20.
	Dinner, 3 courses, £25-£35.
Closed	Never.
Directions	South from Ryde on B3330. Through Nettlestone and hotel signed left and left again.

Andrew Palmer
Priory Bay Hotel
Priory Road,
Seaview PO34 5BU

Tel	+44 (0)1983 613146
Email	enquiries@priorybay.co.uk
Web	www.priorybay.co.uk

Priory Bay Yurts

The Priory Bay Hotel, with its private beach and award-winning restaurants, has been one of the finest destinations in the south for many years. So it's no surprise that the seaside yurts they have created, set on the slope between the hotel and the beach, are a sumptuous blend of comfort and creativity. The yurts are artfully but softly decorated, with a huge double bed, sofas, and cushions that echo their littoral setting. Out on the deck through the French doors, candle lanterns illuminate your private terrace. The swaying trees frame the beach that waits invitingly below; some yurts are set in woodland glades. Guests have full use of the pool and tennis courts at the hotel, as well as eating breakfast there. If that wasn't enough of a treat for the day, you can always stroll the coastal paths or, for those really special occasions, charter the yacht *Infanta* to take a cruise in the bay. *Minimum stay: 2 nights at weekends. Book through Sawday's Canopy & Stars online or by phone.*

Rooms	Yurts for 2-4: £200-£250. Child £40.
Meals	Breakfast, at hotel, included.
	Lunch from £8. Afternoon tea £20.
	Dinner, 3 courses, £25-£35.
Closed	November-March.
Directions	South from Ryde on B3330. Through Nettlestone and hotel signed left and left again.

Canopy & Stars
Priory Bay Yurts
Priory Bay Hotel, Priory Road,
Seaview PO34 5BU

Tel	+44 (0)117 204 7830
Email	enquiries@canopyandstars.co.uk
Web	www.canopyandstars.co.uk/priorybay

Hever Castle Luxury Bed & Breakfast

Hever is out of this world, a magical slice of English DNA. This 13th-century moated castle was home to Anne Boleyn, second wife to Henry VIII, mother of Elizabeth I. It is one of those places that thrills at every turn. It has all the regal trimmings: 625 acres of green and pleasant land, fabulous formal gardens, a 38-acre lake you can walk around. You stay in the Astor Wing, built in Tudor style in 1903; gorgeous bedrooms, recently refurbished, are fit for a king. Expect period colours, panelled walls, perhaps a golden chaise longue or a glimpse of the castle through leaded windows. Lots have pretty wallpaper, one has a vaulted ceiling, several have four-poster beds, while bigger rooms have sofas. Bathrooms are predictably divine, some with claw-foot baths, others with walk-in power showers; a few have both. But don't linger; entrance to the castle and gardens is included in your very attractive price. You can boat on the lake, have picnic dinners, they even host the odd spot of jousting. There's golf, too, and a good pub in the village for dinner. Unbeatable.

Rooms	13 doubles, 3 twins: £155–£205. 2 singles: £105–£120. Extra bed/sofabed £50 p.p. per night.
Meals	Picnic lunches by arrangement. Restaurants within 0.25 miles.
Closed	Rarely.
Directions	Castle signed west out of Edenbridge.

Roland Smith
Hever Castle Luxury Bed & Breakfast
Hever,
Edenbridge TN8 7NG

Tel	+44 (0)1732 861800
Email	stay@hevercastle.co.uk
Web	www.hevercastle.co.uk

Leicester Arms

A Georgian pub in a Tudor village that sits in a peaceful valley – a beautiful slice of rural Kent. Outside, green hills roll, rivers run and the odd fox breaks cover in pursuit of lunch. Inside, a beautiful renovation has bought this lovely old inn back to life with timber frames, open fires and a Grade II listed bar. Potter about and find stripped boards, noble portraits and original red-brick walls, but it's the honest food in the lovely restaurant that's drawing the crowds, perhaps Mediterranean fish soup, Gloucester Old Spot sausages, pear and almond tart with vanilla ice-cream. Bedrooms upstairs have a lovely fresh feel with pale green walls, waffled throws, perhaps a four-poster or an 1860 walnut bed. Those at the back have long country views, all have sparkling bathrooms and flat-screen TVs. The inn takes its name from the Earls of Leicester who own Penshurst Palace, a sublime old pile in the village that's open to the public; you can also get married here. Walk from the front door, hire bikes, or head south to the Ashdown Forest, home of Pooh Bear.

Rooms	6 doubles, 3 four-posters: £119–£159. 2 family rooms for 4: £159. 2 singles: £99–£119. Extra people over 14 in the family rooms: £25 p.p. per night.
Meals	Continental breakfast included; full cooked £8. Lunch from £4.50. Sunday lunch from £12.95. Dinner, 3 courses, £25–£30.
Closed	Never.
Directions	A26 towards Tunbridge Wells, follow B2176. After 3 miles pub is on left, opposite the Church.

Melissa Porter
Leicester Arms
High Street, Penshurst,
Tonbridge TN11 8BT

Tel	+44 (0)1892 871617
Email	info@theleicesterarmshotel.com
Web	www.theleicesterarmshotel.com

The Tunbridge Wells Hotel

Charles I put Tunbridge Wells on the map when he came to take the waters in 1630. By the end of the century the town had flourished and the great and good gathered to stroll along the Pantiles, the colonnaded terraces in the middle of town. They remain every bit as lovely today, with pavement cafés, antique shops, the odd concert and a weekly farmers' market. Hogging the limelight is this newly refurbished hotel, which spills onto the terrace outside, a lovely spot to eat in summer. Inside, you find a buzzing brasserie that will make you think you've crossed the channel: clumps of lampshades hang from the ceilings, French art is crammed on the walls, a happy vibe runs throughout. The food is excellent, French to its core, perhaps lobster bisque, coq au vin, then tarte tatin, all of which you wash down with impeccable French wines. Bedrooms above have a simple elegance: warm colours, smart beds, pretty furniture, lovely prices. Good bathrooms have power showers, some a roll top bath, one of which is in the room. The Downs wait across the road to work off any excess so come to make merry.

Rooms	15 twin/doubles: £109–£129. 2 suites for 2: £169–£179. 2 family rooms for 4: £139. 1 single: £85.
Meals	Continental breakfast included; cooked dishes from £3.50. Lunch & dinner £5–£30.
Closed	Never.
Directions	Sent on booking.

Julian Leefe-Griffiths
The Tunbridge Wells Hotel
58 The Pantiles,
Tunbridge Wells TN2 5TD

Tel	+44 (0)1892 530501
Email	info@thetunbridgewellshotel.com
Web	www.thetunbridgewellshotel.com

Leeds Castle

This iconic English castle has a just smidgeon of history to it. Six queens of England lived here, it was a favourite haunt of Edward I and a pleasure palace to Henry VIII, who stayed here with Catherine of Aragon before setting off to meet Francis I at the Field of the Cloth of Gold in 1520. It dates back to 1119 and is every bit as spectacular as you'd expect, its 500 acres home to lakes and rivers and beautiful gardens, then a Tudor tithe barn that doubles as a restaurant. In the 18th century the castle was remodelled in country-house style and from the 1930s the great and the good gathered here at weekends for riotous house parties. These days you can stay in the pretty courtyard rooms, on the island in Maiden's Tower with sublime views, or in the castle itself, spilling with history, with spectacular interiors, stately bedrooms and butlers to serve dinner. The castle is mostly for parties taking eight rooms or more, but rooms are available for one-off events: concerts in the park, special weekends. You can punt on the moat, picnic in the grounds, try your hand at falconry. Unbeatable. *Castle bookings 8-room minimum.*

Rooms	5 doubles (Maiden's), 17 twin/doubles (Courtyard rooms): £120-£275. 20 twin/doubles (Castle – includes dinner for 2): £325-£400. Dinner, B&B in Courtyard rooms from £75 p.p. in low season.
Meals	Dinner, 3 courses, about £25 in the Courtyard Restaurant.
Closed	Christmas Eve & Christmas Day.
Directions	M20, junc. 8, then A20 south. Ignore brown signs to castle, pass Park Gate Inn, then 1st right and right again into castle.

	Mark Flavell
	Leeds Castle
	Maidstone ME17 1PL
Tel	+44 (0)1622 767823
Email	accommodation@leeds-castle.co.uk
Web	www.leeds-castle.com

The Milk House

The gardens at Sissinghurst Castle were designed by Vita Sackville-West; they're some of the loveliest in the land and if you stay at this cute village pub, you can walk over after breakfast, strolling through apple orchards and bluebell woods. As for the Milk House, Dane and Sarah have recently refurbished from top to toe, making it a great base from which to explore this deeply rural area. It's also a place for a very good meal, with food taking centre stage, its seasonal fare mostly sourced within 20 miles. Outside, there's a smart dining terrace, a duck pond behind, then lawns for a pint in the sun with views over open country. Airy interiors have an easy style with woven willow lampshades hanging above the bar, then timber frames in the dining room, where you dig into fabulous food, perhaps home-cured smoked salmon, free-range Park Farm beef, chocolate tart with kirsch-soaked cherries or a plate of matchless local cheese. Nicely priced bedrooms are crisply uncluttered. Expect chic fabrics, relaxing colours, excellent bathrooms and a sofa if there's room.

Rooms	3 doubles, 1 twin: £95–£120.
Meals	Lunch from £4.
	Sunday lunch from £12.95.
	Dinner, 3 courses, about £30.
Closed	Rarely.
Directions	East into Sissinghurst on A262. In village, on left.

Dane & Sarah Allchorne
The Milk House
The Street, Sissinghurst,
Cranbrook TN17 2JG

Tel	+44 (0)1580 720200
Email	fresh@themilkhouse.co.uk
Web	www.themilkhouse.co.uk

Cloth Hall Oast

Sweep up the rhododendron-lined drive to this immaculate Kentish oast house and barn. For 40 years Mrs Morgan lived in the 15th-century manor next door where she tended both guests and garden; now she has turned her perfectionist's eye upon these five acres. There are well-groomed lawns, a carp-filled pond, pergola, summer house, heated pool and flower beds full of colour. In fine weather enjoy breakfast on the deck overlooking the pond. Light shimmers through swathes of glass in the dining room; there are off-white walls and pale beams that soar from floor to rafter. Mrs Morgan is a charming and courteous hostess and is always nearby to lend a helping hand. There are three bedrooms for guests: a four-poster on the ground floor, a family room and a queen-size double on the first. Colours are soft, fabrics are frilled but nothing is busy or overdone; you are spoiled with good bathrooms and fine mattresses, crisp linen, flowered chintz... and a Michelin starred restaurant in the village. Return to the guest sitting room, made snug by a log fire on winter nights. *No credit cards.*

Rooms	1 double, 1 four-poster, 1 family room for 3: £90-£125.
Meals	Dinner from £25, by arrangement. Pub & restaurant 1 mile.
Closed	Christmas.
Directions	Leave village with windmill on left, taking Golford Road east for Tenterden. After a mile right, before cemetery. Signed right.

Katherine Morgan
Cloth Hall Oast
Course Horn Lane,
Cranbrook TN17 3NR

Tel	+44 (0)1580 712220
Email	clothhalloast@aol.com
Web	www.clothhalloast.co.uk

Elvey Farm

This ancient farmhouse stands in six acres of blissful peace, half a mile up a private drive. It's a deeply rural position, a nostalgic sweep back to old England. White roses run riot on red walls, a thick vine shades the veranda, trim lawns run up to colourful borders. Inside you find timber frames at every turn, but the feel is airy and contemporary with smart furniture sitting amid stripped boards and old beams. Bedrooms come in similar vein. The two in the main house are big and family-friendly, while those in the stable block have chunky beds, small sitting rooms and excellent wet rooms; two have slipper baths. Best of all are two seriously cool new rooms in the granary. Expect timber-framed walls in state-of-the-art bathrooms and massive beds under original rafters; one room comes with a hot tub in a secret garden. As for the restaurant, locally sourced Kentish fare offers delicious rustic treats: hunter's pâté, slow-roasted pork, tarte tatin with honeycomb ice-cream. The Greensand Way runs through the grounds, Leeds Castle is close, *The Darling Buds of May* was filmed in the village.

Rooms	1 double, 1 four-poster, 2 doubles (Oast), 2 suites for 2 (Granary), 3 suites for 2, 2 suites for 4 (Stables): £105–£245. Singles from £85. Dinner, B&B from £74.50 p.p.
Meals	Dinner, 3 courses, about £30. Sunday lunch from £12.95.
Closed	Never.
Directions	M20 junc. 8; A20 to Lenham. At Charing r'bout 3rd exit for A20 Ashford. Right at lights to Pluckley. Bypass village, down hill, right at pub, right and right again.

Simon Peek
Elvey Farm
Pluckley,
Ashford TN27 0SU

Tel	+44 (0)1233 840442
Email	bookings@elveyfarm.co.uk
Web	www.elveyfarm.co.uk

The Relish

It's not just the super-comfy interiors that make The Relish such a tempting port of call. There's a sense of generosity here: a drink on the house each night in the sitting room; tea and cakes on tap all day; free internet throughout. This is a grand 1850s merchant's house on the posh side of town — lovely old bricks and mortar, softly contemporary interiors. Laura and Rakesh took over recently and have already pulled out the paintbrushes, so wind up the cast-iron staircase to find bedrooms that make you smile. You get Hypnos beds with padded headboards, crisp white linen and pretty throws. There's a sense of space, a sofa if there's room, big mirrors and lovely bathrooms. All are great value for money. Downstairs, candles flicker on the mantelpieces above an open fire, the high-ceilinged dining room comes with stripped floors and padded benches and in summer you can decamp onto the terrace for breakfast, a communal garden stretching out beyond. You're one street back from Folkestone's cliff-top front for big sea views. Steps lead down to smart gardens, the promenade and waterside restaurants. *Minimum stay: 2 nights at weekends in summer.*

Rooms	9 doubles: £98–£150.
	1 single: £75.
Meals	Restaurants nearby.
Closed	22 December to 2 January.
Directions	In centre of town, from Langholm Gardens, head west on Sandgate Road. 1st right into Augusta Gardens/Trinity Gardens. Hotel on right.

Laura & Rakesh Sharma
The Relish
4 Augusta Gardens,
Folkestone CT20 2RR

Tel	+44 (0)1303 850952
Email	reservations@hotelrelish.co.uk
Web	www.hotelrelish.co.uk

Wallett's Court Country House Hotel & Spa

A fine position at the end of England with fields sweeping south towards white cliffs. You can follow paths across to a lighthouse for rather good views – gulls wheel above, wild flowers flourish below. The hotel stands opposite a Norman church on land gifted by William the Conqueror to his brother Odo. The current building dates from 1627, its eight peaceful acres home to free-range chickens, a kitchen garden, a lawn for afternoon tea, then a tennis court, boules pitch and climbing frame. Interiors have contemporary art on ancient brick walls, a fire roars in the sitting-room bar, lovely food waits in the restaurant, perhaps Shetland scallops, haunch of wild boar, a faultless pear tarte tatin. Bedrooms are scattered about. Some in the main house have four-posters and timber frames, others in converted barns are simpler, though two big suites come in contemporary style. There are cabins, wagons and tipis for posh camping in summer, then treatment rooms hidden in the garden and an indoor pool. Canterbury cathedral, golf at Sandwich and Dover Castle all wait. *Dinner, B&B only on Saturday nights.*

Rooms	10 twin/doubles, 3 four-posters: £140–£210. 2 suites for 2: £210–£250. 1 tipi for 2, 1 cabin for 2, 1 wagon for 2: £150–£170. Singles from £110.
Meals	Afternoon tea from £8.95. Sunday lunch from £16.95. Dinner, 3 courses, £39.95.
Closed	Rarely.
Directions	From Dover A2 & A20, then A258 towards Deal. Right, signed St Margaret's at Cliffe. House 1 mile on right, signed.

Chris, Lea & Gavin Oakley
Wallett's Court Country House Hotel
Dover Road, Westcliffe,
Dover CT15 6EW

Tel	+44 (0)1304 852424
Email	mail@wallettscourt.com
Web	www.wallettscourthotelspa.com

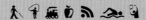

Entry 140   Map 4

The Bell Hotel

Sandwich, a Cinque port, is England's best-preserved medieval town. It's tiny, dates to the 12th century, and timber-framed houses are found all over town. The Bell stands opposite the old toll gate, where the river Stour glides past on its way to the sea. You can follow it down to Sandwich Bay past the famous Royal St George's golf course. Back at the hotel revolving doors propel you into an elegant world of golden sofas, smouldering logs and vintage luggage piled up in a corner. Open-plan interiors flow from restaurant to conservatory to bar. All are smart and airy, with blond wood and halogen lighting giving a contemporary feel. Doors open onto a terrace in summer, while brasserie-style food hits the spot. Bedrooms come in different sizes and mix comfort and style in equal measure. The bigger ones with river views are fabulous, but smaller rooms are nicely priced and all have warm colours, sparkling bathrooms, digital radios and WiFi. Canterbury is close, Turner Contemporary in Margate is unmissable, and Broadstairs, a pretty seaside town, is worth a peek.

Rooms	29 twin/doubles, 4 family rooms for 2–3: £110–£165. 2 suites for 2: £190–£210. 2 singles: £95. Dinner, B&B from £80 p.p.
Meals	Lunch from £5. Dinner £15–£30. Sunday lunch £15.50.
Closed	Never.
Directions	A2, M2, A299, then A256 south. Follow signs into Sandwich. Over bridge, hotel on left by river.

James Redshaw
The Bell Hotel
1 Upper Strand Street,
Sandwich CT13 9EF

Tel	+44 (0)1304 613388
Email	bellhotel@shepherd-neame.co.uk
Web	www.bellhotelsandwich.co.uk

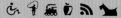

The Royal Harbour Hotel

This quirky townhouse hotel stands on a Georgian crescent with magnificent views of harbour and sea. Simplicity, elegance and eccentricity go hand in hand. The whimsical sitting room has stripped floors, gorgeous armchairs, a crackling fire and an honesty bar. Beautiful things abound: a roll-top desk, lovely art, potted palms, a miniature orange tree bearing fruit. There are binoculars with which to scan the high seas (Ramsgate was home to the Commander of the Channel Fleet), books by the hundred for a good read (Dickens's Bleak House is up the road in Broadstairs) and a library of DVDs for the telly in your room. Bedrooms at the front are tiny, but have the view, those at the back are bigger and quieter. Suites have a coal fire and French windows that open onto small balconies. You get crisp linen, duck down pillows and good little shower rooms. Breakfast is a leisurely feast with cured hams from James's brother, while dinner in the claret-walled Empire room offers proper English cooking: game terrine, Dover sole, apple and gingerbread crumble. *Minimum stay: 2 nights at weekends in high season.*

Rooms	16 doubles, 2 twins: £90–£120. 3 suites for 2: £165–£235. 2 family rooms for 4: £120–£140. 4 singles: £60–£70. Dinner, B&B from £70 p.p.
Meals	Dinner, 3 courses, £25–£30.
Closed	Rarely.
Directions	M2, A299, then A256 into Ramsgate. Follow signs for town centre, pick up coast on right. On left as road drops down hill. Off-street parking.

	James Thomas The Royal Harbour Hotel 10–11 Nelson Crescent, Ramsgate CT11 9JF
Tel	+44 (0)1843 591514
Email	info@royalharbourhotel.co.uk
Web	www.royalharbourhotel.co.uk

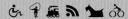

Read's Restaurant with Rooms

A gorgeous country-house restaurant with rooms, Read's stands in five acres of lawned grounds with a half-acre kitchen garden that supplies much for the table. Inside, you find warm elegance at every turn. There's a sitting room bar for pre-dinner drinks, then a couple of beautiful dining rooms where you eat at smartly clothed tables surrounded by ornamental fireplaces and lots of good art. As for the food, it's some of the best in Kent. David and Rona came here 33 years ago, and locals and travellers come for their delicious delights: a hot soufflé of Montgomery Cheddar on a bed of smoked haddock, local venison with pickled pears and walnut croquettes, a chestnut and whisky parfait with toasted hazelnuts and Seville orange curd meringues. The bedrooms are just as good – country-house splendour in spades. Expect decanters of sherry, Roberts radios, huge beds dressed in crisp white linen, wonderful bathrooms with robes to pad about in. Canterbury, Whitstable and Leeds Castle are close, as is Rochester for all things Dickens.

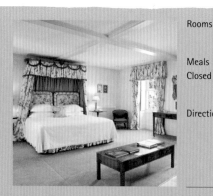

Rooms	5 doubles, 1 twin/double: £165–£195. Singles from £125. Dinner, B&B from £135 p.p.
Meals	Lunch £26. Dinner £60.
Closed	Sunday & Monday. 1st week in January, 1st 2 weeks in September.
Directions	M2, junc. 7, then A2 west into Faversham. Past petrol station and signed left after 400m.

David & Rona Pitchford
Read's Restaurant with Rooms
Macknade Manor, Canterbury Road,
Faversham ME13 8XE

Tel	+44 (0)1795 535344
Email	enquiries@reads.com
Web	www.reads.com

The Cartford Inn

Patrick and Julie know how to run a great little inn: whisk up some fabulous food, throw in a pinch of quirky style, then add lovely bedrooms and serve informally. The inn stands on the banks of the river Wyre – views from the restaurant drift upstream with the Trough of Bowland looming beyond. The front bar, with its cool art, roaring fire and friendly locals is a great place to stop for a pint of local ale, though a courtyard garden will draw you out in good weather. In typically relaxed style you can eat whatever you want wherever you want, perhaps a traditional French tartiflette, venison Wellington with a game jus, then a blackberry curd tart with blackberry sorbet. Bedrooms are just as good – gilded sleigh beds, signature wallpapers, crisp white linen and river views. All have lovely bathrooms with REN lotions, two have roll top baths in the room, the penthouse suite has a shower for two and a rooftop terrace. You can walk by the river – a two-mile circular walk will spin you round – head east into the Yorkshire Dales, or spin off to Blackpool and jump on a rollercoaster. Fantastic.

Rooms	10 doubles, 1 twin: £120–£130. 1 suite for 2-6: £200. 2 family rooms for 3-4: £140. Singles from £65.
Meals	Lunch from £8.50. Dinner, 3 courses, £25–£35. Not Mon lunch.
Closed	Christmas Day.
Directions	M6 junc. 32, M55 junc. 3, then A585 north. Right at T-junction onto A586 for Garstang. Little Eccleston signed left.

Patrick & Julie Beaume
The Cartford Inn
Cartford Lane, Little Eccleston,
Preston PR3 0YP
Tel   +44 (0)1995 670166
Email info@thecartfordinn.co.uk
Web   www.thecartfordinn.co.uk

The Inn at Whitewell

It is almost impossible to imagine a day when a better inn will grace the English landscape. Everything here is perfect. The inn sits just above the river Hodder, and doors in the bar lead onto a terrace where guests can enjoy five-mile views across parkland to rising fells. Inside, fires roar, newspapers wait, there are beams, sofas, maps and copies of *Wisden*. Bedrooms, some in the Coach House, are exemplary and come with real luxury, perhaps a peat fire, a lavish four-poster, a fabulous Victorian power shower. All have beautiful fabrics, top linen and gadgets galore; many have the marvellous view – you can fall asleep at night to the sound of the river. There are bar meals for those who want to watch their weight (the Whitewell fish pie is rightly famous) or a restaurant for splendid food, so dig into seared scallops, Bowland lamb, a plate of local cheese (the Queen once popped in for lunch). Elsewhere, a wine shop in reception, seven miles of private fishing and countryside as good as any in the land. Dogs and children are very welcome. Magnificent.

Rooms	17 doubles, 5 twin/doubles: £120–£215. 1 suite for 2: £210–£240. Singles from £88.
Meals	Lunch & bar meals from £8. Dinner £25–£35.
Closed	Never.
Directions	M6 junc. 31A, B6243 east through Longridge, then follow signs to Whitewell for 9 miles.

Old favourite

Charles Bowman
The Inn at Whitewell
Dunsop Road, Whitewell,
Clitheroe BB7 3AT
Tel +44 (0)1200 448222
Email reception@innatwhitewell.com
Web www.innatwhitewell.com

Entry 145 Map 6

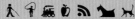

The Spread Eagle

If you're on a budget, but want something special, you'll find it here. The Spread Eagle is one of those rare places that scores ten out of ten on all counts. Its position on the banks of the Ribble is dreamy, the pub itself is a small-scale pleasure dome, its fabulous bedrooms are an absolute steal. It's predictably popular with locals and walkers, who come for tasty food, well-kept ales, and helpful staff. Inside: Farrow & Ball colours, sofas and settles, roaring fires, flagstones and beams. The dining room comes with library wallpaper, but you can eat whatever you want wherever you want, perhaps pressed ham hock terrine, steak and stilton pudding, pear tarte tatin with cider sorbet. Lovely bedrooms have colour and style, pretty linen, big beds and fat mattresses. Some have river views, all have fancy showers, one has a bathtub in the room. You're in the glorious Ribble valley, on the edge of the Yorkshire Dales: Malham is close for walking, Settle for antiques. There's a film club, pie nights, zumba classes – it all happens here. To quote a reader: "I couldn't fault anything." Wonderful.

Rooms	4 doubles, 2 twin/doubles: £85–£110. 1 suite for 2: £135. Dinner, B&B £85 p.p.
Meals	Lunch & bar meals from £8.95. Dinner from £9.95. Sunday lunch from £14.95.
Closed	Never.
Directions	A59 north past Clitheroe. Sawley & Sawley Abbey signed left after 2 miles.

Greig & Natalie Barnes
The Spread Eagle
Sawley,
Clitheroe BB7 4NH

Tel   +44 (0)1200 441202
Email   spread.eagle@zen.co.uk
Web   www.spreadeaglesawley.co.uk

The Castle Hotel

Lincoln, a medieval powerhouse, has been at the centre of British life for 2,000 years. Romans, Vikings and Normans ruled here, the cathedral is one of the finest in Europe, an original copy of the Magna Carta sits in its castle. As for the hotel, it's a great base from which to explore the city. It stands in the old town with views to the front of the castle's enormous walls and the cathedral's towers soaring two streets east. Paul and Saera renovated from top to toe, rescuing it from neglect. Now there's an airy bar in reception, an attractive restaurant for fancy food and a clutch of bedrooms waiting above. Expect contemporary colours, smart fabrics, padded bedheads, excellent bathrooms. Lincoln's wonders wait: the castle and its dungeon, the jaw-dropping cathedral, then Steep Hill (old-world charm with lots of tearooms) which leads down to Brayford Pool, where you can sit on café terraces and watch the world go by. The Christmas market in early December is one of the best in Britain. Come by train, it's only two hours from London.

Rooms	16 twin/doubles: £110–£130.
	1 suite for 2: £140.
	1 single: £90.
	Dinner, B&B from £90 p.p.
Meals	Lunch & bar meals from £10.
	Dinner £30–£35.
Closed	Rarely.
Directions	Sent on booking.

Paul Catlow & Saera Ahmad
The Castle Hotel
Westgate, Lincoln LN1 3AS

Tel	+44 (0)1522 538801
Email	info@castlehotel.net
Web	www.castlehotel.net

The William Cecil

This attractive townhouse hotel stands yards from the gates of the Burghley estate. Inside, interiors offer a pleasing mix of English quirkiness and splendour. Downstairs, informality reigns. There are armchairs in front of the fire in the bar, smart wicker tables in the conservatory, doors onto a lovely terrace in summer, then hanging lamps and half-panelling in the colourful restaurant. The food is fresh and local with seasonal delights that include game from the Burghley estate. You might find lobster mousse with avocado ice-cream, slow-cooked Burghley venison casserole, lemon curd pie with lime sorbet. You can walk it all off with a stroll through historic Stamford or spin over to Burghley for one of the finest Elizabethan houses in the realm. Come back to country-house bedrooms that mix eclectic Rajasthan furniture with a little English decorum. You'll find beautiful art, a wall of paper, perhaps a day bed or a ceiling rose. Some have views onto the estate, all have excellent bedrooms, the best with roll top tubs and vast walk-in showers. Dogs don't fare badly either with Union Jack beds.

Rooms	20 doubles, 7 twin/doubles: £125.
Meals	Lunch from £6.50. Dinner from £12.
	Sunday lunch, 3 courses, £24.50.
Closed	Never.
Directions	Sent on booking.

Paul Brown
The William Cecil
St Martins, Stamford PE9 2LJ

Tel	+44 (0)1780 750070
Email	enquiries@thewilliamcecil.co.uk
Web	www.thewilliamcecil.co.uk

Magpies Restaurant Horncastle

This is a charming restaurant with rooms in a little-known corner of rural England and it's a huge treat to stay. It's a family affair and delightfully homespun – a warm welcome, no airs and graces, just remarkable food and lovely rooms. Andrew is self-taught and follows his nose to extraordinary flavours – a mere glance at one of his menus is enough to make you hungry. Caroline runs front of house with unpretentious charm, somehow managing to whisk up the puddings, too. Lunch and dinner are both irresistible, as is afternoon tea, a feast of scrumptious cakes, stilton scones and red velvet cupcakes. As for the main event, you sit with a drink and some delicious nibbles, then wrestle over what to choose, plumping perhaps for escabeche of red mullet, partridge stuffed with chestnut and foie gras, dark chocolate terrine with Turkish Delight sorbet. Bedrooms above are lovely: pretty colours, comfy beds, fabulous bathrooms; they're also a steal. As for Horncastle, once famous for its medieval horse fair, it's now popular for its Christmas markets and the Viking Way. Don't miss Lincoln Cathedral. *Pets by arrangement.*

Rooms	2 doubles, 1 twin/double: £110–£130. Singles from £70.
Meals	Lunch from £20. Dinner £41–£47. Not Monday, Tuesday or Saturday lunch.
Closed	First week in January & Monday-Tuesday.
Directions	East into Horncastle on A158. Across junction with A153 and on right after 400m.

Caroline & Andrew Gilbert
Magpies Restaurant Horncastle
71-73 East Street,
Horncastle LN9 6AA
Tel   +44 (0)1507 527004
Web   www.magpiesresturant.co.uk

SACO Holborn – Lamb's Conduit Street

Lamb's Conduit Street is cool, quirky and pedestrianised with a sprinkling of cafés and restaurants and the legendary bookshop Persephone. A recent refurbishment has made these serviced apartments a great central base. You get the equivalent of a hotel suite, then excellent kitchens thrown in for free. Sparkling top-floor apartments open onto vast decked terraces while those below have walls of glass overlooking the street. It's all a big surprise given the utilitarian 60s exterior: there's space and style, with open-plan living rooms, excellent bathrooms, comfy bedrooms and lots of appealing extras such as washing machines, dishwashers and flat-screen TVs; the reception staff are great, too. The building stands directly opposite Great Ormond Street Hospital – quiet at night and devoid of the crowds. It's also extremely central: you can walk to St Paul's, Covent Garden, Oxford Street and the British Museum. Waitrose for shopping and Russell Square for the tube are a step away, as is the Renoir, a small London cinema for great independent film. Off-road parking available by arrangement.

Rooms	24 apartments for 2: £201–£232.
	10 apartments for 4: £264–£306.
	2 apartments for 6: £398–£462.
Meals	Self-catered. Restaurants nearby.
Closed	Never.
Directions	Train: Liverpool Street.
	Tube: Russell Square.
	Bus: 19, 38, 55, 243.
	Private parking from £15 a day.

Tim Ripman
SACO Holborn – Lamb's Conduit Street
Spens House, 72-84 Lamb's Conduit
Street, Holborn, London WC1N 3LT

Tel	+44 (0)20 7269 9930
Email	london@sacoapartments.com
Web	www.sacoapartments.com

22 York Street

The Callis family lives in a Regency townhouse in W1 – not your average London residence and one that defies all attempts to pigeonhole it. There may be ten bedrooms, but you should still expect the feel of home: Michael is determined to keep things friendly and easy-going. This might explain the salsa dancing lessons that once broke out at breakfast, a meal of great conviviality taken communally around a curved wooden table in the big and bright kitchen/dining room. Here, a weeping ficus tree stands next to the piano, which, of course, you are welcome to play. There's always something to catch your eye, be it the red-lipped oil painting outside the dining room or the old boots on the landing. Wooden floors run throughout, and the house has a huge sitting room, with sofas, books and backgammon. Expect silk eiderdowns, good beds and lots of space in the bedrooms: all are spotless and very comfy. This is Sherlock Holmes country and Madame Tussauds, Regent's Park and Lord's are all close, as are hundreds of restaurants. A very friendly place.

Rooms	5 doubles, 2 twins: £150. 3 singles: £95-£120.
Meals	Continental breakfast included. Pubs/restaurants nearby.
Closed	Never.
Directions	Train: Paddington (to Heathrow). Tube: Baker Street (2-minute walk). Bus: 2, 13, 30, 74, 82, 113, 139, 274. Parking: £25 a day, off-street.

Michael & Liz Callis
22 York Street
Marylebone, London W1U 6PX

Tel	+44 (0)20 7224 2990
Email	mc@22yorkstreet.co.uk
Web	www.22yorkstreet.co.uk

The Portobello Hotel

In 1969, in the days of Bowie and the Rolling Stones, this small hotel opened its doors, making it London's first boutique hotel. It was a new idea, a hip little place, not dull and formal like other hotels, but relaxed and friendly with lots of colour and a bohemian feel. These days, not much has changed, and it remains a popular base for artists and movie stars, designers and musicians, a star-studded list of regulars who come for its seductive combination of privacy, informality and style. It stands in the middle of Notting Hill, peacefully hidden away on a side street yet close to the tube, with Portobello Road and the shops and cafés of Westbourne Grove a short stroll. Inside, a beautiful sitting room has pine bay windows and carved ceiling roses, then fresh flowers, big art and views onto communal gardens. Bedrooms vary in size, not style. Lots have claw-foot baths in the room, one has a small terrace, another a high four-poster with library steps to help you up. Bigger rooms have sofas, all have cool colours, antique furniture, coffee machines and robes for the bathroom.

Rooms	19 doubles: £175-£385. 2 singles: £125-£175.
Meals	Continental breakfast included; cooked dishes from £5. Light bites from £6. Restaurants within 500m.
Closed	24 December (midday) – 27 December (10am).
Directions	Tube: Notting Hill Gate. Bus: 12, 27, 28, 52, 70, 94. Parking: Nearest car park £25 per 24 hrs.

David Smith
The Portobello Hotel
22 Stanley Gardens,
Notting Hill Gate, London W11 2NG

Tel	+44 (0)20 7727 2777
Email	stay@portobellohotel.com
Web	www.portobellohotel.com

Temple Lodge Club

Temple Lodge, once home to the painter Sir Frank Brangwyn, is sandwiched between a courtyard and a lushly landscaped garden. The peace is remarkable making it a very restful place – simple yet human and warmly comfortable, a nourishing experience. Michael and his devoted team run it with quiet energy. You breakfast overlooking the garden, there are newspapers to browse, a library instead of TVs. Bedrooms are surprisingly stylish: pretty art, crisp linen, no clutter, a hint of country chic. They're exceptional value for money, too, so book well in advance. Some rooms have garden views, only two have their own bathrooms and loo; if you don't mind that, you'll be happy. The Thames passes by at the end of the road, the Riverside Studios is round the corner for theatre and film, and the Gate Vegetarian Restaurant is across the courtyard, a well-known eatery, its food so good even committed carnivores can't resist. It was also Brangwyn's studio, hence the artist's window. The house is a non-denominational Christian centre with two services a week, which you may take or leave as you choose.

Rooms	1 double; 1 double (en suite with separate wc); 1 double with separate bathroom; 1 double, 2 twins sharing baths: £76–£120. 5 singles sharing baths: £58–£72. Extra bed/sofabed available £12–£14 p.p. per night.
Meals	Continental breakfast included. Vegetarian restaurant across courtyard.
Closed	Never.
Directions	Tube: Hammersmith (5-minute walk). Bus: 9, 10, 27, 295.

Michael Beaumont
Temple Lodge Club
51 Queen Caroline Street,
Hammersmith, London W6 9QL

Tel	+44 (0)20 8748 8388
Email	templelodgeclub@btconnect.com
Web	www.templelodgeclub.com

The Georgian House

Serena's great-great grandfather was commissioned by Thomas Cubitt to build this row of houses, and liked the results so much he kept one for himself. They were built to rival Belgravia and have the same august credentials: pillars at the door, porticos and friezes, then high-ceilinged interiors as befits elegant Georgian architecture. Fast forward 160 years and the house, still in the same family, is now a B&B hotel, with a friendly brigade of international staff and a lovely sitting room in reception, where you can make a coffee and read the papers. As for the bedrooms, they come in two styles: rooms that haven't been recently refurbished and those that have. The former are due to be upgraded soon, but are simpler altogether: compact with blond wood. The latter are lovely: bigger, with white walls, a roll of paper, pretty fabrics, perhaps a sofa. Breakfast hits the spot with free-range eggs and Musk's sausages (also popular with Her Majesty). You're close to Victoria (and the train to Gatwick) and Buckingham Palace. A couple of Harry Potter themed rooms are popular with younger guests.

Rooms	23 doubles; 2 doubles sharing 2 bathrooms with 2 singles: £99–£199. 9 family rooms for 3; 9 family rooms for 4: £139–£249. 10 singles; 2 singles sharing 2 bathrooms with 2 doubles: £79–£165. 4 apartments for 5-6, (self-catering): £159–£349 p.w.
Meals	Pubs/restaurants within walking distance.
Closed	Never.
Directions	Tube: Victoria, Pimlico, Sloane Square. Train: Victoria (for Gatwick). Bus: 6, 11, 16, 24, 38, 52, 73, 82, 185, 211, 239, C10

Serena von der Heyde
The Georgian House
35-37 St. Georges Drive, Pimlico,
London SW1V 4DG

Tel	+44 (0)20 7834 1438
Email	reception@georgianhousehotel.co.uk
Web	www.georgianhousehotel.co.uk

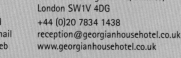

Artist Residence London

This cool London base is a phoenix from the ashes, a down-at-heel pub recently transformed into a 21st-century pleasure dome. It sits on a quiet back street between the Thames and Victoria Station, a five-minute walk to Pimlico Road, another five to Sloane Square and the Kings Road. Inside, an 18-month renovation has touched every corner. There's a groovy bar in the enormous cellar, a sitting room/breakfast room that opens onto a terrace, then excellent food in the high-ceilinged restaurant. Fires smoulder, art hangs on every wall, check-in is a breeze, with kind staff on hand to smooth your way. Chic, uncluttered rooms have cool colours, smart fabrics, the best beds and vintage tiles in power-showered bathrooms. Smaller rooms have bedside lamps that hang from the ceilings, bigger rooms have sofas, perhaps an exposed brick wall. Suites – one is enormous – have free-standing baths and walk-in showers. Back downstairs, sit at the bar and watch the chefs prepare your food, perhaps lamb with clams and mango or wild sea bass with oysters. Victoria Station (for Gatwick) is close.

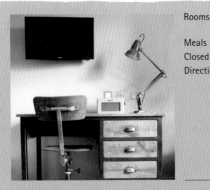

Rooms	8 doubles: £160–£240.
	2 suites for 4: £180–£300.
Meals	Lunch & dinner about £30.
Closed	Never.
Directions	Tube: Victoria, Pimlico, Sloane Square.
	Train: Victoria (for Gatwick).
	Bus: 6, 11, 16, 24, 38, 52, 73, 82, 185, 211, 239, C10.

Charlie Newey & Justin Salisbury
Artist Residence London
52 Cambridge Street, Pimlico,
London SW1V 4QQ

Tel	+44 (0)20 7828 6684
Email	london@artistresidence.co.uk
Web	www.artistresidencelondon.co.uk

Lime Tree Hotel

You'll be hard pressed to find better value in the centre of town. The Lime Tree – two elegant Georgian townhouses – stands less than a mile from Buckingham Palace, with Westminster, Sloane Square and Piccadilly easy strolls. Add warm interiors, kind owners and one of the capital's loveliest pubs waiting round the corner and you've unearthed a London gem. There's Cole & Son wallpaper in the airy dining room, so dig into an excellent breakfast (included in the price), then drop into the tiny sitting room next door for guide books and a computer for guests to use. Rooms – one on the ground floor with doors onto the garden and the quietest at the back – are just the ticket: smart without being lavish. Expect warm colours, crisp linen, pretty wallpaper and excellent bathrooms (most have super showers). Those at the front on the first floor have high ceilings and fine windows, those at the top (a few stairs!) are cosy in the eaves. Charlotte and Matt are hands-on and will point you in the right direction. Don't miss the Thomas Cubitt pub (50 paces from the front door) for seriously good food. *Minimum stay: 2 nights at weekends.*

Rooms	12 doubles, 4 twins: £165–£195. 1 family room for 4: £225. 6 singles: £110–£145. 2 triples: £205.
Meals	Restaurants nearby.
Closed	Never.
Directions	Train: Victoria (for Gatwick). Tube: Victoria or Sloane Square. Bus: 11, 24, 38, 52, 73, C1. Parking: £34 a day off-street.

Charlotte & Matt Goodsall
Lime Tree Hotel
135 Ebury Street, Victoria,
London SW1W 9QU

Tel	+44 (0)20 7730 8191
Email	info@limetreehotel.co.uk
Web	www.limetreehotel.co.uk

The Levin Hotel

A great London base for shopaholics – Harrods waits at one end of the street, Harvey Nicks at the other. As for the hotel, it sits quietly on Basil Street, a peaceful retreat in the middle of Knightsbridge. There's no sitting room, but a lively café/bar/restaurant, which acts as the social hub. Bedrooms spread over four floors with a lift to carry you up, though you may prefer to walk – a contemporary chandelier with an 18-metre drop fills the stairwell. As for the rooms, some are bigger, others smaller, but all have the same chic style: bold colours, Art Nouveau furnishings, hand-stitched beds, white marble bathrooms. Bigger rooms have sofas, all have Bose radios, flat-screen TVs, white robes and beautiful linen. You can breakfast on croissants from the owner's bakery, nip back early for afternoon tea, or dine on lovely comfort food, perhaps salmon fishcakes, shepherd's pie, Eton Mess with mixed berries. If that's not enough, there's a Michelin star next door at the Capital (their sister hotel). All rooms are air conditioned, there's a full concierge service and iPads are available at reception. *Pets by arrangement.*

Rooms	3 doubles, 3 twin/doubles, 5 twin/doubles: £240-£479. 1 suite for 2: £375-£619. Extra beds for under 12s, £30.
Meals	Lunch from £5.50. Dinner, 3 courses, about £30. Afternoon tea from £15.95.
Closed	Never.
Directions	Tube: Knightsbridge. Bus: 09, 10, 19, 22, 52, 137, C1. Car parks £45 a day.

Harald Duttine
The Levin Hotel
28 Basil Street, Knightstbridge,
London SW3 1AS

Tel	+44 (0)20 7589 6286
Email	reservations@thelevinhotel.co.uk
Web	www.thelevinhotel.co.uk

The Troubadour

Bob Dylan played here in the 60s, so did Jimi Hendrix, Joni Mitchell and the Rolling Stones. The Troubadour is a slice of old London cool, a quirky coffee house/bar in Earls Court with a magical garden and a small club in the basement where bands play most nights. Outside, pavement tables make the best of the weather; inside, rows of teapots elegantly adorn the windows, as they have done since the bar opened in 1954. The ceiling drips with musical instruments, you find tables and booths, the odd pew. The kitchen is open all day (if you wear a hat on Tuesday nights, pudding is free), so try deep-fried calamari or rib-eye steak; in summer, you can eat in the garden. Next door, above their fabulous wine shop, charming suites up in the eaves – no lift! – give views of London rooftops. Expect big colour, a super bed, an alcoholic fridge, a small sofabed in front of a flat-screen TV. There's a kitchen, too; wake before 9am and make your own breakfast, or come down after for bacon and eggs served late into the afternoon. "Character pours out of every hidden cupboard," says a guest. Brilliant. *Pets by arrangement.*

Rooms	2 suites for 2-4, each with sofabed: £175-£225. Singles from £160.
Meals	Continental breakfast included; cooked extras from £4.50. Lunch & dinner £5-£25.
Closed	25 & 26 December; 1 January.
Directions	Tube: Earl's Court or West Brompton (both 5-minute walk). Bus: 74, 328, 430, C1, C3. Car parks £35 a day.

Simon & Susie Thornhill
The Troubadour
263-267 Old Brompton Road,
Earls Court, London SW5 9JA

Tel	+44 (0)20 7370 1434
Email	susie@troubadour.co.uk
Web	www.troubadour.co.uk

The Royal Foundation of St Katharine

London is full of surprises and this is one of them. St Katharine's was founded by Queen Matilda in 1147, a hospital for the poor and infirm that originally stood next to the Tower of London. In 1273, after a dispute over its control, it passed into the hands of English queens, in whose patronage it has remained ever since (the Queen Mother was a frequent visitor). It moved East and grew into a village on the banks of the Thames, giving its name to St Katharine's Docks (a short walk). In 1825 it moved to Regents Park, returning to the East End in 1948; it now sits between Tower Bridge and Canary Wharf. Inside, you find a world at odds with the roar of the city: a courtyard garden where roses ramble, a beautiful chapel that fills with light, a fine old house with muralled meeting rooms. There's a sitting room with comfy sofas, a dining room for a simple breakfast, then straightforward bedrooms that do the trick, some with garden views, all with comfy beds, power showers and blond wood furniture. Limehouse station (DLR) is a two-minute walk, the London marathon passes outside. There's free parking, too.

Rooms	20 doubles, 2 twins: £90–£185. 3 family rooms for 4: £140–£245. 11 singles: £75–£125.
Meals	Continental breakfast included. Restaurants nearby.
Closed	Christmas.
Directions	Docklands Light Railway: Limehouse. Tube: Stepney Green (0.75 mile). Bus: 15, 100, 115, D3. Free parking.

Mark Aitken
The Royal Foundation of St Katharine
2 Butcher Row, Limehouse,
London E14 8DS

Tel	+44 (0)300 111 1147
Email	reservations@rfsk.org.uk
Web	www.rfsk.org.uk

The Boundary

A beautiful bolthole in Shoreditch, epicentre of cool London. Designed by Terence Conran, it's much more than a mere hotel – its bars, restaurants, deli and roof terrace are a magnet for locals, who come for great food, loads of style and an informal vibe to hang out in. Big, airy bedrooms are exemplary, each the work of a different designer, each themed to an artist or art movement. Original furniture and beautiful art, much from Conran's private collection, come as standard. Beds are dressed in white linen, bathrooms pack a designer punch, corner rooms have six huge windows, enormous suites open onto terraces. Three restaurants guarantee happiness. The vine-shaded roof terrace serves grilled fish and meat amid rather good views; Albion offers old English favourites (lamb hot pot, fish pie) and doubles as a deli and bakery; Boundary, theatrically adorned in the original printworks, is French to its core (lobster bisque, Pyrenean lamb, lemon soufflé). Brick Lane, Columbia Road and Hoxton Square are all close, while Shoreditch High Street overground station is on your doorstep. Très chic.

Rooms	10 doubles, 2 twin/doubles: £228-£330. 5 suites for 2: £372-£660.
Meals	Breakfast from £5. Lunch from £6.50. Sunday lunch from £19.50. Dinner from £13.50 in Albion; from £21.95 in Boundary (not Sun night).
Closed	Never.
Directions	Overground: Shoreditch High Street. Tube: Old Street, Liverpool Street, Bethnal Green. Train: Liverpool Street. Bus: 35, 47, 78.

Manisha Rajawat
The Boundary
2-4 Boundary Street,
Shoreditch, London E2 7DD

Tel	+44 (0)20 7729 1051
Email	sawdays@Theboundary.co.uk
Web	www.theboundary.co.uk

Strattons

Strattons isn't a hotel, it's a place that tickles your senses. First there's the house, a beautiful Queen Anne villa that wouldn't look out of place in the French countryside. Then you step inside and you're immediately surrounded by art, not one or two interesting pieces, but a treasure trove of wonderful stuff that spills from every corner, sits on every wall or dangles from the odd ceiling. You'll find august busts, contemporary chandeliers, murals by the dozen. Bedrooms are just as good: a carved four-poster in priestly red, Botticelli's angels hovering on a wall, bedside lights that hang from the ceiling. Some have double-ended baths in the room, others a roof terrace with sun loungers. As for the food, there's a deli across the courtyard for homemade treats: naughty cakes, sweet smelling bacon rolls, local cheeses and oils to take home. The restaurant (turn right at the chaise longue), is another art-filled room where local food follows the seasons, perhaps game pie with honey and fennel, slow-cooked beef with roasted roots, hazelnut tart with crème fraîche. Don't miss the Brecks for magical walking. *Pets by arrangement.*

Rooms	6 doubles, 1 twin/double: £99–£180. 5 suites for 2: £155–£275. 2 apartments for 2: £172–£275. Singles £92–£175.
Meals	Lunch (deli), Mon–Sat, from £6. Sunday lunch (hotel) from £12. Dinner, 3 courses, about £30.
Closed	Never.
Directions	Ash Close runs off north end of market place between W H Brown estate agents & fish & chip restaurant.

Vanessa & Les Scott
Strattons
4 Ash Close,
Swaffham PE37 7NH

Tel	+44 (0)1760 723845
Email	enquiries@strattonshotel.com
Web	www.strattonshotel.com

Chalk & Cheese

Andrew and Bridget's quirky Victorian schoolhouse stands on the village green. If its exterior gives the impression of rural decorum, then its interiors do the opposite – this is a whimsical world of antiques and vintage collectibles. It's all refreshingly original, a poke in the eye to the minimalist movement. The big room takes centre stage, its high ceiling and stained glass windows giving an ecclesiastic feel. Mismatching sofas wait below, there's a rocking chair in front of the fire, a bust of Aristotle draped in a feather boa and a lovely bar with lampshades descending from on high. Homely bedrooms are warmly simple and nicely priced. One has a four-poster, another a slipper bath, two next door in a cute cottage can be taken together to self-cater. As for the food, lunch menus are written by hand, a wood-fired pizza oven works overtime at weekends, and you can sup on pea and ham soup, homemade cottage pie and sticky toffee pudding for under £20. There's a conservatory breakfast room, a terrace for summer, even a farm shop and art gallery. Lovely local walking waits as does the coast.

Rooms	3 doubles, 1 twin, 1 four-poster: £70–£95. Singles from £60. Extra beds from £10. Self-catering option.
Meals	Lunch from £4.50. Dinner, 3 courses, £20–£25 (not Mon or Tues).
Closed	Never.
Directions	North of A1122 between Swaffham and Downham Market. In village, on green.

Andrew & Bridget Archibald
Chalk & Cheese
1 Eastgate Street, Shouldham,
King's Lynn PE33 0DD

Tel	+44 (0)1366 348039
Email	info@chalkandcheesenorfolk.co.uk
Web	www.bed-and-breakfast-west-norfolk.co.uk

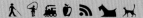

Congham Hall

This is a lovely old Georgian merchant's house set in 30 acres of parkland, but it's also a cool little spa hotel with an indoor pool and treatment rooms, a perfect blend of old and new. Inside, a recent refurbishment has brought contemporary elegance into this smart country house. Outside, three gardeners grow flowers for the house, vegetables for the kitchen and keep the gardens looking utterly lovely. There's an open fire and beautiful art in the sitting room, a cool little bar with low-hanging lampshades, then an airy dining room for tasty food, perhaps Norfolk asparagus with a soft poached egg, Breckland duck with carrots and parsnips, lemon panna cotta with raspberry sorbet. After which you'll need to atone, so grab a robe from your room and roast away in the sauna before jumping in the pool for a few lengths; some might prefer the hot tub on the terrace! Bedrooms are lovely. Those in the house are more traditional, those in the courtyard have doors onto private terraces. Sandringham is close, as is the North Norfolk coast. Children are very welcome and have their own menu.

Rooms	25 twin/doubles: £125–£245. 1 suite for 2: £250–£270.
Meals	Lunch from £6.50. Dinner £12.95–£40. Afternoon tea from £8.75.
Closed	Rarely.
Directions	Sent on booking.

Julie Woodhouse
Congham Hall
Grimston, King's Lynn PE32 1AH
Tel   +44 (0)1485 600250
Email   info@conghamhallhotel.co.uk
Web   www.conghamhallhotel.co.uk

The Hoste

Nelson was a local, now it's farmers and film stars who jostle at the bar. In its 300-year history the Hoste has been a court house, a livestock market and a brothel. These days it's a Norfolk institution, a default destination for those in search of a little luxury. It's all things to all men: a fabulous restaurant, a conservatory café, a beautiful country pub. Inside, stylish interiors come as standard with warm colours, panelled walls and beautiful art everywhere. Best of all, it never stands still. The airy new garden room hums with happy guests, a fine spot for breakfast with a wall of glass that opens onto a lawned terrace. Elsewhere, four new bedrooms are predictably lovely, like all rooms at the Hoste, each refurbished every five years. You get sofas, four-posters, sleigh beds and fabulous bathrooms, you can even sleep in a railway carriage over at Railway House. As for the food, it's as local as possible, perhaps Brancaster oysters, Norfolk rib-eye, treacle tart with blood orange ice-cream. There's a beauty spa, live jazz and a magical coastline for windswept walks.

Rooms	52 twin/doubles: £130–£230.
	9 cottages for 6 (self-catering):
	£160–£200.
	1 train carriage for 2 (Railway House):
	£170–£230. Singles from £110.
	Dinner, B&B from £85 p.p.
Meals	Lunch from £6.
	Dinner, 3 courses, from £25.
	Sunday lunch from £14.
Closed	Never.
Directions	On B1155 for Burnham Market.
	By green & church in village centre.

Denis Frucot
The Hoste
The Green, Burnham Market,
King's Lynn PE31 8HD

Tel	+44 (0)1328 738777
Email	reception@thehoste.com
Web	www.thehoste.com

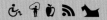

The White Horse

You strike gold at The White Horse. For a start, you get one of the best views on the North Norfolk coast – a long, cool sweep over tidal marshes to Scolt Head Island. But it's not just the proximity of the water that elates: the inn, its pleasant rooms and its fish-abundant menus score top marks. Follow your nose and find a sunken garden at the front, a local's bar for billiards, a couple of sofas for a game of Scrabble, and a conservatory/dining room for the freshest fish. Best of all is the sun-trapping terrace; eat out here in summer. Walkers pass, sea birds swoop, sail boats glide off into the sunset. At high tide the water laps at the garden edge, at low tide fishermen harvest mussels and oysters from the bay. Inside, the feel is smart without being stuffy: stripped boards, open fires, seaside chic with sunny colours. Neat carpeted bedrooms come in seascape colours and bathrooms are spotless. In the main building some have fabulous views, those in the garden open onto flower-filled terraces. The coastal path passes directly outside.
Minimum stay: 2 nights at weekends.

Rooms	11 doubles, 4 twins: £100-£180. Extra beds £30. Cots £5. Dogs £10.
Meals	Lunch & bar meals from £9.95. Dinner from £13.95.
Closed	Never.
Directions	Midway between Hunstanton & Wells-next-the-Sea on A149.

Cliff & James Nye
The White Horse
Brancaster Staithe PE31 8BY

Tel	+44 (0)1485 210262
Email	reception@whitehorsebrancaster.co.uk
Web	www.whitehorsebrancaster.co.uk

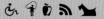

The Globe Inn at Wells-next-the-Sea

Wells is one of the prettiest towns on the North Norfolk coast. Fisherman land their catch on the quay, a sandy beach runs for a mile or two, pine trees soar above local fields. As for the Globe, it sits on The Buttlands, a smart square of Georgian houses that rings the village green. There's a terrace at the front for a pint in the sun, a courtyard to the side for dinner in summer, then an airy bar that floods with light through big bay windows. Inside, you find wooden floors, the odd sofa, seaside colours and a wood-burner for chilly days. Bedrooms, all recently refurbished, have a wall of paper, padded heads, then crisp white linen on excellent beds and waffled robes in pretty bathrooms. Three have views of the green, all have local art and flat-screen TVs. Back downstairs, there's good food in the restaurant, which opens onto the courtyard, perhaps pan-fried fillet of sea bass, a venison burger or Norfolk duck with ginger and rhubarb. Rooms connect for families, dogs are very welcome. Don't miss Titchwell for migrating birds or Blakeney for lounging seals. Boat trips can be arranged, too. *Minimum stay: 2 nights at weekends.*

Rooms	5 doubles, 2 twin/doubles: £95-£160. Singles from £95.
Meals	Lunch from £6. Dinner, 3 courses, £25-£30.
Closed	Rarely.
Directions	A149 east into Wells. In village, above quay, on green.

Antonia & Stephen Bournes
The Globe Inn at Wells-next-the-Sea
The Buttlands,
Wells-Next-The-Sea NR23 1EU

Tel   +44 (0)1328 710206
Email   hello@theglobeatwells.co.uk
Web   www.theglobeatwells.co.uk

The Blakeney Hotel

The view here is matchless, a clean sweep across the salt marshes up to Blakeney Point. The estuary passes five paces from the front door and guests are prone to fall into graceful inertia and watch the boats slide by. You can do this from a sun-trapping terrace, a convivial bar, a traditional restaurant and the stunning first-floor sitting room that comes with binoculars to follow the wildlife. Most bedrooms have been refurbished in a contemporary country-house style with lovely fabrics, cool colours, an armchair or sofa, then gorgeous bathrooms; those at the front have the view. Six traditional rooms remain – simpler, but still pretty, with yellow and red chintz, good beds and crisp linen. There's a bar for light lunches, a drawing room with an open fire, then a stylish indoor pool with steam room and sauna; a snooker room and children's games' room wait too. Outside, paths lead down to the marshes, there are seals to spot, birds to watch, links golf at Sheringham and Cromer. Lovely food awaits your return, perhaps potted brown shrimps, Gressingham duck, sticky toffee pudding.

Rooms	19 doubles, 36 twin/doubles: £182–£322. 8 singles: £91–£149.
Meals	Lunch from £9.50. Dinner, 3 courses, £29–£43.50.
Closed	Never.
Directions	A148 north from Fakenham, then B1156 north to Blakeney. In village on quay.

Stannard Family
The Blakeney Hotel
The Quay, Blakeney,
Holt NR25 7NE

Tel	+44 (0)1263 740797
Email	reception@blakeneyhotel.co.uk
Web	www.blakeneyhotel.co.uk

Cley Windmill

The setting here is magical: rushes flutter in the salt marsh, raised paths lead off to the sea and a vast sky seems to start at your feet. The windmill dates to 1713 and was converted into a house in the 1920s. Square rooms are bigger and suit those who prefer to shuffle, while round rooms in the tower are impossibly romantic (one is for mountaineers only). Six rooms are in the mill and you really want to go for these, though the cottage is set up for self-catering and visiting dogs. Inside, you find the loveliest drawing room – low ceiling, open fire, honesty bar, stripped floorboards and a window seat to beat most others. Bedrooms come in country style with pretty pine, painted wood, colourful walls, super views. Rooms in the tower (with compact shower rooms) get smaller as you rise, but the view improves with every step; there's a viewing platform half way up for all. Meals are taken in a pretty dining room, so drop down for a big breakfast or book for dinner: homemade soups, local fish pie, sinful puddings. There's a lovely walled garden for guests, too. *Minimum stay: 2 nights at weekends.*

Rooms	6 doubles, 2 twin/doubles: £110–£199. 1 cottage for 4 (self-catering): £425–£570 per week; minimum 3 nights £320.
Meals	Dinner, 3 courses, £32.50.
Closed	Christmas.
Directions	Head east through Cley on A149. Mill signed on left in village.

Simon Whatling
Cley Windmill
The Quay, Cley,
Holt NR25 7RP

Tel   +44 (0)1263 740209
Email   info@cleywindmill.co.uk
Web   www.cleywindmill.co.uk

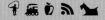

Saracens Head

Lost in the lanes of deepest Norfolk, an English inn that's hard to beat. Outside, Georgian red-brick walls ripple around, encircling a beautiful courtyard where you can sit for sundowners in summer before slipping into the restaurant for a good meal. Tim and Janie came back from the Alps, unable to resist the allure of this inn. A sympathetic refurbishment has brightened things up, but the spirit remains the same: this is a country-house pub with lovely staff who go the extra mile. Downstairs the bar hums with happy locals who come for Norfolk ales and good French wines, while the food in the restaurant is as good as ever: Norfolk pigeon and pork terrine, wild sea bass, treacle tart and caramel ice-cream. Upstairs you'll find a sitting room on the landing, where windows frame country views, and six pretty bedrooms. All have been redecorated and have smart carpets, blond wood furniture, comfy beds and sparkling bathrooms. Breakfast sets you up for the day, so explore the coast at Cromer, play golf on the cliffs at Sheringham, or visit Blickling Hall, a Jacobean pile. Blissful stuff.

Rooms	5 twin/doubles: £100–£110.
	1 family room for 4: £110–£140.
	Singles from £70.
Meals	Lunch from £6.50.
	Dinner, 3 courses, £25–£35.
	Not Mon; or Tue lunch Oct–June.
Closed	Christmas.
Directions	From Norwich A140 past Aylsham, then 3rd left for Erpingham. Right into Calthorpe, through village, straight out the other side (not right). On right after about 0.5 miles.

Tim & Janie Elwes
Saracens Head
Wolterton,
Norwich NR11 7LZ

Tel	+44 (0)1263 768909
Email	info@saracenshead-norfolk.co.uk
Web	www.saracenshead-norfolk.co.uk

The Pheasant Inn

A super little inn lost in beautiful country, the kind you hope to chance upon. The Kershaws run it with great passion and an instinctive understanding of its traditions. The bars are wonderful. Brass beer taps glow, 100-year old photos of the local community hang on stone walls, the clock above the fire keeps perfect time. Fires burn, bowler hats and saddles pop up here and there, varnished wood ceilings shine. House ales are expertly kept, Timothy Taylor's and Wylam waiting for thirsty souls. Fruit and vegetables come from the garden, while Robin's lovely food hits the spot perfectly, perhaps twice-baked cheese soufflé, slow-roasted Northumberland lamb, brioche and marmalade bread and butter pudding; as for Sunday lunch, *The Observer* voted it 'Best in the North'. Bedrooms in the old hay barn are light and airy, cute and cosy, great value for money. You're in the Northumberland National Park – no traffic jams, not too much hurry. You can sail on the lake, cycle round it or take to the hills and walk. For £10 you can also gaze into the universe at the Kielder Observatory (best in winter). Brilliant. *Minimum stay: 2 nights at weekends.*

Rooms	4 doubles, 3 twins: £95-£100. 1 family room for 4: £95-£140. Singles £65-£70. Dinner, B&B £70-£75 p.p. Extra bed/sofabed available £15 p.p. per night.
Meals	Bar meals from £9.95. Dinner, 3 courses, £20-£30.
Closed	Christmas.
Directions	From Bellingham follow signs west to Kielder Water & Falstone for 9 miles. Hotel on left, 1 mile short of Kielder Water.

Walter, Irene & Robin Kershaw
The Pheasant Inn
Stannersburn,
Hexham NE48 1DD
Tel   +44 (0)1434 240382
Email   stay@thepheasantinn.com
Web   www.thepheasantinn.com

Nicely priced

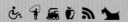

Eshott Hall

An utterly gorgeous Palladian mansion set in 35 acres of medieval woodlands and pasture. Wisteria fans out at the front, there's an ancient fernery, paths that weave past rare trees, an extremely productive kitchen garden. Inside is equally grand, and all the better for a recent refurbishment. You find Corinthian columns and a fine ornate ceiling in the drawing room, a roaring fire and leather sofas in the striking library, then a panelled dining room from which you may spot the odd deer tucking into the garden roses. Nip up the stairs, passing a stained-glass window designed by William Morris, and find a clutch of light-filled bedrooms. A couple come with free-standing baths in the room, others have high ceilings, garden views, perhaps a sofa or a four-poster bed. Chic bathrooms have natural stone, white robes and spoiling oils. There's tennis in the garden, peace at every turn, then white beaches, Hadrian's Wall, Holy Island and Alnwick Castle. Come back for a good dinner, perhaps potted Craster crab, Ingram Valley lamb, pear tarte tatin with mascarpone ice-cream. Fabulous.

Rooms	11 twin/doubles, 5 doubles: £120–£250. Singles from £110. Dinner, B&B from £95 p.p.
Meals	Lunch from £6. Dinner, 3 courses, about £35. Sunday lunch from £17.50.
Closed	Never.
Directions	East off A1 7 miles north of Morpeth, 9 miles south of Alnwick, at Eshott signpost. Hall gates approx. 1 mile down lane.

	Mark Alderson
	Eshott Hall
	Eshott,
	Morpeth NE65 9EN
Tel	+44 (0)1670 787454
Email	info@eshotthall.co.uk
Web	www.eshotthall.co.uk

Hart's Nottingham

A small enclave of good things. You're on the smart side of town at the end of a cul-de-sac, thus remarkably quiet. You're also at the top of the hill and close to the castle with exceptional views that sweep south for ten miles; at night, a carpet of light sparkles. Inside, cool lines and travertine marble greet you in reception. Bedrooms are excellent, not huge, but perfectly adequate and extremely well designed. All come with wide-screen TVs, Bose sound systems, super little bathrooms and king-size beds wrapped in crisp white cotton. Those on the ground floor open onto a fine garden, each with a terrace where you can breakfast in good weather; rooms on higher floors have better views (six overlook the courtyard). A cool little bar, the hub of the hotel, is open for breakfast, lunch and dinner, but Hart's Restaurant across the courtyard offers fabulous food, perhaps pan-fried wood pigeon with blackberries, free-range chicken with wild garlic, tarte tatin with caramel ice-cream. There's a private car park for hotel guests and a small gym, too.

Rooms	29 doubles, 1 family room for 4: £125–£175. 2 suites for 2: £265.
Meals	Continental breakfast £9; full English £14. Bar snacks from £3.50. Lunch from £14.95. Dinner, 3 courses, £24–£40.
Closed	Never.
Directions	M1 junc. 24, then follow signs for city centre and Nottingham Castle. Left into Park Row from Maid Marian Way. Hotel on left at top of hill. Parking £8.50/night.

Adam Worthington
Hart's Nottingham
Standard Hill, Park Row,
Nottingham NG1 6GN

Tel	+44 (0)115 988 1900
Email	reception@hartshotel.co.uk
Web	www.hartsnottingham.co.uk

Langar Hall

Langar Hall is one of the loveliest places in this book – reason enough to come to Nottinghamshire – and Imogen's exquisite style and natural joie de vivre make this a mecca for those in search of an informal country-house with a touch of bohemian flair. The house sits at the top of a hardly noticeable hill in glorious parkland, bang next door to the church. Imo's family came 150 years ago, building on the site of Admiral Lord Howe's burned-down home. Much of what fills the house arrived then and it's easy to feel intoxicated by beautiful things: statues and busts, a pillared dining room, ancient tomes in overflowing bookshelves, an eclectic collection of oil paintings. Bedrooms are wonderful, some resplendent with antiques, others with fabrics draped from beams or trompe l'œil panelling. Heavenly food is a big treat, too, perhaps wild garlic soup, local venison, pistachio soufflé with lemon sorbet. There's a pretty conservatory for afternoon tea that opens onto a terrace, then grounds all around for medieval fishponds, an adventure play area and, once a year, Shakespeare on the lawn. One of a kind.

Rooms	7 doubles, 2 twins, 1 four-poster, 1 suite for 2, 1 chalet for 2: £100–£199.
Meals	Lunch from £18.50. Dinner, 3 courses, £25–£35.
Closed	Never.
Directions	From Nottingham A52 towards Grantham. Right, signed Cropwell Bishop, then straight on for 5 miles. House next to church on edge of village, signed.

Imogen Skirving
Langar Hall
Church Lane, Langar,
Nottingham NG13 9HG
Tel   +44 (0)1949 860559
Email info@langarhall.co.uk
Web   www.langarhall.com

AWARD WINNER
Hotel of the Year
England

Entry 173   Map 6

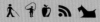

Old Bank Hotel

You're in the heart of old Oxford, with Merton College and Christ Church Meadows to the south, the Radcliffe Camera and the Bodleian Library to the north, and University College and the Botanic Gardens at Magdalen Bridge to the east. As for the Old Bank, its stylish interiors are home to an exceptional collection of modern art and photography. The hub is the old tiller's hall, now a cocktail bar and brasserie, with six arched windows overlooking the high street. Food flies from the kitchen all day, anything from a pizza or a steak to afternoon tea, with meat from the owner's farm and fish from the Channel Islands. Bedrooms are gorgeous: fine beds, piles of cushions, original art, robes in chic bathrooms. Some have padded window seats, others have sofas, all have flat-screen TVs and good WiFi. Staff are lovely, beds are turned down, the daily papers delivered to your door. There's a decked courtyard for breakfast in summer, free off-street parking, then daily walking tours for guests. The University Church of St Mary stands opposite, so climb its tower for the best views of Oxford. *Minimum stay: 2 nights at weekends.*

Rooms	20 doubles, 21 twin/doubles: £170-£290. 1 suite for 5: £305-£500.
Meals	Breakfast £5-£15. Lunch & dinner £5-£30. Afternoon tea from £6.95.
Closed	Never.
Directions	Cross Magdalen Bridge for city centre. Straight through 1st set of lights, then left into Merton St. Follow road right; 1st right into Magpie Lane. Car park 2nd right.

	Ben Truesdale Old Bank Hotel 92-94 High Street, Oxford OX1 4BJ
Tel	+44 (0)1865 799599
Email	info@oldbank-hotel.co.uk
Web	www.oldbank-hotel.co.uk

Old Parsonage Hotel

The Old Parsonage has been at the centre of Oxford live for over 350 years. It stands in the middle of town on land owned by University College and was once home to Oscar Wilde. It is the loveliest place to stay in town, not least due to a spectacular refurbishment that has touched every corner. Chief among its virtues are its shaded dining terrace, its exceptional art collection, and its first-floor library (curated by Philip Blackwell), which opens onto a small roof terrace. Inside, logs smoulder in an ancient fireplace, newspapers wait by mullioned windows, fresh flowers scent the air. The restaurant doubles as an art gallery, its charcoal walls crammed with portraits. It's a theatrical setting for a good meal, perhaps Jersey crab, duck with dandelion, rhubarb crumble with rhubarb ice-cream. Bedrooms are delicious: pale greys, Oxford art, sublime white marble bathrooms with robes and pots of spoiling oils. Expect the best beds, the crispest linen, pretty throws and padded bedheads. There are free guided walking tours for guests every day and picnics for lunch by the river. *Minimum stay: 2 nights at weekends.*

Rooms	24 doubles, 5 twins: £195-£405. 6 suites for 3: £315-£485.
Meals	Breakfast £5-£15. Lunch from £18.50. Afternoon tea from £9. Dinner, 3 courses, about £35.
Closed	Never.
Directions	From A40 ring road, south onto Banbury Road; thro' Summertown and hotel on right just before St Giles church.

Rebecca Mofford
Old Parsonage Hotel
1 Banbury Road,
Oxford OX2 6NN
Tel   +44 (0)1865 310210
Email   info@oldparsonage-hotel.co.uk
Web   www.oldparsonage-hotel.co.uk

The Trout at Tadpole Bridge

A 17th-century Cotswold inn on the banks of the Thames; pick up a pint, drift into the garden, watch the world float by. Inside you find all the trimmings of a lovely old pub: timber frames, exposed stone walls, a wood-burner to keep things toasty, local ales on tap at the bar. Logs are piled high in alcoves, good art hangs on the walls, pretty rugs cover old flagstones. Delicious food flies from the kitchen – anything from posh fish and chips or steak and ale pie to rack of lamb with a rosemary crust or Gressingham duck with ginger purée. Bedrooms at the back are away from the crowd; three open onto a small courtyard where wild roses ramble. You get smart fabrics, trim carpets, monsoon showers (one room has a claw-foot bath), DVD players, flat-screen TVs and a library of films. Sleigh beds, brass beds, smartly upholstered armchairs... one room even has a roof terrace. You can watch boats pass from the breakfast table, feast on local sausages, tuck into homemade marmalade courtesy of Helen's mum. Oxford is close, there are maps for walkers, you can even get married in the garden. *Minimum stay: 2 nights at weekends.*

Rooms	2 doubles, 3 twin/doubles: £130. 1 suite for 2: £160. Singles from £85.
Meals	Lunch from £5. Dinner, 3 courses, about £30. Sunday lunch from £14.95.
Closed	Christmas Day & Boxing Day.
Directions	A420 southwest from Oxford for Swindon. After 13 miles right for Tadpole Bridge. Pub on right by bridge.

Gareth & Helen Pugh
The Trout at Tadpole Bridge
Buckland Marsh,
Faringdon SN7 8RF

Tel	+44 (0)1367 870382
Email	info@trout-inn.co.uk
Web	www.trout-inn.co.uk

The Feathers Hotel

Woodstock is hard to beat, its golden cottages stitched together seamlessly. It's intrinsically linked to Blenheim Palace, one of Britain's finest houses, seat of the Dukes of Marlborough, birthplace of Winston Churchill. You can stroll up in five minutes, drop your jaw, then come back for afternoon tea. The hotel sits serenely on the high street with a carriage arch leading into a stone courtyard where you sit in summer sipping Pimm's; just heavenly. Inside, elegant, uncluttered interiors keep things simple: beautiful art, smouldering fires, a wall or two of original panelling, flowers everywhere. Ancient windows flood the place with light, there are colourful rugs on polished wooden floors, then more gin than you can shake a stick at in the sitting-room bar (181 different bottles). Bedrooms are dreamy with beautiful fabrics, lovely beds, mohair throws, delicious wallpapers. Some have sofas, all come with robes in fancy bathrooms. Back downstairs you'll find delicious food in the restaurant, perhaps crab risotto, grilled lemon sole, treacle tart with chocolate ice-cream. Oxford is close. *Minimum stay: 2 nights at weekends in summer.*

Rooms	13 doubles, 3 twin/doubles: £169–£229. 5 suites for 2: £259–£319. Singles from £129.
Meals	Lunch from £5. Dinner, 3 courses, £39.95–£49.95 (not Sunday eve).
Closed	Never.
Directions	North from Oxford on A44. In Woodstock left after traffic lights & hotel on left.

Pete Saunders
The Feathers Hotel
Market Street, Woodstock OX20 1SX

Tel	+44 (0)1993 812291
Email	enquiries@feathers.co.uk
Web	www.feathers.co.uk

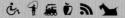

The Kings Head Inn

The sort of inn that defines this country: a 16th-century cider house made of ancient stone that sits on the green in a Cotswold village with free-range hens strutting their stuff and a family of ducks bathing in the pond. Inside, locals gather to chew the cud, scoff great food and wash it down with a cleansing ale. The fire burns all year, you get low ceilings, painted stone walls, country rugs on flagstone floors. Bedrooms, all different, are scattered about; all are well priced. Those in the main house have more character, those in the courtyard are bigger (and quieter). You'll find painted wood, lots of colour, pretty fabrics, spotless bathrooms; most have great views, too. Breakfast and supper are taken in a pretty dining room (exposed stone walls, pale wood tables), while you can lunch by the fire in the bar on Cornish scallops, steak and ale pie, then a plate of British cheeses. There are lovely unpompous touches like jugs of cow parsley in the loo, and loads to do: antiques in Stow, golf at Burford, walking and riding through gorgeous terrain. The front terrace teems with life in summer.

Rooms	10 doubles, 2 twin/doubles: £95-£135. Singles from £70.
Meals	Lunch from £7.50. Dinner, 3 courses, about £30. Sunday lunch from £12.95.
Closed	Christmas Day & Boxing Day.
Directions	East out of Stow-on-the-Wold on A436, then right onto B4450 for Bledington. Pub in village on green.

Archie & Nicola Orr-Ewing
The Kings Head Inn
The Green, Bledington,
Chipping Norton OX7 6XQ
Tel   +44 (0)1608 658365
Email   info@kingsheadinn.net
Web   www.kingsheadinn.net

AWARD
WINNER

Nicely priced

The Feathered Nest Country Inn

The village is tiny, the view is fantastic, the bar is lively, the rooms are a treat. This 300-year-old malthouse recently had a facelift and now shines. Interiors mix all the old originals – stone walls, timber frames, beamed ceilings, open fires – with a contemporary, rustic style. The net result is an extremely attractive country inn, one of the best in the south. Downstairs, one room flows into another. You get beautiful bay windows, roaring fires, saddled bar stools, green leather armchairs. Everywhere you go something lovely catches the eye, not least the view – the best in the Cotswolds; it will draw you to the terrace where your eyes drift off over quilted fields to a distant ridge. You get beds of lavender, swathes of lawn, a vegetable garden that serves the kitchen. Bedrooms upstairs are gorgeous. One is enormous, two have the view, beds are dressed in crisp linen. Most have power showers, one has a claw-foot bath, all have robes. There's even a Nespresso machine in every room. Super food waits downstairs: Old Spot terrine, Fairford chicken, rhubarb and champagne jelly. *Minimum stay: 2 nights at weekends.*

Rooms	4 doubles: £180-£230. Singles from £105. Cots £15. Under 12s in family room, £30.
Meals	Lunch & dinner £6.50-£30. Not Sunday eve.
Closed	Mondays (except Bank Holidays).
Directions	North from Burford on A424 for Stow-on-the-Wold. After 4 miles right for Nether Westcote. In village.

Tony & Amanda Timmer
The Feathered Nest Country Inn
Nether Westcote,
Chipping Norton OX7 6SD

Tel   +44 (0)1993 833030
Email reservations@thefeatherednestinn.co.uk
Web   www.thefeatherednestinn.co.uk

Burford House

Burford was made rich by 14th-century mill owners. Its golden high street slips downhill to the river Windrush, where paths lead out into glorious country, passing a church that dates to Norman times; Cromwell held a band of Levellers here in 1649 and their murals survive inside. Halfway up the hill, this 17th-century timber-framed house stands bang in the middle of town. Interiors sweep you back to the soft elegance of old England: a couple of cosy sitting rooms, a whispering wood-burner, exposed stone walls, a courtyard for summer dining. Slip into the restaurant and find Farrow & Ball colours, freshly cut flowers, rugs on wood boards, theatre posters on the wall. The food is delicious so come for ham hock terrine, a trio of Cotswold lamb, a plate of rhubarb puddings. Bedrooms are delightful, two across the courtyard in the coach house. Some have oak beams, others a claw-foot bath. All come with super beds, woollen blankets and robes in good bathrooms; those at the back have rooftop views. Wake on Sunday to the sound of pealing bells.
Minimum stay: 2 nights at weekends during summer.

Rooms	5 twin/doubles, 2 four-posters: £125-£225. 1 family room for 4: £175-£250.
Meals	Light lunch from £4.95. Dinner (Wed-Sat) about £35 (if pre-booked, £30).
Closed	Rarely.
Directions	In centre of Burford, halfway down hill. Free on-street parking, free public car park nearby.

	Ian Hawkins
	Burford House
	99 High Street,
	Burford OX18 4QA
Tel	+44 (0)1993 823151
Email	stay@burfordhouse.co.uk
Web	www.burford-house.co.uk

The Swan

Free-range bantams strut in the garden, a pint of Hooky waits at the bar. This lovely old pub sits in glorious country with the river Windrush passing ten paces from the front door and the village cricket pitch waiting beyond. It started life as a water mill and stands on the Devonshire estate, hence all the pictures of the Mitford sisters hanging on the walls. Outside, wisteria wanders along golden stone and creepers blush red in the autumn sun. Interiors are delicious: low ceilings, open fires, beautiful windows, stone walls. Over the years thirsty feet have worn grooves into 400-year-old flagstones, so follow in their footsteps and stop for a drink at the bar, then eat from a seasonal menu that brims with local produce: curried sweet potato soup, Foxbury Farm chargrilled steak, dark chocolate and ginger pot. Doors in the conservatory restaurant open onto the garden terrace in fine weather. Bedrooms in the old forge hit the spot: very pretty, nicely priced, super-comfy beds. Expect 15th-century walls, 21st-century interior design and a pink chaise longue in the suite. Burford is close.

Rooms	4 doubles, 1 twin, 5 twin/doubles: £120-£140. 1 suite for 2: £150-£180. Singles from £70.
Meals	Lunch from £5. Dinner, 3 courses, about £30. Sunday lunch from £14.95.
Closed	Christmas Day & Boxing Day.
Directions	West from Oxford on A40 for Cheltenham/Burford. Past Witney & village signed right at 1st r'bout.

Archie & Nicola Orr-Ewing
The Swan
Swinbrook,
Burford OX18 4DY
Tel +44 (0)1993 823339
Email info@theswanswinbrook.co.uk
Web www.theswanswinbrook.co.uk

The Olive Branch

A lovely pub in a sleepy Rutland village, where bridle paths lead out across peaceful fields. It dates to the 17th century and is built of Clipsham stone, as is York Minster. Inside, a warm, informal, rustic chic hits the spot perfectly with open fires, old beams, stone walls and choir stalls in the bar. But there's more here than cool design. This is a place to come and eat great food, the lovely, local seasonal stuff that's cooked with passion by Sean and his brigade, perhaps potted pork and stilton with apple jelly, haunch of venison with a juniper fondant, then a boozy rhubarb trifle. Bedrooms in Beech House across the lane are gorgeous. Three have terraces, one has a free-standing bath, all come with crisp linen, pretty beds, Roberts radios and real coffee. Super breakfasts – smoothies, boiled eggs and soldiers, the full cooked works – are served in a stone-walled barn with flames leaping in the wood-burner. The front garden fills in summer, the sloe gin comes from local berries, and Newark is close for the biggest antiques market in Europe. Picnic hampers can be arranged. A total gem.

Rooms	5 doubles, 1 family room for 4: £115–£195. Singles from £97.50.
Meals	Lunch from £6.25. Dinner, 3 courses, £25–£35. Sunday lunch from £16.95.
Closed	Rarely.
Directions	A1 5 miles north of Stamford, then exit onto B668. Right & right again for Clipsham. In village (Beech House across the road from The Olive Branch).

Ben Jones & Sean Hope
The Olive Branch
Main Street, Clipsham,
Oakham LE15 7SH

Tel	+44 (0)1780 410355
Email	info@theolivebranchpub.com
Web	www.theolivebranchpub.com

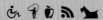

Hambleton Hall Hotel & Restaurant

A sublime country house, one of the loveliest in England. The position here is matchless. The house stands on a tiny peninsular that juts into Rutland Water. You can sail on it or cycle around it, then come back to the undisputed wonders of Hambleton: sofas by the fire in the panelled hall, a pillared bar in red for cocktails, a Michelin star in the dining room. French windows in the sitting room (beautiful art, fresh flowers, the daily papers) open onto fine gardens. Expect clipped lawns and gravel paths, a formal parterre garden that bursts with summer colour and a walled swimming pool with views over grazing parkland to the water. Bedrooms are the very best. Hand-stitched Italian linen, mirrored armoires, Roberts radios, fabulous marble bathrooms; Stefa's eye for fabrics, some of which coat the walls, is faultless. The Pavilion, a supremely comfortable two-bedroom suite, has its own terrace. Polish the day off with incredible food, perhaps breast of wood pigeon, fallow venison with Asian pear, passion fruit soufflé with banana sorbet. Don't miss the hotel's bakery up the road. Irreproachable. *Minimum stay: 2 nights at weekends.*

Rooms	15 twin/doubles: £265-£440.
	1 suite for 4: £400-£630.
	Singles from £195.
Meals	Lunch from £25.50. Sunday lunch £55.
	Dinner, 3 courses, £65.
	Tasting menu £75.
Closed	Never.
Directions	From A1, A606 west towards Oakham for about 8 miles, then left, signed Hambleton. In village bear left and hotel signed right.

Tim & Stefa Hart
Hambleton Hall Hotel & Restaurant
Ketton Road, Hambleton,
Oakham LE15 8TH

Tel	+44 (0)1572 756991
Email	hotel@hambletonhall.com
Web	www.hambletonhall.com

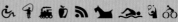

The Castle Hotel

This thriving medieval market town sits amid some of the loveliest country in the land, a launch pad for walkers and cyclists, with Offa's Dyke, Long Mynd and the Kerry Ridgeway all close. After a day in the hills what better than to roll back down to this quirky hotel for a night of genteel carousing. You'll find heaps of country comforts: hearty food, an impeccable pint, cosy rooms with honest prices. Downstairs, there's a coal fire in the pretty snug, oak panelling in the breakfast room, and Millie the short-haired dachshund who patrols the corridors with aplomb. Spotless bedrooms upstairs have good beds, warm colours, flat-screen TVs, an armchair if there's room. Some are up in the eaves, several have views of the Shropshire hills, two are seriously fancy. Back downstairs you find the sort of food you hanker for after a day in the open air, perhaps broccoli and stilton soup, beef and ale pie, sticky toffee pudding (all for a song). Don't miss the hugely popular real ale festival in July, the beer drinker's equivalent of Glastonbury. There's a lovely garden, too, perfect for sundowners in summer.

Rooms	7 doubles, 1 twin: £85–£130.
	2 family rooms for 4: £85–£105.
	Singles from £60.
	Dinner, B&B from £70 p.p.
Meals	Lunch from £4.50.
	Dinner, 3 courses, about £25.
Closed	Christmas Day.
Directions	At top of hill in town, off A488.

Henry Hunter
The Castle Hotel
Bishop's Castle SY9 5BN

Tel	+44 (0)1588 638403
Email	stay@thecastlehotelbishopscastle.co.uk
Web	www.thecastlehotelbishopscastle.co.uk

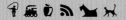

Pen-y-Dyffryn Country Hotel

In a blissful valley lost to the world, a small country house that sparkles on the side of a peaceful hill. This is one of those lovely places where guests return again and again, mostly due to Audrey and Miles, who run a very happy ship. Outside, fields tumble down to a stream that marks the border with Wales. Daffodils erupt in spring, the lawns are scattered with deckchairs in summer, paths lead into the hills for fine walking. Lovely interiors are just the ticket: Laura Ashley wallpaper and an open fire in the quirky bar; colourful art and super food in the pretty restaurant; the daily papers and the odd chaise longue in the sitting room. Bedrooms hit the spot. Most have the view, one has a French sleigh bed, a couple have jacuzzi baths for two. Four lovely rooms outside are dog-friendly and have their own patios. You get warm colours, crisp linen, pretty fabrics and sparkling bathrooms. After a day in the hills come back for a good dinner, perhaps wild mushroom risotto, pan-fried wood pigeon, hot chocolate fondant with vanilla ice-cream. Offa's Dyke and Powis Castle are close. *Minimum stay: 2 nights at weekends.*

Rooms	8 doubles, 4 twins: £120-£190. Singles from £86.
Meals	Light lunch (for residents) by arrangement. Dinner, 3 courses, £30-£37.
Closed	Rarely.
Directions	From A5 head to Oswestry. Leave town on B4580, signed Llansilin. Hotel 3 miles up. Approach Rhydycroesau, left at town sign, first right.

Miles & Audrey Hunter
Pen-y-Dyffryn Country Hotel
Rhydycroesau,
Oswestry SY10 7JD

Tel	+44 (0)1691 653700
Email	stay@peny.co.uk
Web	www.peny.co.uk

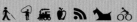

Sebastian's

This lovely little restaurant with rooms occupies an old merchant's house that dates from 1640. Michelle and Mark have been at the helm for 23 years cooking up a fine reputation – not only for their delicious food, but for the quirky, old-world interiors in which they serve it. Step off the street to find huge beams, timber frames, half panelling and stripped floors. In between you get smartly clothed tables, fairy lights and candles, exotic screens and fresh flowers. Old posters of the Orient Express hang on the walls (Mark supplies the train with canapés and desserts). Back in the restaurant there are sofas in front of a cavernous fire that smoulders from morning to night in winter. Here you drool over the menu before digging into fabulous food, perhaps scallop ravioli with lemon grass and ginger, loin of lamb with a goat's cheese tart, limoncello mousse. Five delightful rooms wait, one in the main house (timber frames, lots of colour), four off the courtyard (comfy sofas, lovely bathrooms). Montgomery, the prettiest town in Wales, is close.

Rooms	4 doubles, 1 twin/double: £75. Singles £65.
Meals	Continental breakfast £6.95; full English £11.95. Dinner, set menu, 3 courses, £22.50; 5 courses, £44.50 (Tue-Sat).
Closed	Rarely.
Directions	In middle of Oswestry on B4580.

Michelle & Mark Sebastian Fisher
Sebastian's
45 Willow Street,
Oswestry SY11 1AQ
Tel   +44 (0)1691 655444
Email   sebastians.rest@virgin.net
Web   www.sebastians-hotel.co.uk

The Swan

The Swan is gorgeous, a contemporary take on a village local. It's part of a new wave of cool little pubs that open all day and do so much more than serve a good pint. The locals love it. They come for breakfast, pop in to buy a loaf of bread, then return for afternoon tea and raid the cake stands. It's set back from the road, with a sprinkling of tables and chairs on the pavement in French-café style. Interiors mix old and new brilliantly. You get Farrow & Ball colours and cool lamps hanging above the bar, then lovely old rugs on boarded floors and a wood-burner to keep things toasty. Push inland to find an airy restaurant open to the rafters that overlooks the garden. Here you dig into Tom Blake's fabulous food (he's ex-River Cottage), anything from a Cornish crab sandwich with lemon mayo to a three-course feast, maybe Wye valley asparagus, Wedmore lamb chops, bitter chocolate mousse with chocolate cookies. Bedrooms are lovely. Two have fancy baths in the room, you get vintage French furniture, iPod docks, colourful throws and walk-in power showers. Glastonbury is close, as are the Mendips.

Rooms	4 doubles, 2 twin/doubles: £85–£120. Extra bed £20. Cots available.
Meals	Lunch from £5. Dinner, 3 courses, about £25. Sunday lunch from £14. Bar meals only Sun night.
Closed	Rarely.
Directions	M5, junc. 22, then B3139 to Wedmore. In village.

Jen Edwards
The Swan
Cheddar Road,
Wedmore BS28 4EQ

Tel	+44 (0)1934 710337
Email	info@theswanwedmore.com
Web	www.theswanwedmore.com

The Talbot Inn at Mells

A timeless village – ancient church, manor house, unspoilt stone cottages – with this 15th-century coaching inn hogging the limelight. It's an absolute stunner, with huge oak doors that lead into a cobbled courtyard, where life gathers in good weather. There's a tithe-barn sitting room with big sofas and a Sunday cinema, then the Coach House Grill, where you eat at weekends under hanging beams. As for the main house, it's a warren of ancient passageways, nooks and crannies and low doorways – the décor may be contemporary, but the past lives on. You'll find rugs on wood floors, crackling log fires, a lovely bar for a pint of Butcombe, then cosy rooms where you dig into tasty food, perhaps leek and potato soup, lemon sole with greens and beets, apple and rosemary tarte tatin. Bedrooms are the best, some small, others huge with claw-foot baths beside modern four-posters. Nothing is too much trouble for the spoiling staff. There's a colourful garden, then further afield some great local walking, so bring your boots. The First World War poet, Siegfried Sassoon, is buried in the churchyard.

Rooms	8 doubles: £95-£150.
Meals	Lunch & dinner £5-£30. Sunday lunch, 2 courses, £15.
Closed	Open all day.
Directions	From Frome A362 for Radstock; left for Mells. At mini-roundabout right to Mells. After 1 mile right to Mells.

Matt Greenlees
The Talbot Inn at Mells
Selwood Street, Mells,
Frome BA11 3PN
Tel   +44 (0)1373 812254
Email   info@talbotinn.com
Web   www.talbotinn.com

At The Chapel

Every now and then you walk into a small hotel and immediately know you've struck gold. That's what happens here. You cross the threshold and suddenly your pleasure receptors erupt in delight. At the front, you find an intoxicating wine shop on one side, then an irresistible bakery on the other (if you stay, they leave freshly baked croissants outside your room in the morning, a pre-breakfast snack). Back downstairs your eyes draw you through to an enormous room. This is an old Baptist chapel that Catherine and Ahmed bought ten years ago; the chapel itself, now a restaurant/café/art gallery/theatre was once their sitting room. You get white walls, vast windows, contemporary art and a rather cool bar. The food is perfect, nothing too posh, just seriously tasty stuff: fabulous pizza, fish from Lyme Bay, an ambrosial baked aubergine with parmesan and basil. Outside, a gorgeous terrace looks over the town to green hills; above, fabulous bedrooms come with flawless white marble bathrooms. We've run out of space, so come to see for yourself; expect something very special.

Rooms	8 doubles: £100-£250.
Meals	Breakfast from £2.50.
	Lunch & dinner £5-£35.
Closed	Rarely.
Directions	Bruton is 5 miles north of the A303 at Wincanton. On high street.

Catherine Butler & Ahmed Sidki
At The Chapel
High Street,
Bruton BA10 0AE

Tel	+44 (0)1749 814070
Email	mail@atthechapel.co.uk
Web	www.atthechapel.co.uk

The Pilgrims Restaurant with Rooms

Medieval pilgrims in search of King Arthur's tomb would stop here for sustenance before heading out across the marshes on their way to Glastonbury abbey. These days, the food, the welcome and the rooms are all so lovely you're more likely to suffer a crisis of faith and stay put. Jools is to blame – his food is far too good to miss, good enough to alter the DNA of these walls – the Pilgrims is not an inn these days, but a restaurant with rooms. All the lovely old stuff survives – stone walls, timber frames, panelled walls and a couple of sofas in front of the fire. Tables in the restaurant are nicely spaced apart with subtle lighting and service that hits the spot. As for the food, expect local ingredients cooked to perfection, perhaps Lyme Bay scallops, rack of lamb, smooth dark chocolate with a hint of stem ginger. Five lovely bedrooms wait in the old skittle alley. Three have cathedral ceilings, all come with exposed stone walls, flat-screen TVs and crisp linen on good beds. As for the bathrooms, expect double-ended baths, separate power showers, fluffy robes. Wells and Glastonbury are close.

Rooms	4 doubles, 1 twin/double: £95–£120.
Meals	Lunch from £8.
	Dinner, 3 courses, about £30.
	Sunday lunch £19.
	Not Monday.
Closed	Rarely.
Directions	On B3153 between Castle Cary & Somerton. In village by traffic lights.

Julian & Sally Mitchison
The Pilgrims Restaurant with Rooms
Lovington,
Castle Cary BA7 7PT

Tel	+44 (0)1963 240597
Email	jools@thepilgrimsatlovington.co.uk
Web	www.thepilgrimsatlovington.co.uk

The White Hart

Cool inns with lovely rooms in interesting parts of the land are a big hit with lots of us – we like the easy style, the local food, the good prices and the happy staff. The White Hart is a case in point, a beautifully refurbished inn. It sits on Somerton's ancient market square, 16th-century bricks and mortar, 21st-century lipstick and pearls. Inside, old and new mix beautifully: stone walls and parquet flooring, lovely sofas in front of the fire, funky lamps hanging above the bar. You'll find soft colours, padded window seats, country rugs, antler chandeliers. There's a cute booth in a stone turret, then cathedral ceilings in the airy restaurant, where lovely food waits, perhaps a chargrilled steak, smoked mackerel fishcakes, a pizza cooked in the wood-fired oven. In summer, you spill onto a smart courtyard or into the garden for views of open country. Upstairs, fabulous bedrooms await. You might find timber frames, a claw-foot bath, a wall of paper or stripped boards. All have super beds, flat-screen TVs, lovely bathrooms and a nice price. Beautiful Somerset is all around, don't miss it.

Rooms	8 doubles: £85–£130.
Meals	Lunch from £6.
	Dinner, 3 courses, £25–£30.
	Sunday lunch from £15.
Closed	Never.
Directions	South from Glastonbury on B3151. Right for Somerton, left into village and on left in square.

Natalie Patrick
The White Hart
Market Place,
Somerton TA11 7LX

Tel	+44 (0)1458 272273
Email	info@whitehartsomerton.com
Web	www.whitehartsomerton.com

The Devonshire Arms

A lively English village with a well-kept green; the old school house stands to the south, the church to the east and the post office to the west. The inn (due north) is over 400 years old and was once a hunting lodge for the Dukes of Devonshire; a rather smart pillared porch survives at the front. These days open-plan interiors are warmly contemporary with high ceilings, shiny blond floorboards and fresh flowers everywhere. Hop onto brown leather stools at the bar and order a pint of Moor Revival, or sink into sofas in front of the fire and crack open a bottle of wine. In summer, life spills onto the terrace at the front, the courtyard at the back and the lawned garden beyond. Super bedrooms run along at the front; all are a good size, but those at each end are huge. You get fresh light rooms, natural flooring, crisp white linen and freeview TV. Two have free-standing baths, some have compact showers. Delicious food is on tap in the restaurant – chargrilled scallops, slow-cooked lamb, passion fruit crème brûlée – so take to the nearby Somerset levels and walk off your indulgence in style.

Rooms	9 doubles: £95-£140. Singles £85-£140. Extra bed/sofabed £20 p.p. per night.
Meals	Lunch from £6.95. Dinner, 3 courses, about £30. Sunday lunch from £12.95.
Closed	Rarely.
Directions	A303, then north on B3165, through Martock to Long Sutton. On village green.

Philip & Sheila Mepham
The Devonshire Arms
Long Sutton,
Langport TA10 9LP

Tel	+44 (0)1458 241271
Email	mail@thedevonshirearms.com
Web	www.thedevonshirearms.com

Little Barwick House

A beautiful restaurant with rooms lost in peaceful lanes south of Yeovil. Tim and Emma rolled west 14 years ago and now have a legion of fans who come to feast on their ambrosial food. Their small Georgian country house stands privately in three acres of peace. Horses graze in the paddock below, afternoon tea is served in the garden to the sound of birdsong in summer. Inside, chic interiors flood with light thanks to fine windows that run along the front. There's an open fire in the bar, eclectic reading in the sitting room, then contemporary art in the high-ceilinged dining room. Gorgeous bedrooms have a country-house feel and come with warm colours, pretty fabrics, Roberts radios, a sofa if there's room. You'll find fresh garden flowers, antique furniture, then White Company oils in compact bathrooms. Dinner is the main event, heaven in three courses. Everything is homemade and cooked by Tim and Emma, an equal partnership in the kitchen – perhaps Lyme Bay scallops, saddle of wild venison, dark chocolate tort with armagnac ice-cream. Posh wines by the glass come courtesy of clever technology. *Children over 5 welcome.*

Rooms	4 doubles, 2 twins: £100–£170. Singles £75–£140. Dinner, B&B £105–£130 p.p. Extra bed/sofabed available £25 p.p. per night.
Meals	Lunch, 3 courses, £29.95. Dinner, 3 courses, £47.95.
Closed	Mondays & Sunday nights.
Directions	From Yeovil A37 south for Dorchester; left at 1st r'bout. Down hill, past church, left in village and house on left after 200 yds.

Emma & Tim Ford
Little Barwick House
Rexes Hollow Lane, Barwick,
Yeovil BA22 9TD
Tel   +44 (0)1935 423902
Email   reservations@barwick7.fsnet.co.uk
Web   www.littlebarwickhouse.co.uk

AWARD
WINNER

Fabulous food

Entry 193   Map 2

Lord Poulett Arms

In a ravishing village, an idyllic inn, French at heart and quietly groovy. Part pub, part country house, with walls painted in reds and greens and old rugs covering flagged floors, the Lord Poulett gives a glimpse of a 21st-century dream local, where classical design fuses with earthy rusticity. A fire burns on both sides of the chimney in the dining room; on one side you can sink into leather armchairs, on the other you can eat under beams at antique oak tables while candles flicker. Take refuge with the daily papers on the sofa in the locals' bar or head past a pile of logs at the back door and discover an informal French garden of box and bay trees, with a piste for boules and a creeper-shaded terrace. Bedrooms upstairs come in funky country-house style, with fancy flock wallpaper, perhaps crushed velvet curtains, a small chandelier or a carved-wood bed. Two rooms have slipper baths behind screens in the room; two have claw-foot baths in bathrooms one step across the landing; Roberts radios add to the fun. Delicious food includes summer barbecues, Sunday roasts and the full works at breakfast.

Rooms	2 doubles; 2 doubles with separate bath: £85–£95. Singles from £60.
Meals	Lunch from £5.50. Dinner, 3 courses, £25–£30.
Closed	Never.
Directions	A303, then A356 south for Crewkerne. Right for West Chinnock. Through village, 1st left for Hinton St George. Pub on right in village.

Steve & Michelle Hill
Lord Poulett Arms
High Street,
Hinton St George TA17 8SE

Tel	+44 (0)1460 73149
Email	reservations@lordpoulettarms.com
Web	www.lordpoulettarms.com

Farmers Arms

A lovely inn lost in peaceful hills on the Somerset Levels – a great base for a night or two of affordable luxury. Outside, cockerels crow, cows graze and glorious views from the beer garden drift downhill for a couple of miles – a perfect spot for a pint in summer. Inside, you'll find friendly natives, sofas in front of an open fire and a timber-framed bar, where one airy room rolls into another giving a sense of space and light. There are beamed ceilings, tongue-and-groove panelling, logs piled high in the alcoves. Bedrooms – some big, some huge – are just the ticket. They come with whitewashed walls, cast-iron beds, varnished floors, power showers or double-ended baths. One has a daybed, others have sofas, another has a private courtyard. Delicious food flies from the kitchen, perhaps half a pint of Atlantic prawns, West Country lamb with dauphinoise potatoes, orange and mango cheesecake; in summer you can eat in a courtyard garden. There are local stables if you want to ride and great walking, so bring your boots. Five berths for camper vans wait above the beer garden, too.

Rooms	4 doubles, 1 twin/double: £105-£125. Singles from £75.
Meals	Lunch & dinner £5-£35.
Closed	Never.
Directions	M5 junc. 25, then south on A358. On dual carriageway, right, signed West Hatch. Follow signs to RSPCA centre up hill for two miles. Signed on left.

Dionne Walsh
Farmers Arms
West Hatch, Taunton TA3 5RS

Tel	+44 (0)1823 480980
Email	farmersarmswh@gmail.com
Web	www.farmersarmssomerset.co.uk

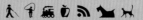

The Oaks Hotel

Another old-school charmer. This Edwardian house sits above the village, a winning position on the side of the hill. A beautiful garden wraps around you; views to the front shoot out to sea, those to the side skim over rooftops and land on Exmoor hills. Tim and Anne do it all themselves and practise the art of old-fashioned hospitality with great flair: they stop to chat, carry bags, ply you with tea and cake on arrival. Logs smoulder on the fire in the hall, hot coals glow in the sitting room. There's a snug bar, parquet flooring, floral fabrics, masses of books. Spotless bedrooms, all with sea views, are lovely: deeply comfy, lots of colour, great value for money. You get bowls of fruit, crisp white linen, fluffy bathrobes and Roberts radios; most have sofas, while beds are turned down every evening. As for dinner, Anne whisks up a four-course feast, perhaps smoked duck and almond salad, Cornish crab cakes with lime and ginger, Somerset pork with prunes and sherry, hot treacle tart with marmalade ice-cream. Exmoor, the coast and Dunster Castle all wait.

Rooms	1 double, 6 twin/doubles: £155–£175. Dinner, B&B from £115 p.p.
Meals	Dinner, 4 courses, £37.50.
Closed	November–April.
Directions	A39 west to Porlock. Keep left down hill into village and hotel on left after 200m.

Anne & Tim Riley
The Oaks Hotel
Porlock TA24 8ES

Tel	+44 (0)1643 862265
Email	info@oakshotel.co.uk
Web	www.oakshotel.co.uk

Cross Lane House

A medieval farmhouse in a National Trust village, where a 500-year-old bridge sweeps you across to ancient woodland. Outside, a cobbled courtyard leads up to a hay barn that's open on one side – not a bad spot for breakfast in good weather. Inside, original panelling is the big architectural draw, but Max and Andrew's lovely design gives a warm country-house feel, making this an intimate bolthole in which to linger. You'll find a sitting room packed with beautiful things – books galore, a wood-burner, sofas and armchairs to take the strain. There's a spy hole in the panelling, some ancient graffiti, too, then a pretty dining room with candles and low ceilings for nicely priced food, perhaps scallops with wild garlic, chicken wrapped in prosciutto, lemon tart with amaretto cream. Bedrooms upstairs are deeply satisfying: lovely beds, bowls of fruit, timber frames, super bathrooms. One is smaller, two are bigger, the family suite comes with a separate bedroom for children (or adults). Expect Roberts radios, Cowshed oils, a sofa if there's room. Exmoor waits. The road passes quietly at night. *Minimum stay: 2 nights at weekends.*

Rooms	3 doubles, 1 suite for 3: £110–£195. Dinner, B&B £120 p.p.
Meals	Lunch from £6 (Thur-Sat). Dinner, 3 courses, £29. Sunday lunch £18–£24.
Closed	January.
Directions	A39 west from Minehead. On right after 5 miles, 1 mile before Porlock.

Max Lawrence & Andrew Stinson
Cross Lane House
Allerford,
Minehead TA24 8HW

Tel	+44 (0)1643 863276
Email	max@crosslanehouse.com
Web	www.crosslanehouse.com

Netherstowe House

This quirky hotel is full of surprises, not least its wonderful bedrooms that are an absolute steal, but also for its peculiar location on the edge of a 1970s housing estate. If the latter puts you off, don't let it – the house is hidden by fine beech hedging and once up the drive you forget the outside world. Inside you fall immediately under the spell of some rather eccentric interiors that mix country-house style with 19th-century colonial overtones. You'll find varnished wood floors, roaring fires, tropical plants erupting with style, the odd chandelier. Gorgeous bedrooms are great value for money and come in an elegant clean style: beautiful beds, cool colours, old armoires. Bathrooms are fabulous. If you want something more contemporary, nip across the courtyard to the serviced apartments with sofabeds for children. They come with fancy kitchens but breakfast is included and the hotel is yours to roam. As for the food, it's served in a couple of smart dining rooms, perhaps wild mushroom risotto, slow-cooked spicy pork belly, roast pineapple with mango salsa. There are good steaks in the colourful cellar bistro, too.

Rooms	7 doubles, 1 twin: £95-£159.
	1 suite for 2-4: £195.
	8 apartments for 2: £130.
Meals	Lunch from £19.95.
	Dinner, 3 courses, about £30.
Closed	26 December to 2 January.
Directions	Sent on booking.

Ben Heathcote
Netherstowe House
Netherstowe Lane,
Lichfield WS13 6AY

Tel   +44 (0)1543 254270
Email   info@netherstowehouse.com
Web   www.netherstowehouse.com

The Packhorse Inn

The rise of the cool country inn continues apace and the most recent member to join the club is the Packhorse, a beautifully renovated country pub that was rescued from abject neglect. These days it's a small-scale pleasure dome – striking interiors, ambrosial food, bedrooms and bathrooms that elate – yet it remains a village local with a lovely bar that welcomes all. The downstairs is open plan with a fire that burns on two sides and the odd armchair to take the strain. You'll find varnished floorboards, beautiful art, low-hanging lamps at the cool little bar. Chic bedrooms have beautiful beds, cashmere throws, walk-in showers, perhaps a double-ended bath in the room. Back downstairs irresistible food waits, maybe truffled goat's cheese with quince and figs, Suffolk venison and kidney pudding, plum tarte tatin with fruit-cake ice-cream. There's a terrace for good weather and a private dining room turns into a very cool meeting room. This is prime horse-racing country three miles east of Newmarket (the peerless Frankel is at stud nearby). Cambridge and Bury St Edmunds are also close.

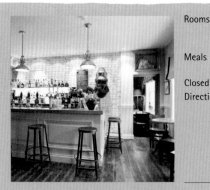

Rooms	6 doubles, 2 twin/doubles: £100–£140. Singles from £85. Extra beds for children £10.
Meals	Lunch from £6. Dinner, 3 courses, about £35.
Closed	Christmas day.
Directions	A14, junc. 38, then north onto A11. Take 1st exit and east on B1085. Through Kentford and into Moulton. Left at green and on left.

AWARD
WINNER

Favourite
newcomer

Hayley & Chris Lee
The Packhorse Inn
Bridge Street, Moulton,
Newmarket CB8 8SP

Tel	+44 (0)1638 751818
Email	info@thepackhorseinn.com
Web	www.thepackhorseinn.com

The Bildeston Crown

A 15th-century village inn owned by the local farmer – his roast rib of beef on Sundays is hard to beat. Outside, there's a terrace overlooking the village, then a small courtyard for a pint in the sun. Inside, timber frames, sagging ceilings and heavy beams are all original. A contemporary feel runs throughout with bold colours, comfy sofas and big art on the walls. There's an open fire in the pretty bar, a good spot for afternoon tea, but the big draw here is the restaurant with Suffolk lamb, Red Poll beef and Nedging pork all from the fields around you; vegetables come from the farm's kitchen garden, too. A couple of menus run side by side: one for dishes like fish pie or chargrilled steak, then another for fancier food altogether, perhaps duck consommé, Suffolk venison, chocolate fondant with vanilla ice-cream (an eight-course tasting menu is an extension of the à la carte). Upstairs, lovely bedrooms wait. One has a four-poster, another comes in black with a funky bath, all have robes in good bathrooms. Bury St Edmunds, medieval Lavenham and the Suffolk coast are close.

Rooms	10 doubles, 1 twin: £100–£195. Singles from £70.
Meals	Lunch from £6.50. Bar meals from £12.50. Dinner, 3 courses, £27–£45. Tasting menu £65. Sunday lunch from £17.
Closed	Never.
Directions	A12 junc. 31, then B1070 to Hadleigh. A1141 north, then B1115 into village & on right.

Alice Gibbons
The Bildeston Crown
104 High Street,
Bildeston IP7 7EB

Tel	+44 (0)1449 740510
Email	reception@thebildestoncrown.com
Web	www.thebildestoncrown.com

The Great House

Lavenham is a Suffolk gem, a medieval wool town trapped in aspic. The Great House stands across the market place from the Guildhall, its Georgian façade giving way to airy 15th-century interiors, where timber frames and old beams mix with contemporary colours and varnished wood floors. The poet Stephen Spender and his brother Humphrey – famous artist and photographer – once lived here and the house became a meeting place for artists, but these days it's the ambrosial food that draws the crowd. French to its core – the cheese board must qualify as one of the best in Britain – so dig into something delicious, perhaps venison, pistachio and sultana terrine, sea bass served with olives and white wine, then tarte tatin with cinnamon ice-cream. Fabulous bedrooms – all recently refurbished in lavish style – come with delicious bed linen, suede sofas, coffee machines, and robes in magnificent bathrooms. Four are huge, but even the tiniest is a dream. One has a regal four-poster, another has a 14th-century fireplace in its bathroom. All come with an array of gadgets: hi-fi, surround-sound, flat-screen TV... *Minimum stay: 2 nights at weekends.*

Rooms	4 doubles, 1 twin/double: £95–£195. Dinner, B&B from £112.50 p.p.
Meals	Breakfast £10–£15. Lunch, 2 courses, from £18.50 (not Mon/Tues). Dinner, 3 courses, £33.50 (not Sun/Mon).
Closed	First 4 weeks in January; 2 weeks in summer.
Directions	A1141 to Lavenham. At High Street 1st right after The Swan or up Lady Street into Market Place. On-site parking.

AWARD WINNER

Fabulous food

Régis & Martine Crépy
The Great House
Market Place, Lavenham,
Sudbury CO10 9QZ

Tel	+44 (0)1787 247431
Email	info@greathouse.co.uk
Web	www.greathouse.co.uk

Entry 201   Map 4

The Swan at Lavenham

The Swan is ancient, 600 years old, a spectacular tangle of medieval timber and sagging beams. Refurbished in epic style, it has never looked better. Inside, fires roar, ceilings soar and the loveliest staff weave through the mix delivering sinful plates of afternoon tea or cocktails before supper. Potter about and find a minstrel's gallery in the vaulted dining room, a fabulous old bar that was a favourite haunt of WWII airmen, then a lawned courtyard garden, where you can stop for a glass of Pimm's in summer. Bedrooms are lovely, some vast with four-posters and timber-framed walls, others more contemporary with cool colours and good sofas. All have super-comfy beds, crisp white linen, sparkling bathrooms and fluffy robes; bowls of fruit come as standard, beds are turned down during dinner. Elsewhere, there's a 14th-century hall for private dinners and weddings, and you can eat in an open-plan brasserie if you want something lighter. Finally, medieval Lavenham is a sight to behold; don't miss it. *Minimum stay: 2 nights at weekends. Some on-site parking. Ask about special offers.*

Rooms	32 twin/doubles, 2 four-posters: £195–£350. 10 suites for 2: £290–£350. 1 single: £105. Dinner, B&B from £122 p.p.
Meals	Lunch, 2 courses, from £16.95. Dinner, 3 courses, £35.95. Brasserie, 2 courses, from £16.
Closed	Never.
Directions	In village.

Ingo Wiangke
The Swan at Lavenham
High Street ,
Lavenham CO10 9QA

Tel	+44 (0)1787 247477
Email	info@theswanatlavenham.co.uk
Web	www.theswanatlavenham.co.uk

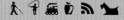

The Crown

The Crown is all things to all men, a lovely country pub, a popular local restaurant, a small boutique hotel, a cool little bolthole in Constable country. It sits in a pretty village with long views from its colourful terrace over the Box Valley, not a bad spot for a glass of Pimm's after a day exploring the area. It dates to 1560 and has old beams and timber frames, though interiors have youthful good looks: warm colours, tongue-and-groove panelling, terracotta-tiled floors, a fancy wine cellar behind a wall of glass. You'll find rugs and settles, the daily papers, leather armchairs in front of a wood-burner. Four ales wait at the bar, 30 wines come by the glass and there's seasonal food that will make you smile, perhaps mussel chowder, steak and kidney pie, steamed orange pudding with marmalade ice-cream. Airy bedrooms are hidden away at the bottom of the garden, all exemplary with super bathrooms, excellent beds, lovely linen and a dash of colour. All have armchairs or sofas, three have French windows that open onto private terraces with fine views. A great place to eat, sleep and potter.

Rooms	10 doubles: £135–£225.
	1 suite for 2: £195–£245.
Meals	Lunch & dinner £5–£25.
Closed	Rarely.
Directions	North from Colchester on A134, then B1087 east into Stoke-by-Nayland. Right at T-junction; pub on left.

Richard Sunderland
The Crown
Park Street, Stoke-by-Nayland,
Colchester CO6 4SE

Tel	+44 (0)1206 262001
Email	info@crowninn.net
Web	www.crowninn.net

Kesgrave Hall

This Georgian mansion sits in 38 acres of woodland and was built for an MP in 1812. It served as home to US airmen during WWII, becoming a prep school shortly after. Refurbished in 2008, it was an instant hit with locals, who love the style, the food and the informal vibe, and despite its country-house good looks, it is almost a restaurant with rooms, the emphasis firmly on the food. Find Wellington boots in the entrance hall, high ceilings in the huge sitting room, stripped boards in the humming bistro and doors that open onto a terrace in summer. Excellent bedrooms have lots of style. One is huge and comes with a faux leopard-skin sofa and free-standing bath. The others might not be quite as wild, but they're lovely nonetheless, some in the eaves, others in beautifully refurbished outbuildings. Expect warm colours, crisp linen, good lighting and fancy bathrooms. Back downstairs tasty bistro food flies from the kitchen, perhaps goat's cheese panna cotta, cottage pie with red cabbage, pear tart with rosemary and vanilla ice-cream. Suffolk's magical coast waits.

Rooms	10 doubles, 7 twin/doubles: £130–£230. 6 suites for 2: £275–£300.	
Meals	Breakfast £10–£16. Lunch & dinner, 3 courses, £25–£30.	
Closed	Never.	
Directions	Skirt Ipswich to the south on A14, then head north on A12. Left at 4th r'bout; signed right after 0.25 miles.	

Oliver Richards
Kesgrave Hall
Hall Road, Kesgrave,
Ipswich IP5 2PU
Tel   +44 (0)1473 333741
Email   reception@kesgravehall.com
Web   www.milsomhotels.com

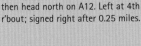

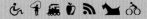

The Crown at Woodbridge

This cool little hotel in the middle of Woodbridge slopes down Quay Street, its rainbow of pastel colours now a landmark in town. Inside, open-plan interiors flood with light courtesy of a glass ceiling. A Windermere skiff hangs above the bar, you find painted panelling, comfy sofas, slate floors and a wood-burner roaring in the fireplace. Dining rooms sprawl, one in red, another in pale olive; you get leather banquettes, contemporary art, the odd window seat. Beautiful bedrooms upstairs vary in size, but all have the same smart feel: cool colours, duck-down duvets, padded headboards, Hypnos beds. You'll find panels of entwined willow, pitchforks hanging on the wall, super bathrooms that go the whole hog. Back downstairs, Stephen's rustic food is the big draw, perhaps potted shoulder of venison with walnuts and sloe jelly, steamed mussels in white wine and garlic, toffee apple tart with vanilla ice-cream. As for breakfast, everything is brought to your table: poached fruits, flagons of juice, the best sausages in Suffolk. Don't miss Snape Maltings, Sutton Hoo or the Aldeburgh food festival in October.

Rooms	8 twin/doubles; 2 family rooms for 4: £120–£160. Singles from £95.
Meals	Lunch & dinner £6–£30. Sunday roast from £12.50.
Closed	Never.
Directions	A12 north from Ipswich, then B1438 into town. Pass station & left into Quay St. On right.

Garth Wray
The Crown at Woodbridge
Thoroughfare,
Woodbridge IP12 1AD

Tel	+44 (0)1394 384242
Email	info@thecrownatwoodbridge.co.uk
Web	www.thecrownatwoodbridge.co.uk

The Crown & Castle

Orford is unbeatable, a sleepy Suffolk village blissfully marooned at the end of the road. River, beach and forest wait, as does the Crown & Castle, a fabulous English hostelry where the art of hospitality is practised with great flair. The inn stands in the shadow of Orford's 12th-century castle. The feel is warm and airy with stripped floorboards, open fires, eclectic art and candles at night. Rooms come with Vi-Spring beds, super bathrooms, lovely fabrics, the odd armchair. Four in the main house have watery views, the suite is stunning, the garden rooms big and light, the courtyard rooms (the latest addition) utterly sublime. All have crisp white linen, TVs, DVDs and digital radios. Wellington boots wait at the back door, so pull on a pair and explore Rendlesham Forest or hop on a boat and chug over to Orfordness. Ambrosial food awaits your return, perhaps seared squid with coriander and garlic, slow-cooked pork belly with a shellfish broth, crushed pistachio meringue with a chocolate ice-cream sundae. A great place to wash up for a few lazy days. Sutton Hoo is close. Very dog-friendly. *Minimum stay: 2 nights dinner, B&B, at weekends.*

Rooms	18 doubles, 2 twins: £130–£190. 1 suite for 2: £245. Dinner, B&B from £99.50 p.p.
Meals	Lunch from £8.50. À la carte dinner around £35.
Closed	Never.
Directions	A12 north from Ipswich, A1152 east to Woodbridge, then B1084 into Orford. Right in square for castle. On left.

David & Ruth Watson
The Crown & Castle
Orford,
Woodbridge IP12 2LJ
Tel   +44 (0)1394 450205
Email info@crownandcastle.co.uk
Web   www.crownandcastle.co.uk

Wentworth Hotel

The Wentworth has the loveliest position in town, the beach literally a pebble's throw from the garden, the sea rolling east under a vast sky. Inside, fires smoulder, clocks chime and seaside elegance abounds. It's all terrifically English, with vintage wallpapers, kind local staff and an elegant bar that opens onto a terrace garden. The restaurant looks out to sea, spilling onto a sunken terrace in summer for views of passing boats. Delicious English fare flies from the kitchen: stilton soup, breast of guinea fowl, lemon posset with raspberries and shortbread. The hotel has been in the same family since 1920 and old-fashioned values mix harmoniously with interiors that are refreshed often to keep things sparkling. Spotless bedrooms are deeply comfy, those at the front have huge sea views (and binoculars). Expect warm colours, wicker armchairs, padded headboards and comfortable beds. Bathrooms, all refurbished, are excellent. Sofas galore in the sitting room, but you may want to spurn them to walk by the sea. Joyce Grenfell was a regular. The Snape Maltings are close. *Minimum stay: 2 nights at weekends.*

Rooms	24 twin/doubles, 7 doubles: £140–£220. 4 singles: £85–£119. Dinner, B&B from £79 p.p.
Meals	Bar meals from £5. Lunch from £12. Dinner, 3 courses, £18.50–£24.
Closed	Never.
Directions	A12 north from Ipswich, then A1094 for Aldeburgh. Past church, down hill, left at x-roads; hotel on right.

Michael Pritt
Wentworth Hotel
Wentworth Road,
Aldeburgh IP15 5BD

Tel	+44 (0)1728 452312
Email	stay@wentworth-aldeburgh.com
Web	www.wentworth-aldeburgh.com

The Brudenell Hotel

The Brudenell stands bang on the beach in one of England's loveliest seaside towns. It makes the most of its view: a dining terrace at the front runs the length of the building; a glass-fronted restaurant swims in light; an elegant sitting room looks the right way. The hotel mixes a contemporary style and an informal feel. You'll find coastal art, sunny colours, driftwood sculptures on display. Beautiful bedrooms come in different shapes and sizes. Those at the back look onto open country and river marsh, those at the front have hypnotic views of sea and sky. A chic style runs throughout: seaside colours, good fabrics, blond wood furniture, sofas if there's room; bathrooms are excellent. Back downstairs the open-plan brasserie is the hub of the hotel. It serves good comfort food with lots of fish on the menu, but you can always grab a burger or a steak if that's what you want. Try crispy fried goat's cheese, Harwich crab tart, sticky toffee pudding with clotted cream. Elsewhere, there are beach towels, deckchairs or golf up the road at Thorpeness, and on clear nights the starry sky will amaze you. *Minimum stay: 2 nights at weekends.*

Rooms	12 doubles, 30 twin/doubles: £150–£325. 2 singles: £80.
Meals	Lunch from £5. Dinner, 3 courses, about £30.
Closed	Never.
Directions	A1094 into Aldeburgh. Right at T-junction, down high street, last left in village before car park & yacht club.

Peter Osborne
The Brudenell Hotel
The Parade,
Aldeburgh IP15 5BU

Tel	+44 (0)1728 452071
Email	info@brudenellhotel.co.uk
Web	www.brudenellhotel.co.uk

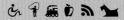

The Westleton Crown

This is one of England's oldest coaching inns, with 800 years of continuous service under its belt. It stands in a village two miles inland from the sea at Dunwich, with Westleton Heath running east towards Minsmere Bird Sanctuary. Inside, stripped floors, smouldering fires, exposed brickwork and ancient beams sweep you back 200 years. Weave about and find nooks and crannies in which to hide, flames flickering in open fires, a huge map on the wall for walkers. You can eat wherever you want, there's a conservatory breakfast room with fine local photography, then a colourful terraced garden for barbecues in summer. Fish comes straight off the boats at Lowestoft, local butchers provide local meat, perhaps wild rabbit and ham hock, spiced sea bass with curried cockles, coconut panna cotta with roasted pineapple. Bedrooms are scattered about (Will and Kate loved theirs!), some in the main house, others in converted stables. Expect lime whites, comfy beds, crisp linen, flat-screen TVs. Pretty bathrooms come courtesy of Fired Earth, some with claw-foot baths. Aldeburgh and Southwold are close. *Minimum stay: 2 nights at weekends.*

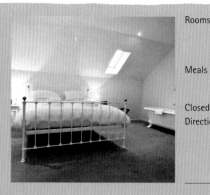

Rooms	26 doubles, 2 twins: £95-£180. 3 suites for 2: £185-£215. 2 family rooms for 4: £160-£180. 1 single: £90-£100.
Meals	Lunch & bar meals from £5.50. Dinner, 3 courses, about £30. Sunday lunch from £14.95.
Closed	Never.
Directions	A12 north from Ipswich. Right at Yoxford onto B1122, then left for Westleton on B1125. On right in village.

Gareth Clarke
The Westleton Crown
The Street, Westleton,
Saxmundham IP17 3AD

Tel	+44 (0)1728 648777
Email	info@westletoncrown.co.uk
Web	www.westletoncrown.co.uk

The Anchor

The Anchor is one of those wonderful places that has resisted the urge to be precious. This is a cool little seaside inn where relaxed informality reigns; kids are welcome, staff are lovely, dogs fall asleep in the bar. You're 500 yards from the sea with a vast sky hovering above and waves breaking in the distance. Outside, a big terrace fills with happy locals in summer, while a lawned garden stretches off towards the water. Inside, a beautiful simplicity abounds – Cape Cod meets English country local. You'll find books everywhere, wonderful art, roaring fires, scrubbed pine tables, old leather benches and painted tongue-and-groove. Sophie's local food is the big draw, perhaps fish soup with rouille and baguette, roast cod with lentils and chorizo, then a warm chocolate fondant. Bedrooms are great value and those in the house have a warm, homely feel. The garden chalet suites are different altogether – big and airy with sofas inside, and terraces that overlook nearby dunes and beach huts. Mark's bottled beers are exceptional, as is his lovely wine list. Starry skies amaze. Unmissable.

Rooms	9 doubles, 1 single/double: £95–£150.
Meals	Lunch from £5.25.
	Sunday lunch, 2 courses, £20.
	Dinner, 3 courses, about £30.
Closed	Christmas Day.
Directions	From A12 south of Southwold, B1387 to Walberswick.

Mark & Sophie Dorber
The Anchor
Main Street, Walberswick,
Southwold IP18 6UA

Tel	+44 (0)1502 722112
Email	info@anchoratwalberswick.com
Web	www.anchoratwalberswick.com

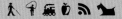

The Swan House

Once a 16th-century tavern, now a 21st-century pleasure dome, Swan House is a magical little place – quirky, intimate, deeply beautiful. It sits opposite a 14th-century church, the river Waveney passing below. In summer life spills onto the pedestrianised Walk; in winter you sink into sofas in front of the fire. Interiors are perfect: timber frames, ancient walls, beamed ceilings, striking colours. It's a tiny place which adds greatly to its charm. A movie plays in the front hall every day, you get fresh flowers and lovely art everywhere. One restaurant comes in red with pretty rugs and logs in the alcove; the other doubles as a gallery and has a fine oval table. Faultless bedrooms mix low ceilings, contemporary panelling, creaky floorboards and piles of books. Two have open fires, one a mezzanine for children, another a small balcony; all have magnificent bathrooms. Breakfast is extraordinary, one delicious course after another: Irish tea loaf, hams and cheese, plates of fruit, the full cooked works. Dinner is equally splendid: fresh mussels, confit of duck, amaretto ice-cream. One of the best. *Minimum stay: 2 nights at weekends. Children over 6 welcome.*

Rooms	4 doubles: £90–£145. 1 family room for 4: £140–£165.
Meals	Lunch from £6. Dinner: table d'hôte, £14–£17.50; à la carte, £25–£35. Sunday lunch from £14.
Closed	Rarely.
Directions	In centre of town at foot of clock tower. Car parks nearby.

Roland Blunk & Carmela Sabatini
The Swan House
By the tower,
Beccles NR34 9HE

Tel	+44 (0)1502 713474
Email	info@swan-house.com
Web	www.swan-house.com

Park House Hotel & Spa

A blissful pocket of rural Sussex. Park House sits in 12 acres of glorious English gardens with quilted fields circling the grounds and the South Downs rising beyond. Potter about outside and find a croquet lawn, a grass tennis court and a six-hole golf course that slips into the country. Fine shrubberies burst with colour while Wellington boots wait at the front door for long country walks. You may prefer to stay put; the newest addition is its fabulous spa. It comes with a very swanky indoor pool to go with its outside partner, four treatment rooms, a sauna and steam room, then a proper gym and a terraced bar for lazy afternoons. As for the house, it's just as good. Beautiful interiors abound mixing country-house style with contemporary colours. The pavilion bar overlooks the gardens, you breakfast in the conservatory or out on the terrace, there are flagstones in reception, the daily papers in the sitting room, great food in the dining room. Gorgeous bedrooms are the final luxury: heavenly beds, big country views, fancy bathrooms, iMac TVs. Exceptional.

Rooms	6 doubles, 10 twin/doubles: £160-£224. 4 family rooms for 4; 1 cottage for 2-4: £230-£360.	
Meals	Lunch, 2 courses, from £20.95. Afternoon tea £19.95. Dinner, 3 courses, £37.50.	
Closed	Rarely.	
Directions	South from Midhurst on A286. At sharp left bend, right (straight ahead), signed Bepton. Hotel on left after 2 miles.	

Rebecca Coonan
Park House Hotel & Spa
Bepton,
Midhurst GU29 0JB

Tel	+44 (0)1730 819000
Email	reservations@parkhousehotel.com
Web	www.parkhousehotel.com

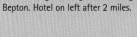

Halfway Bridge Inn

Sam's gorgeous inn wasn't quite as lovely when he took over the reins a few years ago, but after pouring in love and money in equally large amounts, the place now shines. It sits back from the A272, with Goodwood to the south for the races, Petworth to the east for antiques and the South Downs all around for exhilarating walking. Step inside to find a smart, cosy world of original wood floors, whitewashed walls, smouldering fires, the odd mind-your-head beam. It's a deeply pretty place, small but certainly sweet, with snug rooms giving a Dickensian feel, albeit with a 21st-century makeover. Spin round to the bar and find three local ales, 25 wines by the glass, the daily papers and beautifully upholstered bar stools; there's a door onto the terrace for lunch in summer. Big stylish bedrooms wait across the lane in an old stone barn, where old and new mix beautifully – smart bathrooms and lovely furniture amid beams and panelled walls. As for the food, it's a big draw with the locals, perhaps Cornish scallops with tiger prawns, canon of lamb with a mead-scented jus, a prune and armagnac tart.

Rooms	6 doubles: £120–£150.
	1 suite for 2: £170–£190.
	Singles (Sun–Thurs) from £80.
Meals	Lunch & dinner £14.50–£28.
	Bar meals £6.50–£12.50.
Closed	Never.
Directions	On A272 halfway between Midhurst & Petworth.

Sam Bakose
Halfway Bridge Inn
Halfway Bridge,
Petworth GU28 9BP

Tel	+44 (0)1798 861281
Email	enquiries@halfwaybridge.co.uk
Web	www.halfwaybridge.co.uk

The Royal Oak Inn

This pretty inn sits in a sleepy Sussex village with the South Downs rising above and the coast at the Witterings waiting below. Inside, an attractive rusticity prevails: stripped floors, low ceilings and the odd racing print (the inn was once part of the Goodwood estate). There's a small bar for a pint in front of an open fire, but these days it's a mostly dining pub, the restaurant spreading itself far and wide, through the conservatory and out onto the terrace in summer. A small army of chefs conjure up irresistible food, perhaps Selsey crab mousse with a Vermouth foam, roast guinea fowl with a prune terrine, whisky Mac jelly with cinnamon oats. Elegant bedrooms are sprinkled about, some in garden cottages, others upstairs. All come in contemporary style with smart fabrics, leather armchairs, comfy beds and good bathrooms. CD players, plasma screens, and DVD libraries keep you amused. Staff are attentive, complimentary newspapers arrive with breakfast. The South Downs are all about, Goodwood is a mile up the road, Chichester Theatre and Bosham are close. *Minimum stay: 2 nights at weekends.*

Rooms	2 doubles, 3 twin/doubles: £110–£190. 3 suites for 2-4: £180–£280. Singles from £85.
Meals	Lunch from £7.95. Dinner, 3 courses, about £35. Sunday lunch £25–£29.
Closed	Never.
Directions	From Chichester A286 for Midhurst. First right at first mini roundabout into E. Lavant. Down hill, past village green, over bridge, pub 200 yds on left. Car park opposite.

Charles Ullmann
The Royal Oak Inn
Pook Lane, East Lavant,
Chichester PO18 0AX

Tel	+44 (0)1243 527434
Email	rooms@royaloakeastlavant.co.uk
Web	www.royaloakeastlavant.co.uk

The Crab & Lobster

This tiny arrowhead of land south of Chichester is something of a time warp, more 1940s than 21st century. The Crab & Lobster is older still – 350 years at last count. It sits on Pagham Harbour, a tidal marsh that teems with preening birds. Outside, you find a smart whitewashed exterior and a small garden for views across fields of sheep to the water. Inside, flagged floors, whitewashed walls, a fire at one end, a wood-burner at the other. There's a lovely alcove with banquette seating, candles flicker in the evening, in summer you decant onto the back terrace for lunch in the sun. Upstairs, four super rooms come in duck-egg blue with crisp white linen, flat-screen TVs and gorgeous little bathrooms. Three have views of the water, one is up in the eaves and has a telescope to scan the high seas. There's much to explore: Bosham, where King Canute tried to turn back the waves; Fishbourne, for its Roman palace; the Witterings, for miles of beach and dunes. Don't forget dinner, perhaps Selsey crab cakes with chilli jam, fillet of pork with a calvados cream, caramelised plum tart. *Minimum stay: 2 nights at weekends.*

Rooms	4 doubles: £145.1 cottage for 4: £230.
Meals	Bar meals from £11.85.
	Lunch from £16.50.
	Dinner, 3 courses, about £30.
	Sunday lunch from £24.
Closed	Never.
Directions	Mill Lane is off B2145 Chichester to Selsey road, just south of Sidlesham. Pub close to Pagham Harbour.

Sam Bakose
The Crab & Lobster
Mill Lane, Sidlesham,
Chichester PO20 7NB

Tel	+44 (0)1243 641233
Email	enquiries@crab-lobster.co.uk
Web	www.crab-lobster.co.uk

The Bull

Stepping into The Bull is like travelling back in time to Dickensian England; little seems to have changed in 200 years. Electricity has been introduced, but even that is rationed on aesthetic grounds; as a result, light plays beautifully amid old timbers. Elsewhere, fires roar, beams sag, candles twinkle, tankards dangle. You might call it 'nostalgic interior design', but whatever it is, the locals love it; the place was packed on a Sunday afternoon in late January. Well-kept ales are on tap in the bar, excellent food flies from the kitchen, perhaps caramelised parsnip and apple soup, a magnificent plate of rare roast beef, then chilled white chocolate and vanilla fondue. Upstairs, four pretty rooms await (two larger, two above the bar) with more planned. You may find timber-framed walls, leather sleigh beds or statues of eastern deities, while the 21st century delivers digital radios, contemporary art and very good compact bathrooms. Bring walking boots or mountain bikes and take to the high trails on the South Downs National Park, which rise beyond the village. Brighton is close.

Rooms	3 doubles, 1 twin/double: £100–£140.
Meals	Lunch from £5.50.
	Dinner, 3 courses, about £30.
Closed	Never.
Directions	Leave A23 just north of Brighton for Pyecombe. North on A273, then west for Ditchling on B2112. In centre of village at crossroads.

Dominic Worrall
The Bull
2 High Street, Ditchling,
Hassocks BN6 8TA

Tel	+44 (0)1273 843147
Email	info@thebullditchling.com
Web	www.thebullditchling.com

The Griffin Inn

A proper inn, posh with a hint of scruffiness, a community local that draws a devoted crowd. You get open fires, 400-year-old beams, oak panelling and prints on the walls. There's a lively bar, an attractive restaurant and a club room for racing on Saturdays. In summer, life spills onto a pretty terrace for local meat cooked in a wood-fired oven. There are weekend barbecues, too, and deckchairs scattered across the lawns for ten-mile views over Pooh Bear's Ashdown Forest to Sheffield Park. Bedrooms are nicely priced and full of country-inn elegance: uneven floors, the odd four-poster, lovely old furniture and free-standing baths. Rooms in the coach house are quieter, those in Griffin House quieter still. Some in the main house have timber frames, all have robes and colourful art. Back downstairs, seasonal menus do the trick, perhaps rabbit gnocchi, local pheasant, dark chocolate tort with honey ice-cream; breakfast sausages are divine. The pub has three cricket teams that travel the world in pursuit of glory — you may find them in the bar on a summer evening after a hot day in the field. *Minimum stay: 2 nights on bank holiday weekends.*

Rooms	6 doubles, 7 four-posters: £85–£145. Singles £70–£80 (Sun–Thur).
Meals	Bar meals from £6.50. Dinner, 3 courses, £30–£40.
Closed	Christmas Day.
Directions	From East Grinstead A22 south, right at Nutley for Fletching. On for 2 miles into village.

Nigel & James Pullan
The Griffin Inn
Fletching,
Uckfield TN22 3SS

Tel	+44 (0)1825 722890
Email	info@thegriffininn.co.uk
Web	www.thegriffininn.co.uk

Wingrove House

If you need proof that small hotels are infinitely lovelier than their big brothers, here's the evidence. This gorgeous bolthole stands at the end of a pretty village with an ancient church on one side and the South Downs Way passing on the other. At the front a small walled garden leads up to a stone terrace, a great spot to linger in summer; in winter you grab a sofa in front of the wood-burner and roast away in the cool little sitting room bar (wood floors, interesting art, chic colonial feel). Upstairs, delicious bedrooms have smart fabrics, vibrant colours, iPod docks and fancy bathrooms. Two at the front open onto a veranda, the biggest at the back overlooks the churchyard (the bell chimes rarely). There's lots to do. Great walks start from the front door with Cuckmere Haven, Friston Forest and Beachy Head all within range, so work up an appetite, then return to feast on excellent local food, perhaps potted South Coast crab, Sussex lamb with garlic and rosemary, French lemon tart with local raspberry sorbet. Come by train and Nick will pick you up from the station. Brilliant.

Rooms	5 doubles: £95-£175.
Meals	Lunch from £10 (Sat and Sun only). Dinner, 3 courses, £28-£32.
Closed	Rarely.
Directions	M23, A23, then A27 east from Brighton. Past Berwick, then south at r'bout for Alfriston. In village on left.

Nicholas Denyer
Wingrove House
High Street, Alfriston,
Polegate BN26 5TD

Tel	+44 (0)1323 870276
Email	info@wingrovehousealfriston.com
Web	www.wingrovehousealfriston.com

The Tiger Inn

The Tiger sits on a village green that has hardly changed in 50 years and in summer life spills onto the terrace to soak up an English sun. It's all part of a large estate that hugs the coast from Beachy Head to Cuckmere Haven with Birling Gap in between; some of the best coastal walking in the south lies on your doorstep. Back at the inn a fabulous renovation has breathed new life into old bones. Downstairs has bags of character with low beams, stone floors, ancient settles and a roaring fire. Beer brewed on the estate pours from the tap, so try a pint of Legless Rambler before digging into hearty food – Beachy Head beer-battered catch of the day, sausage and mash with a sweet onion gravy, treacle tart with vanilla ice-cream. Five country-house bedrooms are the big surprise. Find beautiful fabrics, padded bedheads, funky bathrooms, the odd beam. Beds are dressed with lambswool throws, warm colours hang on the walls. Back outside, white cliffs wait, as do the South Downs. Finally, Arthur Conan Doyle knew the village and a blue plaque on one of the cottages suggests Sherlock Holmes retired here.

Rooms	4 doubles, 1 twin: £110–£120.
Meals	Lunch & dinner from £8.95.
	Sunday lunch, 3 courses, around £20.
Closed	Never.
Directions	West from Eastbourne on A259.
	Left in village. Parking on right near
	village hall.

Janice Avis
The Tiger Inn
The Green, East Dean,
Eastbourne BN20 0DA

Tel	+44 (0)1323 423209
Email	Tiger@beachyhead.org.uk
Web	www.beachyhead.org.uk

Belle Tout Lighthouse

On top of a white cliff, a fabulous lighthouse with rather good views. To your left, Beachy Head, to your right, Birling Gap – it's a magical position with the South Downs rolling into the English Channel. As for the lighthouse, it dates to 1832, was recently moved backwards 57 feet to stop it crumbling into the sea and featured prominently in the BBC's production of *The Life and Loves of a She-Devil*. It re-opened in 2010 after a splendid renovation as a lovely little B&B hotel. Bedrooms are rather wonderful: not huge, but most with double-aspect windows that bring the outside in. You find white walls to soak up the light, fantastic views of rolling hills, pretty fabrics, lovely linen, the odd exposed brick wall; shower rooms are small but sweet, and one room has a bath. Ian's legendary breakfasts are served on high with views of sea and cliff. There's a fabulous sitting room up here, too, where guests gather each night before climbing up to explore the lantern room. You'll eat well in the village pub, magnificent walking waits. *Minimum stay: 2 nights. Over 15s welcome.*

Rooms	6 doubles: £145–£220.
	Singles from £101.50.
Meals	Pub/restaurant within 1 mile.
Closed	Christmas & New Year.
Directions	A259 to East Dean, then south for Beach Head. Keep left at Birling Gap and on right above sea.

Ian Noall
Belle Tout Lighthouse
Beachy Head Road, Beachy Head,
Eastbourne BN20 0AE

Tel	+44 (0)1323 423185
Email	info@belletout.co.uk
Web	www.belletout.co.uk

Strand House

As you follow the Royal Military Canal down to miles of sandy beach, bear in mind that 600 years ago, you'd have been swimming in the sea. This is reclaimed land and Strand House, built in 1425, originally stood on Winchelsea Harbour. Outside, you find wandering wisteria, colourful flowerbeds and a woodland walk that leads up to the village. Inside, medieval interiors have low ceilings, timber frames and mind-your-head beams. There are reds and yellows, sofas galore, a wood-burner in the sitting room, an honesty bar from which to help yourself. It's a home-spun affair: Hugh cooks breakfast, Mary conjures up tasty meals at weekends. Attractive bedrooms are warm and colourful. One has an ancient four-poster, some have wonky floors, all have comfy beds and compact shower rooms. Airy rooms in the cottage have more space, and the suite, with its balcony and views across the fields, is a treat. The house, once a work house, was painted by Turner and Millais. Local restaurants wait: Webb's Fish Café, The Globe in Rye, a Michelin star at the Curlew in Odium. Dogs are very welcome. *Minimum stay: 2 nights at weekends & high season.*

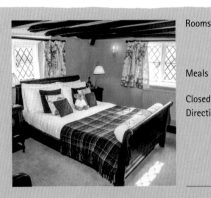

Rooms	6 doubles, 1 twin/double, 5 triples: £80–£150. 1 suite for 4: £180. Singles from £60. Dogs £7.50.
Meals	Dinner, 3 courses, £34.50. Fridays & Saturdays, on request.
Closed	Rarely.
Directions	A259 west from Rye for 2 miles. House on the left at foot of hill, opposite Bridge Inn pub.

Mary Sullivan & Hugh Davie
Strand House
Tanyards Lane, Winchelsea,
Rye TN36 4JT

Tel	+44 (0)1797 226276
Email	info@thestrandhouse.co.uk
Web	www.thestrandhouse.co.uk

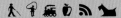

Jeake's House

Rye is utterly gorgeous, one of those lovely English country towns that's been around for centuries, but has never lost its looks. The same is true of Jeake's House. It's spent 300 years on this steep cobbled street in the old town accruing a colourful past as a wool store, a school, and the home of American poet Conrad Potter Aiken. Inside: timber frames, ancient beams and smartly carpeted corridors that weave along to cosy bedrooms, the latter generously furnished, deeply comfortable and excellent value for money. Some have four-posters, all have rich fabrics, one has a telly concealed in the wood-burner. The galleried dining room – once an old Baptist chapel, now painted deep red – is full of busts, books, clocks and mirrors – a fine setting for a full English breakfast. There's also a lovely cosy honesty bar, where a fire burns in winter. Outside, you'll find art galleries, antiques shops, old churches and river walks. All this would be blossom in the wind without Jenny, whose natural friendliness has created a winning atmosphere. Don't miss it. *Children over 8 welcome.*

Rooms	7 twin/doubles; 1 double with separate bath: £90–£116. 3 four-poster suites for 2: £126–£140. Singles from £79.
Meals	Restaurants within walking distance.
Closed	Never.
Directions	From centre of Rye on A268, left off High St onto West St, then 1st right into Mermaid St. House on left. Private car park, £3 a day for guests.

Jenny Hadfield
Jeake's House
Mermaid Street,
Rye TN31 7ET

Tel   +44 (0)1797 222828
Email   stay@jeakeshouse.com
Web   www.jeakeshouse.com

AWARD WINNER

Old favourite

The George in Rye

Ancient Rye has a big history. It's a reclaimed island, a Cinque Port which held its own army. Henry James lived here, too, and the oldest church clock in England chimes at the top of the hill. The George stands serenely on the cobbled high street. Built in 1575 from reclaimed ships' timbers, its exposed beams and panelled walls remain on display. Inside, beautiful interiors mix contemporary and classical styles to great effect – expect Jane Austen in the 21st-century. There's a roaring fire in the bar, screen prints of the Beatles on the walls in reception, a first-floor ballroom with a minstrels' gallery. Gorgeous bedrooms come in all shapes and sizes – make sure you check – but chic fabrics, Frette linen and Vi-Spring mattresses are standard, as are cashmere covers on hot water bottles. Finally, excellent brasserie-style food waits in the lovely new George Grill restaurant – perhaps Spanish charcuterie, half a lobster, treacle tart and stem ginger ice-cream; you can wash it all back with delicious wines, some English. Festivals abound: scallops in February, art in September.

Rooms	8 doubles, 21 twin/doubles: £135–£195. 5 suites for 2: £295–£325. Singles from £95.
Meals	Lunch & dinner £6–£35.
Closed	Never.
Directions	Follow signs up hill into town centre. Through arch; hotel on left, below church. 24-hour parking 5 minutes down hill.

Alex & Katie Clarke
The George in Rye
98 High Street, Rye TN31 7JT

Tel	+44 (0)1797 222114
Email	stay@thegeorgeinrye.com
Web	www.thegeorgeinrye.com

The Gallivant

This cute seaside restaurant with rooms stands across the road from Camber Sands, its five miles of pristine beach the best in the south. Kite surfers, beach cricketers and sun worshippers all gather and at low tide vast tracts of land appear, making it a great place to walk. As for the Gallivant, it's a quirky little pad, a boutique motel with fantastic food. The restaurant, recently refurbished, has a cool New England feel with seaside colours, comfy sofas and a wood-burner that burns on both sides. Uncluttered bedrooms – some big, some small – have lots of style: the best linen, Hypnos beds, driftwood furniture. Two in the main house open onto private terraces, four outside are perfect for families, all have good bathrooms, digital radios and flat-screen TVs (and a DVD library), But it's the food that takes the biscuit, much sourced within 30 miles: porridge for breakfast, fish soup for lunch, afternoon tea 'on the house', then a good dinner, perhaps Rye Bay scallops, salt marsh lamb, caramelised banana with toffee sauce. Visiting chefs – Tom Aikens, Mitch Tonks – come up to cook, too. *Minimum stay: 2 nights at weekends.*

Rooms	18 doubles, 2 doubles with terraces: £115–£170.
Meals	Lunch from £12.50. Dinner, 3 courses, about £30.
Closed	Rarely.
Directions	A259 east from Rye, then B2075 for Camber & Lydd. On left after 2 miles.

Mark O'Reilly
The Gallivant
New Lydd Road, Camber,
Rye TN31 7RB

Tel	+44 (0)1797 225057
Email	enquiries@thegallivanthotel.com
Web	www.thegallivanthotel.com

The Howard Arms

The Howard buzzes with good-humoured babble as well-kept beer flows from the flagstoned bar. Logs crackle contentedly in a vast open fire; a blackboard menu scales the wall above; a dining room at the far end has unexpected elegance, with great swathes of bold colour and some noble paintings. Gorgeous bedrooms are set discreetly apart from the joyful throng, mixing period style and modern luxury beautifully: one with a painted antique headboard and bleached beams, another more folksy, while the five newer rooms in the annexe come in more contemporary style with fancy bathrooms. All are individual, all huge by pub standards. The village is a surprise, too, literally tucked under a lone hill, with an unusual church surrounded by orchards and an extended village green. Round off an idyllic walk amid buzzing bees and wild flowers with a meal at the inn, perhaps salmon trio with celeriac remoulade and orange dressing, then beef, ale and mustard pie before spiced pear and apple flapjack crumble. From a menu with seasonal local produce, the food is inventive, upmarket and very good.

Rooms	5 doubles, 3 twin/doubles: £95–£145. Singles from £85.
Meals	Lunch from £4.50. Dinner from £10.50
Closed	Never.
Directions	From south take A429 Fosse Way through Moreton-in-Marsh. After 5 miles left to Ilmington.

Grant Owen
The Howard Arms
Lower Green, Ilmington,
Shipston-on-Stour CV36 4LT

Tel	+44 (0)1608 682226
Email	info@howardarms.com
Web	www.howardarms.com

The Bell Alderminster

A lively inn on the Alscot estate with gardens that run down to a small river – rugs and picnic hampers are available, so you can decamp in good weather. There's a pretty courtyard terrace, too, with wicker armchairs and sofas, not a bad spot for a pint of home-brewed ale. Inside, you find that happy mix of old and new – low beamed ceilings and exposed brick walls, cool colours and the odd sofa. There are armchairs in front of the fire, a cute sail-shaded conservatory, live music on the last Friday of the month. There's good food, too, with lamb and beef straight from the estate; you might find duck liver pâté, sea bream with saffron, caramel and chocolate cheesecake. Bedrooms are scattered about, some in the main house, a new batch in the converted barn that flanks the terrace. They vary in size (two are small), but all have comfort and style with smart fabrics, crisp linen and sofas or armchairs if there's room. The suites are enormous with exposed beams and fabulous bathrooms. A road passes to the front, quietly at night. Stratford waits up the road for all things Shakespeare.

Rooms	5 doubles, 2 twins: £95-£140.
	2 suites for 2: £145-£165.
	Singles from £70 (Sun-Thur).
Meals	Bar meals from £7.
	Lunch, 2 courses, from £14.50 (Mon-Fri).
	Dinner, 3 courses, from £18 (Mon-Thurs).
	Sunday lunch, 3 courses, £25.
Closed	Never.
Directions	On A3400 in Alderminster.

Ken Taylor
The Bell Alderminster
Shipston Road, Alderminster,
Stratford-upon-Avon CV37 8NY

Tel	+44 (0)1789 450414
Email	info@thebellald.co.uk
Web	www.thebellald.co.uk

Methuen Arms Hotel

Built around the remains of a 14th-century nunnery, converted into a brewery and coaching inn in 1608, and with an impressive Georgian façade, the Methuen has history in spades. Restyled as a boutique inn following a sympathetic restoration, its doors swung open in November 2010 to reveal a stunning interior. From a grand tiled hallway a sweeping staircase leads to a dozen ultra-stylish rooms, those in the former nunnery oozing character with wonky beams and other fascinating features. All have colourful headboards on big beds, wonderfully upholstered armchairs, funky rugs and some rather swish bathrooms, the best with roll top tubs and walk-in showers. Back downstairs are rugs on stone and wood floors, crackling logs in old stone fireplaces, glowing candles on tables and vintage photos of Corsham; the traditional bar and informal dining rooms are truly inviting. A seasonal modern British menu is a further enticement, so tuck into pasta with game ragù, fish pie, or lamb marinated in oregano and garlic. This grand almost Tardis-like inn promises to delight.

Rooms	11 doubles, 2 twin/doubles: £140–£175. 1 family room for 4: £150–£220. Singles from £90.
Meals	Lunch from £5.95. Early supper £18.50–£21.50. Sunday lunch from £18.50. Dinner, 3 courses, about £30.
Closed	Never.
Directions	M4 junc. 17, then A350 south & A4 west. B3353 south into Corsham. On left.

Martin & Debbie Still
Methuen Arms Hotel
2 High Street,
Corsham SN13 0HB
Tel   +44 (0)1249 717060
Email   info@themethuenarms.com
Web   www.themethuenarms.com

The Muddy Duck

In 1125 Cluniac monks founded a monastery in the village; this venerable building was their sleeping quarters. It turned into an alehouse in the 19th-century to satisfy the miners who dug Bath stone from under these hills. These days, it's a gorgeous old inn with an ancient wisteria gracing the stone courtyard at the front, then a smart terraced garden with views across open farmland behind. Inside, old and new mix gracefully: wooden floors, the odd beam and half-panelled walls, red leather bar stools, armchairs in front of the fire and low-hanging lamps in the restaurant. The bar plays host to a colourful cast of farmers and shoot parties, who come for a pint of Butcombe and some great food. Three bedrooms in the house vary in size. All have warm colours, comfy beds and robes in good bathrooms, but the suite is huge with a sofa in front of an open fire and a claw-foot bath in the room. Two new suites wait beyond the car park with smart bathrooms, snug sitting rooms and small terraces, too. Don't miss the food, perhaps grilled sardines, local duck, honey panna cotta. Bath is close.

Rooms	2 doubles: £95–£150. 3 suites for 2: £195.
Meals	Lunch from £4.95. Dinner, 3 courses, about £30.
Closed	Never.
Directions	M4 junction 18, then A46/A4 to Bathford. South on A363 for two miles, then left for Monkton Farleigh. Left at x-roads and on left.

Joe Holden
The Muddy Duck
Monkton Farleigh,
Bradford-on-Avon BA15 2QH

Tel	+44 (0)1225 858705
Email	joe.holden@themuddyduckbath.co.uk
Web	www.themuddyduckbath.co.uk

The Lamb at Hindon

The Lamb has been serving ale on Hindon's high street for 800 years. It is a yard of England's finest cloth, a place where shooting parties come for lunch and farmers meet to chew the cud. Step inside and find huge oak settles, heavy old beams, then deep red walls and roaring fires. A clipped Georgian country elegance lingers; you almost expect Mr Darcy to walk in, give a tormented sigh, then turn on his heels and vanish. There are flagstone floors and stripped wooden boards, window seats and gilded mirrors; old oils entwined in willow hang on the walls, a bookshelf is stuffed with aged tomes of poetry. At night, candles come out, as do some serious whiskies, and in the restaurant you can feast on ham hock and foie gras ballotine, game pie or Dover sole, then local cheeses. Revamped bedrooms come with mahogany furniture, rich colours, tartan throws, the odd four-poster, and some rather smart bathrooms. Splash out and stay in one of the cosy new rooms in the converted coach house. Fishing can be arranged, or you can shoot off to Stonehenge, Stourhead, Salisbury or Bath. *Minimum stay: 2 nights at weekends April-September.*

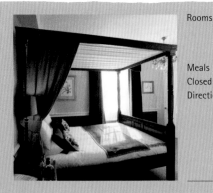

Rooms	10 doubles, 2 twin/doubles, 5 four-posters: £75-£135. 2 suites for 2: £100-£165. Singles from £65.
Meals	Lunch & dinner £5-£30.
Closed	Never.
Directions	M3, A303 & signed left at bottom of steep hill 2 miles east of junction with A350.

The Manager
The Lamb at Hindon
High Street, Hindon,
Salisbury SP3 6DP

Tel	+44 (0)1747 820573
Email	lambhindon@youngs.co.uk
Web	www.lambhindon.co.uk

The Beckford Arms

A country-house inn on the Fonthill estate – you sweep in under the Triumphal Arch. Outside, a pretty half-acre garden for hammocks in the trees, parasols on the terrace and a church spire soaring beyond. Georgian interiors are no less lovely. There's a drawing room with facing sofas in front of a roaring fire; a restaurant with a wall of glass that opens onto the terrace; a bar with parquet flooring for an excellent local pint. Follow your nose and chance upon the odd chandelier, roaming wisteria and a rather grand mahogany table in the private dining room. Bedrooms are small but perfectly formed with prices to match: white walls, the best linen, sisal matting, super bathrooms. If you want something bigger try the pavilions on the estate; former guests include Byron and Nelson, though we doubt they had it so good (small kitchens, claw-foot baths, chic country style). As for the food, it's lovely stuff, perhaps marrow fritters with lemon mayo, local partridge with bread sauce, chocolate bread and butter pudding. There are film nights most Sundays, the cricket team comes to celebrate.

Rooms	7 doubles, 1 twin/double: £95–£120. 2 pavilions for 2: £175–£195.
Meals	Dinner, 3 courses, about £30.
Closed	Never.
Directions	On the road between Tisbury & Hindon, 3 miles south of A303 (Fonthill exit).

Charlie Luxton
The Beckford Arms
Fonthill Gifford, Tisbury,
Salisbury SP3 6PX
Tel   +44 (0)1747 870385
Email   info@beckfordarms.com
Web   www.beckfordarms.com

Howard's House

In a gorgeous English village, a wormhole back in time, this Grade-II listed house dates from 1623 and comes with fine gardens in front of fields that sweep uphill to a ridge of old oak. You can walk straight out, so bring your boots. Inside, airy country-house interiors come with exquisite arched windows, flagstones in reception and the odd beam. Deep sofas, fresh flowers and the morning papers wait in the sitting room, where a fire crackles on cold days. When the sun shines, doors open onto a very pretty terrace for breakfasting. Elegant bedrooms mix old and new to great effect. They're not overly plush, but deeply comfortable with warm colours, mullioned windows, bowls of fruit and a sofa if there's room. Expect oak headboards, pretty fabrics, robes in good bathrooms. Spin downstairs for dinner – perhaps fillet of sea bass with parsnip purée, Scottish beef with roasted shallots, apple crème caramel with a calvados jelly – then climb back up to find your bed turned down. Salisbury, Stonehenge and the gardens at Stourhead are all close.

Rooms	6 doubles, 1 twin/double, 1 four-poster: £190–£210. 1 family room for 4: £190. Singles from £120.
Meals	Lunch £29.50. Dinner £29.50; à la carte £45. 6-course tasting menu £65.
Closed	Rarely.
Directions	A30 from Salisbury, B3089 west to Teffont. There, left at sharp right-hand bend following brown hotel sign. Entrance on right after 0.5 miles.

Noele Thompson & Simon Greenwood
Howard's House
Teffont Evias,
Salisbury SP3 5RJ

Tel	+44 (0)1722 716392
Email	enq@howardshousehotel.co.uk
Web	www.howardshousehotel.co.uk

Russell's

A cool little restaurant with rooms in the middle of one of England's prettiest villages. It stands on the green, flanked by posh shops, a great little base in the Cotswolds. Its airy interiors have a contemporary feel with whitewashed walls and a smart bar for the odd cocktail. In summer, you decant onto the terraces, one at the back, one at the front, so follow the sun. Bedrooms are lovely, you don't need to splash out to get something good. Smaller rooms have all the kit: beautiful fabrics, lovely beds, perhaps a walk-in shower or a claw-foot bath. There's good art, waffled bathrobes, gadgetry galore (flat-screen TVs, DVD players, iPod docks). The magnificent four-poster suite has a cross-beamed cathedral ceiling and exposed stone walls, then a spa bath and shower for two. Back downstairs, lovely food awaits (Jay Rayner loved his), perhaps Cornish crab cocktail, rack of local lamb, blood orange soufflé with chocolate ice-cream. Don't miss the Gordon Russell Museum next door; the hotel was his showroom. J.M. Barrie, Vaughan Williams and Edward Elgar all lived in the village. Brilliant. *Pets by arrangement.*

Rooms	4 doubles, 2 twin/doubles: £115–£245. 1 suite for 2: £245–£300.
Meals	Lunch, 2 courses, from £16.50. Sunday lunch from £21.95. Dinner, 3 courses, about £40 (not Sunday night).
Closed	Rarely.
Directions	A44 from Oxford & Evesham, then B4632 from Cheltenham. In centre of Broadway on High Street.

Andrew Riley
Russell's
20 High Street,
Broadway WR12 7DT

Tel	+44 (0)1386 853555
Email	info@russellsofbroadway.co.uk
Web	www.russellsofbroadway.co.uk

Dormy House Hotel & Spa

A 17th-century farmhouse on top of Willersey Hill with the Cotswold Way on the doorstep – follow it over to Dover's Hill for views that stretch for miles. First, you'll have to pull yourself away from this small-scale pleasure dome, no mean feat. Dormy has recently thrown off its 'old-school' mantle, re-emerging as a 21st-century country-house hotel with a chic spa and gorgeous rooms. Interiors sparkle: a wall of Jacobean panelling, three sitting rooms with open fires, beautiful art and flowers everywhere. An airy restaurant overlooks a garden that fills with colour in summer. You can eat on the terrace in good weather or hop across to the in-house gastropub, where golden stone walls give a smart-rustic feel and delicious comfort food awaits, perhaps sardines on toast, boeuf Bourguignon, treacle tart with vanilla ice-cream. Bedrooms are stunning: delicate wallpapers, the best linen, fabulous bathrooms, tablets and coffee machines. As for the spa… there's a cool pool, a hot tub, treatment rooms and a sauna, then a café/bar with a contemporary wood-burner and big views from its terrace. *Minimum stay: 2 nights at weekends.*

Rooms	12 doubles, 22 twin/doubles: £230–£330. 6 suites for 2: £440. Children under 3 free; under 7's £40; under 13's £60.
Meals	Lunch from £4.75. Sunday lunch £28. Afternoon tea from £8.50. Dinner £12.95–£40.
Closed	Never.
Directions	A44 east from Broadway for two miles. Turn left halfway up Fish Hill. Keep right at folk, then 1st left and hotel on left.

Stephanie Galvin
Dormy House Hotel & Spa
Willersey Hill,
Broadway WR12 7LF

Tel	+44 (0)1386 852711
Email	reservations@dormyhouse.co.uk
Web	www.dormyhouse.co.uk

The Grange Hotel

York Minster, the oldest Gothic cathedral in northern Europe, is utterly imperious, its Great East Window the largest piece of medieval stained glass in the world. It stands less than half a mile from the front door of this welcoming Regency townhouse – a five-minute stroll after your bacon and eggs. Inside, country-house elegance runs throughout: marble pillars in the flagged entrance hall, an open fire in the morning room and a first-floor drawing room that opens onto a small balcony. Bedrooms come in different shapes and sizes with smart fabrics, period colours and good bathrooms. The bigger rooms have high ceilings, perhaps a four-poster bed, but new rooms in the eaves are lovely too. York racecourse brings a happy crowd to the bar, you'll find an airy elegance and some rather fancy food in the Ivy Restaurant, then a vaulted brasserie with red banquettes for simpler dishes, perhaps French onion soup, boeuf bourguignon, chocolate fondant with chocolate chip ice-cream. Castle Howard for all things *Brideshead* and the North Yorkshire Moors for exhilarating walking are both close. *Pets by arrangement.*

Rooms	11 doubles, 18 twin/doubles, 3 four-posters: £137-£235. 1 suite for 2: £284. 3 singles: £123.
Meals	Lunch from £10. Dinner, 3 courses, £30–£35 (early bird discount).
Closed	Never.
Directions	South into York from ring road on A19. On right after two miles, 500 yards north of York Minster.

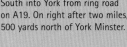

Jackie Millan
The Grange Hotel
1 Clifton,
York YO30 6AA

Tel	+44 (0)1904 644744
Email	info@grangehotel.co.uk
Web	www.grangehotel.co.uk

The Black Swan at Oldstead

Recent years have seen the Black Swan turn from county pub to Michelin-starred restaurant with rooms, but while the accent is now firmly on the food, the front bar remains as lovely as ever, with flagged floors, bay windows and a crackling fire to boot. It's a lovely spot for pre-dinner drinks, though in summer you can decant onto a terrace and enjoy the evening sun. Then it's back inside for the main event, some seriously good food. It's a family affair. The Banks have farmed here for generations, now they're cooking the best local produce, with Tommy heading the kitchen. You eat upstairs in a pretty dining room with mismatching tables and rugs on stripped boards. As for the food, it's ambrosial stuff, the nine-course tasting menu worthy of a big occasion. Highlights may include nettle soup, rabbit with five spice, halibut with roast onions, rhubarb and champagne, but most dishes are on the à la carte in case you're on a diet! Beautiful rooms wait in a stone building next door. Expect super beds, oak armoires, fabulous bathrooms (one has a copper bath). Doors open onto a peaceful terrace, too.

Rooms	2 doubles, 2 four-posters: £250-£390. Price includes dinner for 2.
Meals	Lunch from £28 (not Mon-Wed). 3-course à la carte dinner included. Non residents: early bird set menu £28 (not Sat); à la carte £48; 9-course tasting menu £75.
Closed	First 2 weeks in January.
Directions	A19 from Thirsk; left to Thirkleby & Coxwold, then left for Byland Abbey; follow signs left for Oldstead.

The Banks Family
The Black Swan at Oldstead
Oldstead,
York YO61 4BL

Tel	+44 (0)1347 868387
Email	enquiries@blackswanoldstead.co.uk
Web	www.blackswanoldstead.co.uk

Inn

Yorkshire

The White Bear Hotel

At five o'clock on a Friday evening there's only one place to be in Masham: the tap room at the White Bear, home of Theakston's beer. The great and the good gather to mark the end of the week, the odd pint is sunk, the air is thick with gossip. Interior design is 1920s trapped in aspic – red leather, polished brass, a crackling fire. But there's more here – a country-house dining room for lovely food; a handsome bar with stripped boards; a flower-filled terrace for lunch in the sun. Bedrooms are lovely, a touch of 21st-century luxury. They occupy the old Lightfoot brewery and come in contemporary style with good fabrics, warm colours, excellent beds and fancy bathrooms. Some have views across town, the vast penthouse is open to the rafters and worth slashing out on. There's a courtyard for guests, a sitting room, too; staff will bring drinks if you want privacy and peace. Delicious food waits in the restaurant, perhaps shellfish soup, steak and ale pie, treacle sponge pudding. Tours of the brewery are easily arranged, with a pint of your choice at the end. The Dales are all around.

Rooms	13 twin/doubles: £110–£120. 1 suite for 2: £200–£220.
Meals	Lunch from £4.95. Dinner, 3 courses, about £30.
Closed	Never.
Directions	North from Ripon on A6108. In Masham up hill (for Leyburn). Right at crest of hill. Signed.

Sue Thomas
The White Bear Hotel
Wellgarth, Masham,
Ripon HG4 4EN

Tel	+44 (0)1765 689319
Email	sue@whitebearmasham.co.uk
Web	www.thewhitebearhotel.co.uk

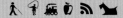

Entry 236   Map 6

Swinton Park

Swinton is utterly glorious, a fabulous old pile that flaunts its beauty with rash abandon. It stands in 200 acres of parkland, part of a 20,000-acre estate. You get the full aristocratic works: five lakes and a huge kitchen garden outside, then stately interiors at every turn. Expect marble pillars, varnished wood floors, vast arched windows, roaring fires. The drawing room is stupendous, a little like the salon of a 17th-century French château, but the dining room is equally impressive, its magnificent ceiling worth the trip alone. The main corridor is an art gallery, there's a bar in the old chapel, a hugely popular cookery school in the old stables, a small spa, too. Bedrooms come in grand style: plush fabrics, huge beds, marble bathrooms, decanters of complimentary gin and whisky. One of the suites occupies the turret, some rooms have sublime views over Home Lake, a couple interconnect, so perfect for families. As for the food, game from the estate and vegetables from the garden are plentiful, while hampers can be left in bothies for walkers wanting a rather good lunch. Magnificent.

Rooms	25 twin/doubles: £195-£380.
	6 suites for 2: £330-£555.
	Dinner, B&B from £132.50 p.p.
Meals	Lunch, 3 courses, from £25.95.
	Dinner £52. Tasting menu £60.
Closed	Never.
Directions	A1(M), Junc. 50, follow signs to Masham on road that runs parallel to motorway. After 3 miles, left onto B6267 to Masham. Hotel signed in village, 1 mile south-west, past golf course.

Mark & Felicity Cunliffe-Lister
Swinton Park
Swinton,
Ripon HG4 4JH

Tel	+44 (0)1765 680900
Email	reservations@swintonpark.com
Web	www.swintonpark.com

The Tempest Arms

A 16th-century ale house three miles west of Skipton with great prices, friendly staff and an easy style. Inside you find stone walls and open fires, six ales on tap at the bar and a smart beamed restaurant. An airy open-plan feel runs throughout with sofas and armchairs strategically placed in front of a fire that burns on both sides. Delicious traditional food is a big draw – the inn is packed for dinner most nights. You can eat wherever you want, so grab a seat and dig into mussels in a white wine sauce, Bolton Abbey lamb with roasted vegetables, treacle tart with pink grapefruit sorbet. Bedrooms are a steal. Those in the main house are simpler, those next door in two stone houses are quietly indulging. You get crisp linen, neutral colours, slate bathrooms and flat-screen TVs. Some have views of the fells, the suites are large and worth the money, a couple have decks with hot tubs to soak in. The Dales are on your doorstep, this is a good base for walkers. Skipton, a proper Yorkshire market town, is worth a look. Hard to fault for the price. Children and dogs are welcome.

Rooms	9 twin/doubles: £90. 10 suites for 2: £120–£130; 2 suites for 2 with hot tubs: £165. Singles from £70. Extra beds £12.99.
Meals	Lunch & bar meals from £8.95. Dinner from £14.95.
Closed	Never.
Directions	A56 west from Skipton. Signed left after two miles.

Martin & Veronica Clarkson
The Tempest Arms
Elslack,
Skipton BD23 3AY

Tel	+44 (0)1282 842450
Email	info@tempestarms.co.uk
Web	www.tempestarms.co.uk

The Traddock

A northern outpost of country-house charm, beautiful inside and out. It's a family affair and those looking for a friendly base from which to explore the Dales will find it here. You enter through a wonderful drawing room – crackling fire, pretty art, the daily papers, cavernous sofas. Follow your nose and find polished wood in the dining room, panelled walls in the breakfast room, then William Morris wallpaper in the sitting room bar, where you can sip a pint of Skipton ale while playing a game of Scrabble. Bedrooms are just the ticket, some coolly contemporary, others deliciously traditional with family antiques and the odd claw-foot bath. Those on the second floor are cosy in the eaves, all have fresh fruit, homemade shortbread and Dales views. Elsewhere, a white-washed sitting room that opens onto the garden and a rug-strewn restaurant for fabulous local food, perhaps Whitby crab, slow-roasted pork, raspberry and white chocolate soufflé. Spectacular walks start at the front door, there are cycle tracks and some extraordinary caves – one is bigger than St Paul's. Brilliant. *Minimum stay: 2 nights at weekends March-November.*

Rooms	7 doubles, 1 twin/double: £95–£195. 2 family rooms for 4: £95–£165. 1 single: £85–£95. Dinner, B&B £78–£128 p.p. Extra bed/sofabed available £15 p.p. per night.
Meals	Lunch from £9.50. Dinner, 3 courses, around £30.
Closed	Never.
Directions	0.75 miles off the A65, midway between Kirkby Lonsdale & Skipton, 4 miles north-west of Settle.

Paul Reynolds
The Traddock
Austwick,
Settle LA2 8BY

Tel	+44 (0)15242 51224
Email	info@thetraddock.co.uk
Web	www.thetraddock.co.uk

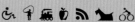

The Burgoyne Hotel

The Burgoyne is one of the loveliest places to stay in the Dales. The view from the front is imperious, a smooth sweep three miles south off to Swaledale; half a dozen benches on the village green look the right way. Inside, the past lives on: an elegant drawing room with a crackling fire where you gather for drinks before dinner; a restaurant in racing green where you feast on delicious Yorkshire-sourced food: hot asparagus wrapped in smoked salmon; Gressingham duck with apple mash and orange liqueur; vanilla panna cotta with red berry coulis. Julia and Mo, who arrived in 2011, are here to keep the traditions alive, updating as they go. Bedrooms come in country-house style: colourful fabrics, excellent beds, thick white linen, a sofa if there's room. A four-poster occupies the old snooker room, all but one room has the view. There are maps for walkers, fishing can be arranged. As for Reeth, it's a gorgeous old traditional village, mentioned in the Domesday Book, with a market every Friday and the best grouse moors in Britain. Dogs are welcome, too. *Extra beds for children under 13: £25. Dogs: £10 a night.*

Rooms	4 doubles, 1 twin, 1 four-poster; 2 doubles, 1 twin, each with separate bathroom: £130-£190. 1 suite for 2: £210. Singles from £112.50.
Meals	Dinner, 2 courses, £27; 4 courses, £40.
Closed	Midweek in January (Monday-Thursday).
Directions	From Richmond A6108, then B6270 to Reeth. Hotel on north side of village green.

Julia & Mo Usman
The Burgoyne Hotel
Reeth,
Richmond DL11 6SN

Tel	+44 (0)1748 884292
Email	enquiries@theburgoyne.co.uk
Web	www.theburgoyne.co.uk

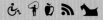

Judges Country House Hotel

This fine old country house is English to its core. It stands in 26 acres of attractive gardens with lawns that sweep down to a small river and paths that weave through private woods. Inside, you find a world that carries you back to grander days. There's an elegant entrance hall that floods with light, a sitting room bar in racing green, then a golden drawing room where doors open to a pretty terrace for lunch in summer. Wander about and find fires primed for combustion, the daily papers laid out in reception, a elegant staircase that rises towards a glass dome. Country-house bedrooms are full of colour. You get bowls of fruit, beautiful beds, gorgeous linen, garden flowers. Bigger rooms have sofas, all have robes in super bathrooms. Back downstairs, there's serious food in the restaurant, perhaps lobster with cardamon and mango, duck with chicory and orange, warm chocolate cake with caramelised banana. If that's not enough, come home early for afternoon tea in front of the fire. The Dales and the Moors are close, while Fountains Abbey and Castle Howard are both within striking distance.

Rooms	14 twin/doubles, 3 four-posters: £130-£220. 2 suites for 2: £160-£220. 2 singles: £99-£110. Dinner, B&B from £102.50 p.p.
Meals	Lunch from £16.95. Dinner, 3 courses, £37.50.
Closed	Never.
Directions	A1(M), then A19 for Middlesbrough. Left onto A67, through Kirklevington, hotel signed left.

Tim Howard
Judges Country House Hotel
Kirklevington Hall, Kirklevington,
Yarm TS15 9LW

Tel	+44 (0)1642 789000
Email	enquiries@judgeshotel.co.uk
Web	www.judgeshotel.co.uk

Broom House at Egton Bridge

As lovely a place to stay on the moors as you could hope for. You wind your way in – up dale, down hill – with a carpet of purple heather in late summer and a golden fleece of bracken in autumn. As for this lovely house, it sits on the edge of one of the prettiest villages on the moors, with fine views of Esk Dale from the garden terrace. Inside, airy interiors are just the ticket – warmly stylish, extremely comfortable – the perfect tonic after a day in the hills. Downstairs, there's a pretty sitting room with garden views, then a dining room for Michael's lovely breakfasts – Whitby kippers, Glaisdale sausage and bacon, smoothies from garden strawberries; in summer, you decant onto the terrace with birdsong, grazing cows and the moors for company. Bedrooms are lovely: warm colours, white cotton, perhaps a sofa if there's room or doors onto the terrace; all have fine bathrooms, one with a free-standing bath. By day you explore the moors, spin over to Whitby or try a leg of the coast-to-coast path (which passes outside). At night, you follow the river into the village for dinner at one of its pubs. Pure bliss.

Rooms	7 doubles, 1 twin: £89–£145. Singles from £68.
Meals	Two pubs in village.
Closed	Christmas.
Directions	Leave A171 for Egton. Through village to Egton Bridge, under bridge, then right into Broom House Lane. Under bridge and on right.

Georgina & Michael Curnow
Broom House at Egton Bridge
Broom House Lane, Egton Bridge,
Whitby YO21 1XD

Tel	+44 (0)1947 895279
Email	mw@broom-house.co.uk
Web	www.broom-house.co.uk

Estbek House

A super find on the Whitby coast. This is a quietly elegant restaurant with rooms ten paces from the beach at Sandsend. It's small, intimate and very welcoming. Tim cooks brilliantly, David talks you through his exceptional wine list and passes on the local news. Cliffs rise to the north, the beach runs away to the south, East Beck river passes directly opposite, ducks waddle across the road. There's a terrace at the front for drinks in summer and a small bar on the lower ground, where you can watch Tim at work in his kitchen. Upstairs, two dining rooms swim in seaside light and come with stripped floors, old radiators and crisp white tablecloths. Grab a window seat for watery views and dig into fresh Whitby crab with avocado and mango salad, local lamb with rhubarb compote, apricot tarte tatin. Bedrooms – bigger on the first floor, smaller on the second – have painted panelling, crisp white linen, colourful throws and shuttered windows. Breakfast is delicious – David's mum makes the marmalade. There are cliff walks, the moors to discover and you can follow the river upstream to Mulgrave Castle.

Rooms	4 doubles, 1 twin/double: £125–£150. Dinner, B&B from £80 p.p.
Meals	Dinner, 3 courses, about £35.
Closed	Occasionally.
Directions	North from Whitby on A174 to Sandsend. On left in village by bridge.

David Cross & Tim Lawrence
Estbek House
Eastrow, Sandsend,
Whitby YO21 3SU

Tel	+44 (0)1947 893424
Email	info@estbekhouse.co.uk
Web	www.estbekhouse.co.uk

The White Swan Inn

A dreamy old inn that stands on Pickering's Market Place, where farmers set up shop on the first Thursday of the month. The exterior is 16th century, with flower baskets hanging from its mellow stone walls. Inside, you find a seriously pretty world: stripped floors, open fires, a tiny bar and a Dickensian feel. There's a restaurant at the back – the heart and soul of the inn – where delicious food flies from the kitchen, perhaps moules marinière, roast rump of local lamb, glazed lemon tart with blood-orange sorbet. Excellent bedrooms are scattered about. Those in the main house have old-world charm, delicious linen, Osborne & Little fabrics and flat-screen TV/DVDs; bathrooms have robes and Bath House oils. Rooms in the courtyard tend to be bigger and come in crisp contemporary style with black-and-white screen prints, mohair blankets and underfloor heating in York stone bathrooms. You'll also find the Bothy, a stylish residents' sitting room with a huge open fire and cathedral ceilings. The moors are all around for fabulous walking, while Castle Howard, Whitby and *Heartbeat* country all wait. *Minimum stay: 2 nights at weekends.*

Rooms	14 doubles, 4 twin/doubles: £149–£179. 3 suites for 2: £149–£189. Singles £115–£179. Dinner, B&B £105–£125 p.p. Extra bed/sofabed available £20 p.p. per night.
Meals	Lunch from £5.25. Dinner £13.95–£27.95. Sunday lunch from £12.95.
Closed	Never.
Directions	From North A170 to Pickering. Entering town left at traffic lights, then 1st right into Market Place. On left.

Victor & Marion Buchanan
The White Swan Inn
Market Place,
Pickering YO18 7AA

Tel	+44 (0)1751 472288
Email	welcome@white-swan.co.uk
Web	www.white-swan.co.uk

The Talbot Hotel

A 17th-century hunting lodge on the Fitzwilliam estate, not far from Castle Howard. It stands on the edge of town with Malton's streets on one side and big views over field and river on the other. Inside, two fires burn in the drawing room, you find fresh flowers, lovely art, the daily papers and cavernous sofas. There's a bar that drops down to an airy conservatory, then a country-house restaurant as well as a private dining room. It's headed up by TV chef James Martin and regulars love the excellent Yorkshire produce, perhaps local wood pigeon with parsnip purée, beef with wild garlic, buttermilk panna cotta with Yorkshire rhubarb. Lovely bedrooms have smart floral fabrics, pale wool carpets and botanical prints on the walls. Bigger rooms have sofas, several have the view, bathrooms are gorgeous and come with robes. You're well positioned for York, the Moors, coastal walks and Castle Howard. Malton, a historic market town, holds a popular farmers' market every other Saturday and a fabulous food festival in May. The hotel has a cookery school, too, with a focus on Yorkshire game and seafood. *Minimum stay: 2 nights at weekends.*

Rooms	23 doubles: £95–£205.
	1 suite for 2, 2 suites for 4: £199–£295.
	Dinner, B&B from £102.50 p.p.
Meals	Dinner, 3 courses, £33–£39.
	Bar meals from £9.
	Sunday lunch from £20.
Closed	Rarely.
Directions	A64 north from York, then B2148 into Malton. Keep right in town and on right after half a mile.

David Macdonald
The Talbot Hotel
45-47 Yorkersgate,
Malton YO17 7AJ

Tel	+44 (0)1653 639096
Email	reservations@talbotmalton.co.uk
Web	www.talbotmalton.co.uk

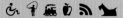

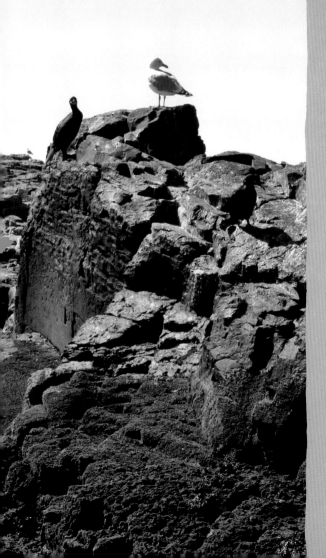

Channel Islands

Photo: Alec Studerus

The Georgian House

Holly's family have been holidaying in Alderney for more than 30 years, now she's come back to take over this treasure of a hotel. Along with her charming young team, she's turned it into the beating heart of the island. Step off the cobbled high street straight into a traditional, cosy bar; grab a bite here or something more extravagant in the light-strewn dining room that opens out to the pretty garden. Vegetables and salad come from their own allotment, the butter is vivid yellow and meat and fish is as local as can be: try the divine head-to-toe pork dish (great for sharing) or a zingy chilli squid. Upstairs three quaint bedrooms, all en suite, are pretty and pristine with locally made soaps and views across the road to the town. The 100-seater cinema opposite shows art house films on reels, during the interval you wander over to The Georgian for a drink. The hotel is packed with locals and visitors alike, and rightly so; there are barbecues, bands, taster evenings, and a blissful atmosphere. Old forts and stunning beaches wait, so hire bikes and explore the island. And book early.

Rooms	2 doubles, 2 twin/doubles: £70-£95. Singles from £45.
Meals	Light lunch from £6. Dinner, 3 courses, £25-£30.
Closed	Mid-January to mid-March.
Directions	Sent on booking. Airport pick-ups.

Holly Fisher
The Georgian House
Victoria Street GY9 3UF
Tel   +44 (0)1481 822471
Email   info@georgianalderney.com
Web   www.georgianalderney.com

White House Hotel

Herm is unique, a tiny island run benignly by the 40 souls lucky enough to live on it. They keep things blissfully simple: no cars, no TVs, just a magical world of field and sky, a perfect place to escape the city. A coastal path rings the island; high cliffs to the south, sandy beaches to the north, cattle grazing the hills between. You get fabulous views at every turn – shimmering islands, pristine waters, yachts and ferries zipping about. There are beach cafés, succulent gardens, an ancient church, even a tavern. Kids love it, so do parents, and the self-catering cottages are extremely popular. As for the hotel, it lingers happily in an elegant past, a great base from which to enjoy the island. You'll find open fires, delicious four-course dinners, a tennis court, a pool to keep you cool. Spotless bedrooms are scattered about, some in the village's colour-washed cottages, others with balconies in the hotel. Several come in contemporary style with fancy bathrooms, but most are warmly traditional as befits the setting. Expect pretty colours, padded headboards and watery views.

Rooms	17 twin/doubles: £138-£218. 21 family rooms for 4: £138-£348. 2 singles: £69-£89. Dinner, B&B £98-£150 p.p. 20 cottages for 2-6 (self-catering): £273-£1,288 per week.
Meals	Lunch from £5. Dinner, 4 courses, £30.
Closed	November-Easter.
Directions	Via Guernsey. Trident ferries leave from the harbour at St Peter Port 8 times a day in summer (£11 return).

	Siôn Dobson Jones White House Hotel Herm Island GY1 3HR
Tel	+44 (0)1481 750075
Email	hotel@herm.com
Web	www.herm.com

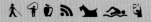

Photo: Hillside, Isle of Wight, entry 129

Scotland

Photo: Grants at Craigellachie,
Highland, entry 273

Darroch Learg Hotel

Welcome to Royal Deeside — river, forest, mountain, sky. There's lots to do — blissful walks, cycle trails, the Dee to fish, Braemar for the Highland Games. Swing back to Darroch and find nothing but good things. This is a lovely old hotel, a country house rooted in a graceful past, with roaring fires, polished brass, Zoffany wallpapers and ambrosial food in the restaurant. Ever-present Nigel and Fiona look after guests with great warmth, many return year after year. Everything is just as it should be: tartan fabrics, Canadian pitch pine windows and doors, fabulous views sweeping south across Balmoral forest. Bedrooms upstairs spoil you rotten with style and comfort in spades. Big rooms at the front have long views, padded window seats, wallpapered bathrooms, perhaps a four-poster bed. Cosy rooms in the eaves are equally lovely, just not quite as big. You get warm colours, pretty furniture, crisp white linen and bathrobes to pad about in. As for the food, don't miss it, perhaps smoked haddock ravioli, Deeside venison, lemon tart with berry sauce. A perfect highland retreat. *Under 12s free, 12+ meals only. Extra beds for adults £25.*

Rooms	2 doubles, 8 twin/doubles, 2 four-posters: £140-£250. Dinner, B&B (obligatory at weekends) £105-£160 p.p.
Meals	Sunday lunch £27.50. Dinner, 3 courses, £45.
Closed	Christmas & last 3 weeks in Jan.
Directions	From Perth A93 north to Ballater. Entering village hotel 1st building on left above road.

Nigel & Fiona Franks
Darroch Learg Hotel
56 Braemar Road,
Ballater AB35 5UX

Tel	+44 (0)1339 755443
Email	enquiries@darrochlearg.co.uk
Web	www.darrochlearg.co.uk

The Creggans Inn

The real James Bond once owned this hotel – Sir Fitzroy MacLean was one of a cast of characters on whom Ian Fleming modelled his hero; the fact the Royal Navy regularly send their big ships into Loch Fyne on exercise is purely coincidental. These days, life at the inn is decidedly restful. Views from the front stretch for miles, the loch eventually giving way to the distant peaks of the Kintyre peninsular. Inside, an airy elegance has spread far and wide. Downstairs, sofas and armchairs are liberally scattered about, there's a locals' bar which doubles as the clubhouse for the village shinty team, then picture windows in the smart restaurant, where you dig into super local fare – perhaps grilled goat's cheese, breast of guinea fowl, chocolate and hazelnut parfait – while watching the sun set over the hills. Traditional country-house bedrooms are lovely: warm colours, pretty fabrics, delicate wallpapers, padded bedheads; most have loch views. There's lots to do: castles and gardens, boat trips and golf, hills for cyclists and walkers. All this an hour and a half from hip Glasgow.

Rooms	4 doubles, 9 twin/doubles: £120–£180. 1 suite for 2: £160–£220. Singles from £85. Dinner, B&B from £80 p.p.
Meals	Bar: lunch & dinner from £4.25. Dinner in restaurant: 4-course table d'hôte menu £37.
Closed	Never.
Directions	From Glasgow, A82 to Tarbert, A83 towards Inverary for 13 miles, then left on A815 to Strachur (10 miles). Hotel on left before village.

Archie & Gillian MacLellan
The Creggans Inn
Loch Fyne, Strachur,
Cairndow PA27 8BX

Tel	+44 (0)1369 860279
Email	info@creggans-inn.co.uk
Web	www.creggans-inn.co.uk

The Manor House

A 1780 dower house for the Dukes of Argyll – their cottage by the sea. Built of local stone, it sits high on the hill with long views over Oban harbour to the Isle of Mull. It's a smart and proper place, not one to bow to fads of fashions, with sea views from the terrace, a roaring fire in the drawing room, beautiful tiles in the entrance hall, an elegant bay window in the bar, then a half-panelled dining room for excellent food. Some bedrooms are on the small side, but all are pretty with warm colours, fresh flowers, crisp linen, bowls of fruit and piles of towels in good bathrooms; those that look seaward have binoculars with which to scour the horizon. Try Loch Fyne kippers for breakfast, seafood risotto for lunch and, if you've room, roast saddle of lamb with shepherds' pie for dinner; there's excellent home baking, too. Ferries leave for the islands from the bottom of the hill – you can watch them sail from the hotel garden. There's a computer for guests to use, afternoon tea can be arranged, and you can watch the sun set from McCaig's Tower overlooking Oban. *Children over 12 welcome.*

Rooms	9 doubles, 2 twins: £120-£235. Dinner, B&B from £87.50 p.p.
Meals	Lunch from £4.25. Dinner, 4 courses, £42.
Closed	Christmas.
Directions	In Oban follow signs to ferry. Hotel on right 0.5 miles after ferry turn-off, signed.

Gregor MacKinnon
The Manor House
Gallanach Road,
Oban PA34 4LS

Tel	+44 (0)1631 562087
Email	info@manorhouseoban.com
Web	www.manorhouseoban.com

The Airds Hotel & Restaurant

This smart country-house hotel on the Appin peninsular stands above Loch Linnhe with views across the water to the Morvern Mountains. It started life in 1750, an inn for passengers taking the paddle steamers up to the Caledonian canal. These days, it's one of the loveliest places to stay on the West Coast, its whitewashed exterior giving no hint of the wonders within. You enter through a small conservatory, then find yourself in a world of smouldering fires, freshly cut flowers, beautiful wallpapers and sofas by the dozen. Bedrooms pack a lovely punch – warm colours, smart fabrics, Frette linen for Vi-Spring beds, sparkling marble bathrooms with Italian robes. Those at the front have the view, bigger rooms have sofas, some at the back have terraces, all spoil you rotten. Best of all is the ambrosial food, perhaps seared scallops with pickled cauliflower, lemon sole with parsley mousse, banana soufflé with passion fruit ice-cream. Outside, there's a garden for croquet and afternoon tea with views of water and mountains. The loveliest staff look after you all the way. Brilliant.

Rooms	8 twin/doubles: £290-£418. 3 suites for 4, each with sofabed: £385-£510. Price includes dinner for 2. Singles from £220. 1 cottage for 5: £575-£875. Extra bed/sofabed £25 p.p per night.
Meals	Lunch from £7. Dinner, 5 courses with coffee, included; non-residents £55. Tasting menu £75. Sunday lunch £18.95.
Closed	Mondays & Tuesdays Nov to Jan.
Directions	A82 north for Fort William, then A828 south for Oban. Right for Port Appin after 12 miles. On left after 2 miles.

Shaun & Jenny McKivragan
The Airds Hotel & Restaurant
Port Appin,
Appin PA38 4DF

Tel	+44 (0)1631 730236
Email	airds@airds-hotel.com
Web	www.airds-hotel.com

Entry 251   Map 8

Bealach House

Good food, a lovely welcome and a fine position in Salachan glen make this an excellent base for those travelling up the west coast. You follow a track through the forest to the only house in the valley. Sheep graze, birds sing, rivers run – other than that you won't hear a thing. Jim and Hilary had a dining pub in the Yorkshire Dales before coming north for a quieter life. Outside, eight acres of gardens have big valley views. Inside, tea and homemade cake is served in front of the wood-burner on colder days or out on the terrace when the sun shines. Bedrooms upstairs aren't huge, but two have room for a sofa and all have warm colours, comfy beds, decanters of sherry and excellent power showers (one has a bath, too). After a hearty breakfast – local eggs, home-made bread – you can climb Ben Nevis, drive up to Loch Ness or take the ferry across to Mull. After which Hilary's food works wonders, perhaps smoked salmon, local venison, chocolate soufflé with a white chocolate sauce (bring your own wine). You can walk from the front door, on clear nights stars fill the sky. *Children over 14 welcome.*

Rooms	2 doubles, 1 twin: £90-£110. Singles from £65.
Meals	Dinner £25-£30.
Closed	Mid-October to mid-February.
Directions	A828 south from Fort William for Oban. Signed left, through gate, 2 miles south of Duror. Follow signs up track for 1 mile to house.

Jim & Hilary McFadyen
Bealach House
Salachan Glen, Duror,
Appin PA38 4BW

Tel	+44 (0)1631 740298
Email	enquiries@bealachhouse.co.uk
Web	www.bealachhouse.co.uk

Kilmeny

Islay is fabulous – easy to get to, seriously pretty, lots to do. It's home to famous whisky distilleries, plays host to 60,000 geese every winter, has spectacular sandy beaches that stretch for miles. You can walk in the hills and spot red deer, or jump in a kayak and glide past seal colonies. As for Kilmeny, it's the perfect island base, part farmhouse B&B, part stylish hotel. It sits in 300 acres of beautiful silence. Blair (from Jura) and Margaret (Islay through and through) have been here for 41 years (they don't look old enough!). Blair runs sheep and cattle (you can wander freely, even help during lambing), while Margaret has perfected the art of spoiling guests rotten. She plies you with tea and cake on arrival, serves a mean breakfast in the pretty dining room, she'll even cook a three-course feast in the evening, perhaps smoked salmon, local lamb, raspberry and almond crumble. Rooms are gorgeous with beautiful beds, delicious fabrics, sofas or armchairs, slipper baths in wonderful bathrooms. As for Islay, Blair and Margaret will share all their secrets, so come to explore. *No credit cards.*

Rooms	4 twin/doubles: £135.
	1 suite for 2: £155.
	Singles from £90.
Meals	Dinner, £35 by arrangement.
Closed	Mid-October to Easter.
Directions	3 miles west from Port Askaig on A846. Signed left.

Margaret & Blair Rozga
Kilmeny
Ballygrant,
Isle of Islay PA45 7QW
Tel   +44 (0)1496 840668
Email   info@kilmeny.co.uk
Web   www.kilmeny.co.uk

Entry 253   Map 8

The Colonsay

Another fabulous Hebridean island, a perfect place to escape the world. Wander at will and find wild flowers in the machair, a golf course tended by sheep and huge sandy beaches across which cows roam. Wildlife is ever present, from a small colony of wild goats to a rich migratory bird population; the odd golden eagle soars overhead, too. At low tide the sands of the south give access to Oronsay. The island's 14th-century priory was one of Scotland's finest and amid impressive ruins its ornate stone cross still stands. As for the hotel, it's a splendid base and brims with an easy style – airy interiors, stripped floors, fires everywhere, friendly staff. There's a locals' bar for a pint (and a brewery on the island), a pretty sitting room packed with books, a dining room for super food, a decked terrace for drinks in the sun. Bedrooms have local art, warm colours, lovely fabrics and the best beds; some have sea views, all have good bathrooms. Spin around on bikes, search for standing stones, lie in the sun and stare at the sky. There's a festival in May for all things Colonsay. Wonderful.

Rooms	4 doubles, 3 twins: £85-£145. 1 family room for 4: £95-£145. 1 single: £70.
Meals	Lunch from £4.50. Packed lunch £7. Bar meals from £11.50. Dinner, 3 courses, about £25.
Closed	November, January (after New Year) & February.
Directions	Calmac ferries from Oban or Kennacraig (not Tue) or Hebridean Airways (Tue & Thur). Hotel on right, half a mile up road from jetty.

Jane Howard
The Colonsay
Scalasaig,
Isle of Colonsay PA61 7YP

Tel	+44 (0)1951 200316
Email	hotel@colonsayestate.co.uk
Web	www.colonsayestate.co.uk

Tiroran House

The setting is magnificent – 17 acres of gardens rolling down to Loch Scridan. Otters and dolphins pass through, buzzards and eagles glide above, red deer visit the garden. As for this 1850 shooting lodge, you'll be hard pressed to find a more comfortable island base, so it's no surprise to discover it was recently voted 'Best Country House Hotel in Scotland' for the second year in a row. There are fires in the drawing rooms, fresh flowers everywhere, games to be played, books to be read. Airy bedrooms hit the spot: crisp linen, beautiful fabrics, the odd chaise longue; some have watery views, all have silence guaranteed. You eat in a smart dining room with much of the delicious food from the island or waters around it, perhaps mussel and oyster broth, saddle of lamb with carrot purée, chocolate tort with vanilla ice-cream. You're bang in the middle of Mull with lots to do: Tobermory, the prettiest town in the Hebrides; Calgary and its magical beach; day trips to Iona and its famous monastery; cruises to Staffa and Fingal's Cave. Come back for afternoon tea – it's as good as the Ritz.

Rooms	5 doubles, 5 twin/doubles: £175-£220.
Meals	Dinner, 4 courses, £48.
Closed	Rarely.
Directions	From Craignure or Fishnish car ferries, A849 for Bunessan & Iona car ferry. Right onto B8035 for Gruline. After 4 miles left at converted church. House 1 mile further.

Laurence & Katie Mackay
Tiroran House
Tiroran,
Isle of Mull PA69 6ES

Tel	+44 (0)1681 705232
Email	info@tiroran.com
Web	www.tiroran.com

Glengorm Castle

Few places defy overstatement, but Glengorm does so with ease. It stands in 5,000 acres at the top of Mull with views that stretch across the sea to Coll and the Uists, Barra and Rhum. Directly in front the land falls away, rolls over lush pasture, then tumbles into the sea. Sheep and cattle graze – Tom wins prizes for his cows. Despite the grandeur, this is a family home with children and dogs pottering about. You feel immediately at ease. First you bounce up a four-mile drive, then you step into a vast hall, where sofas wait in front of the fire and big art hangs on the walls. An oak staircase sweeps you up to wonderful country-house rooms; three have the view, all have warm colours, antique furniture and excellent bathrooms. Elsewhere, a panelled library for guests to use with a selection of whiskies 'on the house', then a vast kitchen garden, coastal paths, even a swimming hole. Breakfast is a feast – grab the table by the window. There's a farm shop, a café and a deli, too, even guided wildlife walks and a hide from which to spot otters. Good restaurants wait in Tobermory.

Rooms	3 doubles, 1 four-poster; 1 twin/double with separate bath: £130-£210.
Meals	Restaurants 5 miles.
Closed	Christmas & New Year.
Directions	North to Tobermory on A848. Straight over roundabout (not right for town). Over x-roads after half a mile and straight ahead for four miles to castle.

Tom & Marjorie Nelson
Glengorm Castle
Tobermory,
Isle of Mull PA75 6QE
Tel   +44 (0)1688 302321
Email   enquiries@glengormcastle.co.uk
Web   www.glengormcastle.co.uk

Cavens

The Solway Firth is a magical spot; overlooked by many, those who come have this patch of heaven to themselves. You swoop down from Dumfries through glorious country, then crest a hill and there it is, vast tracts of tidal sands with a huge sky above. It's a magnet for birdlife, the rich pickings of low tide too tempting to refuse. As for this 1752 shooting lodge, it stands in 20 acres of sweeping lawns, native woodlands and sprawling fields. Inside, elegant interiors come as standard. Two lovely sitting rooms are decked out with busts and oils, golden sofas, smouldering fires, a baby grand piano; in summer, you slip onto the terrace for afternoon tea. Country-house bedrooms have garden views, period furniture, bowls of fruit. One is smaller, others big with room for sofas. One has a stunning bathroom, another has an en suite sunroom. Back downstairs you feast on Angus' delicious food in the smart yellow restaurant, perhaps scallops with lime and Vermouth, Galloway pork in a mustard sauce, lemon panna cotta. There are gardens aplenty and golf at spectacular Southerness.

Rooms	4 doubles, 1 twin: £100-£190. Extra bed/sofabed available £30 per person per night.
Meals	Dinner: 3-course market menu £25; 3-course à la carte about £35. Packed lunch available.
Closed	Rarely.
Directions	From Dumfries A710 to Kirkbean (12 miles). Signed in village on left.

Jane & Angus Fordyce
Cavens
Kirkbean,
Dumfries DG2 8AA
Tel   +44 (0)1387 880234
Email   enquiries@cavens.com
Web   www.cavens.com

Knockinaam Lodge

Lawns run down to the Irish sea, roe deer come to eat the roses, sunsets turn the sky red. This exceptional 1869 shooting lodge is nothing short of glorious: a Michelin star in the dining room, 150 malts in the bar and a level of service you rarely find in such far-flung corners of the realm. There's history, too. Churchill once stayed and you can sleep in his elegant room, read his books and climb the same steps into an ancient bath. Elsewhere, immaculate country-house interiors abound: gorgeous bedrooms, the very best bathrooms, a morning room where the scent of flowers mingles with wood smoke. Outside: cliff walks, nesting peregrine falcons and a rock pool. When it's stormy, waves crash all around. Trees stand guard high on the hill, their branches buffeted by the wind, while bluebells carpet the hills in spring. John Buchan knew the house and described it in *The Thirty-Nine Steps* as the house to which Hannay fled. Remote, beguiling, utterly spoiling – grand old Knockinaam is simply unmissable.

Rooms	4 doubles, 5 twin/doubles: £285-£420. 1 family room for 4: £350-£400. Price includes dinner for 2.
Meals	Lunch, by arrangement, £30-£40. Dinner, 5 courses, included; non-residents £65.
Closed	Never.
Directions	From A77 or A75 pick up signs to Portpatrick. West from Lochans on A77, then left after 2 miles, signed. Follow signs for 3 miles to hotel.

David & Sian Ibbotson
Knockinaam Lodge
Portpatrick,
Stranraer DG9 9AD

Tel	+44 (0)1776 810471
Email	reservations@knockinaamlodge.com
Web	www.knockinaamlodge.com

Trigony House Hotel

A small, welcoming, family-run hotel with good food, nicely priced rooms and a lovely garden, where you may spot red squirrels. The house date to 1700, a shooting lodge for the local castle. Inside, you find Japanese oak panelling in the hall, a wood-burner in the pretty sitting room and an open fire in the dining room, where doors open onto the terrace for dinner in summer. Adam cooks lovely rustic fare, perhaps goat's cheese tart, loin of roe venison, chocolate brownie cheesecake with chocolate ice-cream; there's a small, organic kitchen garden that provides much for the table in summer. Bedrooms vary in size, but not style – all have pretty fabrics, summer colours and good bathrooms. Some are dog-friendly, one has a conservatory/sitting room that opens onto a private lawn, there's a film library downstairs for your TV. After a full cooked breakfast, head west for the Southern Upland Way or the spectacular country between Moniaive and the Galloway Forest. Don't miss Drumlanrig Castle up the road for its gardens, walking trails and excellent mountain bike tracks.

Rooms	4 doubles, 4 twin/doubles: £90-£130. 1 suite for 2: £155. Singles from £85. Dinner, B&B from £82.50 p.p.
Meals	Lunch from £5. Dinner, £25-£35.
Closed	24-26 December.
Directions	North from Dumfries on A76; through Closeburn; signed left after 1 mile.

Adam & Jan Moore
Trigony House Hotel
Closeburn,
Thornhill DG3 5EZ

Tel	+44 (0)1848 331211
Email	info@trigonyhotel.co.uk
Web	www.countryhousehotelsscotland.com

Entry 259   Map 9

Brooks Hotel Edinburgh

Carla and Andrew's third hotel sticks to a simple philosophy: great prices, stylish interiors, happy staff, a central position in town. It is exactly what lots of us want – boutique on a budget – and with Edinburgh's magnetic pull, it's likely to be a big hit. It stands in the West End, a mile from the castle (there are umbrellas at the front door in case it rains). Interiors have been completely renovated. There are sofas, great art and an honesty bar in the sitting room, then doors onto an attractive courtyard, where tables and chairs wait for summer. Back inside, you get a good breakfast in the dining room with lots of choice, too: smoked salmon and scrambled eggs, the full cooked works, even boiled eggs and soldiers. Rooms vary in size, but not style. There's a lift to whizz you up, then Cole & Son wallpapers, Farrow & Ball paints, goose down duvets on pocket-sprung mattresses. You get free WiFi, iPod docks, flat-screen TVs and DVD players. Compact bathrooms have big power showers. Edinburgh waits outside: castle, parliament, cathedral and palace, even the odd bar and restaurant.

Rooms	43 doubles: £59–£149.
	3 family rooms for 4: £99–£169.
	Singles from £55.
Meals	Restaurants nearby.
Closed	Never.
Directions	Sent on booking.

Carla & Andrew Brooks
Brooks Hotel Edinburgh
70-72 Grove Street,
Edinburgh EH3 8AP
Tel   +44 (0)131 228 2323
Email   info@brooksedinburgh.com
Web   www.brooksedinburgh.com

21212

A smart restaurant with rooms in Edinburgh's East End with Holyrood Palace, the Botanic Gardens and lovely Leith all close. Paul left his Michelin star down south, bought this Georgian townhouse, spent a fortune turning it into a 21st-century pleasure dome, then opened for business and won back his star. The house stands at the top of a hill with long views north towards the Firth of Forth. Inside, contemporary splendour waits. High ceilings and vast windows come as standard, but wander at will and find a chic first-floor drawing room, cherubs on the wall, busts and statues all over the place, even a private dining pod made of white leather. Stunning bedrooms have enormous beds, cool colours, fat sofas and iPod docks. Those at the front have the view, all have robes in magnificent bathrooms. As for the restaurant, the kitchen is on display behind a wall of glass and the food it produces is heavenly stuff, perhaps sea bass with cashew nuts, pork with pistachio and onion mustard, lemon curd cheesecake tart with melon juice. Princes Street and its lovely gardens are a short stroll. *Minimum stay: 3 nights at New Year.*

Rooms	4 doubles: £95-£295.
Meals	Lunch from £22. Dinner £49-£69. Not Sunday or Monday.
Closed	Rarely.
Directions	A720 ring road, then A702/A7 into town. Right at T-junc. at Balmoral Hotel, then immediately left with flow. Right at second r'bout and 1st right. On right.

Paul Kitching & Katie O'Brien
21212
3 Royal Terrace,
Edinburgh EH7 5AB

Tel	+44 (0)131 523 1030
Email	reservations@21212restaurant.co.uk
Web	www.21212restaurant.co.uk

23 Mayfield

A great base for all things Edinburgh. Built in 1868, this Victorian villa was once home to a coffee merchant and stands in the shadow of Arthur's Seat. Outside, much prized, off-street parking waits. Inside, you find original fireplaces, ornate ceilings and a stained-glass window on the landing. Ross has added Victorian colours, newspapers on poles, gilt-framed pictures that hang on chains – but best of all is breakfast, served in winter with candelabra on every table. You'll find chesterfield sofas in the sitting room, then old movies playing on the television. Bedrooms offer modern comforts: excellent beds, travertine bathrooms, bold colours, perhaps a panelled wall. You get iPod docks, Bose CD players, the family room has a Nintendo Wii. There's good art throughout, a hot tub in the garden, you can jump on a bus and whizz into town. Breakfast is the best: porridge with honey, free-range eggs, marshmallow pancakes, Stornoway black pudding with the full cooked works. Ross also has an apartment for six in the centre of town if you need more space. *Minimum stay: 2 nights at weekends.*

Rooms	3 twin/doubles, 3 four-posters: £80–£170. 1 family room for 4: £80–£190. 1 triple: £80–£175. Singles from £70.
Meals	Restaurants within 0.5 miles.
Closed	24-26 December.
Directions	A720 bypass, then north onto A722 for Edinburgh. Right onto A721 at T-junction with traffic lights. Over x-roads with main flow, under railway bridge, on right.

Ross Birnie
23 Mayfield
23 Mayfield Gardens,
Edinburgh EH9 2BX

Tel	+44 (0)131 667 5806
Email	info@23mayfield.co.uk
Web	www.23mayfield.co.uk

94DR

Close to Holyrood and Arthur's Seat, this super-friendly design B&B is not only popular for its contemporary style, but for Paul and John, who treat guests like friends and who make sure they see the best of their city. A traditional Victorian exterior gives no hint of the cool interiors that await within. You find original floor tiles and ornate ceilings intact, but other than that it's a clean sweep: deep charcoal downstairs; pure white above. There's a sitting room with iPads in case you want to book a restaurant; an honesty bar too, an espresso machine and lots of handy guide books. Upstairs, stylish, well-priced bedrooms wait. Some are big with claw-foot baths, others smaller with walk-in power showers. All come with comfy beds, bathrobes, beautiful linen and contemporary Scottish art. The family suite (two rooms) has bunk beds and a PlayStation for kids. Delicious breakfasts are served in a conservatory overlooking the back garden, a memorable feast orchestrated by Paul, with lively conversation that travels the world. Majestic Edinburgh is yours to explore. *Minimum stay: 2 nights at weekends.*

Rooms	3 doubles: £100–£145.
	2 suites for 2: £125–£200.
	1 family room for 4: £125–£190.
	Singles from £80.
Meals	Restaurants within 0.5 miles.
Closed	2–15 January.
Directions	Sent on booking.

John MacEwan & Paul Lightfoot
94DR
94 Dalkeith Road,
Edinburgh EH16 5AF

Tel	+44 (0)131 662 9265
Email	stay@94dr.com
Web	www.94dr.com

15 Glasgow

This is a smart Glasgow address – bang in the middle of town, yet beautifully insulated from it. The house, grand Victorian, stands on an attractive square with communal gardens in the middle. Inside, the feel is distinctly contemporary, though you still get a couple of Corinthian pillars in the original tiled entrance hall. Shane and Laura spent a year renovating, and while technically you're in a B&B, the interiors here are a match for any boutique hotel. Downstairs there's a vast sitting room with a couple of sofas in front of a fire. Bedrooms upstairs are no less generous. Those at the back are large, the suites at the front are huge. All come with king-size beds, crisp white linen, handmade bedheads and robes in seriously fancy bathrooms. Suites have a few added extras: big sofas, beautiful windows, one has a double-ended bath overlooking the square. Breakfast is brought to you whenever you want. As for Glasgow, you'll find great restaurants nearby: the Finnieston for seafood and gin cocktails, the Gannet for a flat-iron steak, Ben Nevis for a wee dram and live folk music most nights.

Rooms	2 doubles, 1 twin/double: £99-£135. 2 suites for 2: £129-£165. Singles from £89.
Meals	Restaurants on your doorstep.
Closed	Never.
Directions	West into Glasgow on M8. Exit at junc. 18 for Charing X (outside lane), then double back at lights. 1st left, 1st left, 1st left (really). Follow square round to house.

Shane & Laura McKenzie
15 Glasgow
15 Woodside Place, Glasgow G3 7QL

Tel	+44 (0)141 332 1263
Email	info@15glasgow.com
Web	www.15glasgow.com

The Lime Tree

Quite a few hotels have art galleries, few secure a Matisse exhibition! David, a mountain guide and artist, somehow managed to fill a room with the great man's work. Then, when the Royal Geographical Society came to town, he planted a full-scale replica of Ernest Shackleton's boat on the lawn. These days, he's just finished marking out an epic three-week walk from Fort William up the coast to Cape Wrath – you can plan your own adventures from his lovely map room in the hotel. As for this Macintosh manse, it dates to 1850, though the lime tree itself was planted in 1700, the year the town was settled. Inside, a small, quirky world of stripped floors, open fires and beautiful windows for views of Loch Linnhe. Airy bedrooms are good for the price. Expect white linen, comfy beds, blond wood furniture, neat little bathrooms. There's a rustic bistro for tasty food, perhaps seafood soup, boeuf Bourguignon, Bakewell tart with vanilla ice-cream. Ben Nevis is close, but if you want to do more than walk, climbing, cragging, mountain biking and kayaking can all be arranged.

Rooms	3 doubles, 1 twin: £70–£130.
	5 family rooms for 4: £80–£120.
	Singles from £60. Extra beds in family rooms: under 11s £10, everyone else £25.
Meals	Dinner, 3 courses, £25–£30.
Closed	Rarely.
Directions	North to Fort William on A82. Hotel on right at 1st roundabout in town.

	David Wilson
	The Lime Tree
	Achintore Road,
	Fort William PH33 6RQ
Tel	+44 (0)1397 701806
Email	info@limetreefortwilliam.co.uk
Web	www.limetreefortwilliam.co.uk

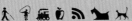

Kilcamb Lodge Hotel & Restaurant

Another beautiful West Coast setting with Loch Sunart at the end of the garden and Glas Bheinn rising beyond. Kilcamb – a barracks during the Jacobite uprising – has a bit of everything: a drawing room with an open fire; an elegant dining room for good food; a cool little brasserie that's recently been refurbished; a handful of lovely bedrooms in chic country-house style. There's a 12-acre garden that rolls down to the sea, where you can spot otters and seals. Ducks and geese fly over, if you're lucky you'll see eagles. Back inside, there's a stained-glass window on the landing, fresh flowers in the drawing room, driftwood lamps and good books. You can eat in the restaurant or the brasserie, either a five-course tasting menu or something simpler, perhaps a plate of seafood, Highland lamb, iced whisky parfait. Bedrooms have warm colours, some with a contemporary feel, others a smart country-house style. All have good bathrooms, crisp linen and comfy beds. Day trips to Mull are easy to arrange. Don't miss Ardnamurchan or Senna Bay at the end of the road. *Minimum stay: 2 nights at weekends in May.*

Rooms	8 doubles: £125-£190. 3 suites for 2: £200-£300. Singles from £85.
Meals	Lunch from £7.50. Afternoon tea £12. Dinner, 3 courses, £25-£45. Tasting menu £55.
Closed	Jan. Limited opening Nov & Feb.
Directions	From Fort William A82 south for 10 miles to Corran ferry, then A861 to Strontian. Hotel west of village on left, signed. A830 & A861 from Fort William takes an hour longer.

David & Sally Ruthven-Fox
Kilcamb Lodge Hotel & Restaurant
Strontian, Acharacle PH36 4HY

Tel	+44 (0)1967 402257
Email	enquiries@kilcamblodge.co.uk
Web	www.kilcamblodge.co.uk

Doune

You arrive by boat – there's no road in – a ferry across to Knoydart, the last great wilderness in Britain. You'll find mountains, sea and beach – a thrilling landscape of boundless peace and ever-changing light. Guillemots race across the water, dolphins and seals come to play, the Sound of Sleat shoots across to Skye. As for Doune, it's a tiny community of happily shipwrecked souls, who rescued this land from ruin; Martin, Jane and Liz look after you with instinctive generosity. The dining room is the hub, pine-clad from top to toe, with a stove to keep you warm and a couple of fiddles for the odd ceilidh. The food is delicious – crab from the bay, roast lamb from the hill, chocolate tart with homemade ice-cream. Bedrooms along the veranda are delightfully simple – pine clad with mezzanine bunks for children, hooks for clothes, armchairs for watching the weather; compact shower rooms sparkle. The walking is magnificent, boat trips can be arranged, the night sky will astound you. There's a lodge for groups, too. A very special place, miss it at your peril. *Minimum stay: 3 nights. 15% off weekly stays.*

Rooms	2 doubles, 1 twin, each with mezzanine bed for children: £93. 1 single with separate shower: £33.
Meals	Packed lunch, £8.50. Dinner, £30.
Closed	October-Easter.
Directions	Park in Mallaig; the boat will collect you at an agreed time.

Martin & Jane Davies
Doune
Knoydart, Mallaig PH41 4PL

Tel	+44 (0)1687 462667
Email	martin@doune-knoydart.co.uk
Web	www.doune-knoydart.co.uk

Grants at Craigellachie

An old factor's house on the banks of Loch Duich with the Five Sisters of Kintail flaunting their beauty to the south; three are munros, views from the top are spectacular. This is a great little base for Highland flings – quirky, homespun, lovely owners. There's lots to do: Glenelg, Applecross and Skye are on your doorstep, Loch Ness is within easy reach, Dornie Castle (the one on the water you see on TV) is on the other side of the loch. After a day pottering through magical landscapes, come home to this cute restaurant with rooms. It's a tiny operation. Tony and Liz do it all themselves: cook, clean, polish and shine, chat to guests after delicious breakfasts, point you in the right direction. There are four rooms, two in the main house (small but sweet, warm colours, fine for a night), then two out back, smarter altogether with neutral colours, lovely linen, robes in fancy bathrooms. One is a suite (with a small kitchen), both have decked terraces. As for Tony's lovely food, don't expect to go hungry. You might have hand-dived scallops and thyme, Glenelg lamb with rosemary, whisky panna cotta.

Rooms	2 doubles, 1 twin: £100–£145. 1 suite for 2: £155–£185. Singles from £70. Dinner, B&B from £82.50 p.p.
Meals	Dinner, 3 courses, about £35. Not Sun or Mon.
Closed	Mid-November to mid-February.
Directions	A87 north from Invergarry to Shiel Bridge. Left in village for Glenleg. First right down to Loch Duich. On left in village.

Tony & Liz Taylor
Grants at Craigellachie
Ratagan, Glenshiel, Kyle IV40 8HP

Tel	+44 (0)1599 511331
Email	info@housebytheloch.co.uk
Web	www.housebytheloch.co.uk

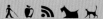

The Torridon

It's hard to beat the top of Scotland, the landscapes here feed the soul. Mountains rise, red deer roam, eagles soar, the light changes every minute. This 1887 shooting lodge was built for the Earl of Lovelace and stands in 58 acres that roll down to the shores of Upper Loch Torridon. Inside, sparkling interiors thrill: a huge fire in the panelled hall, a zodiac ceiling in the drawing room, 350 malts in the pitch pine bar. Big windows pull in the view, while canny walkers pour off the hills to recover in style. Bedrooms are hard to fault, some big, others bigger, with a cool, contemporary style running throughout: bold colours, padded headboards, exquisite linen, magnificent bathrooms; one room has a shower in a turret. Outside, a beautiful two-acre kitchen garden provides much for the table, perhaps lovage and courgette soup, then shoulder of lamb with rosemary gnocchi and passion fruit tart with mango mousse. Dan and Rohaise also own the village inn for simpler food and good rooms from £110. Don't miss the free excursions: kayaking, guided walks, abseiling and mountain biking are all on tap. *Pets by arrangement.*

Rooms	10 doubles, 2 twins, 2 four-posters: £230–£465. 4 suites for 2: £465. Dinner, B&B from £172 p.p. Extra bed £40 per night p.p. 1 boathouse for 4: £925–£1,425.
Meals	Lunch from £5.95. Dinner, 5 courses, £55.
Closed	January.
Directions	A9 to Inverness, A835 to Garve, A832 to Kinlochewe, A896 to Annat (not Torridon). Signed on south shore.

Daniel & Rohaise Rose-Bristow
The Torridon
Annat, By Achnasheen IV22 2EY

Tel	+44 (0)1445 791242
Email	info@thetorridon.com
Web	www.thetorridon.com

Mackay's Rooms

This is the north-west corner of Britain and it's utterly magical: huge skies, sandy beaches, aquamarine seas, cliffs and caves. You drive – or cycle – for mile upon mile with mountains soaring into the heavens and ridges sliding into the sea. If you like big remote landscapes, you'll love it here; what's more, you'll pretty much have it to yourself. Mackay's – they have the shop, the bunkhouse and the garage, too – is the only place to stay in town, its earthy colours mixing with stone walls, open fires and stripped floors to great effect. Bedrooms (some big, others smaller) are extremely comfy. They come with big wooden beds and crisp white linen, while Fiona, a textiles graduate, has a fine eye for fabrics and upholstery. You also get excellent bathrooms, iPod docks, flat-screen TVs and DVD players. Breakfast sets you up for the day – grilled grapefruit, whisky porridge, venison sausages, local eggs – so head east to the beach, west for great golf or catch the ferry across to Cape Wrath and scan the sea for whales. There's surfing for the brave and the beautiful.

Rooms	6 doubles, 1 twin: £125-£165. 4 cottages for 2-6 (self-catering): £800-£1,600 per week. Singles from £110.
Meals	Restaurants in village.
Closed	October-April. Cottages open all year.
Directions	A838 north from Rhiconich. After 19 miles enter Durness village. Mackay's is on right-hand side opposite memorial.

Fiona Mackay
Mackay's Rooms
Durine, Durness, Lairg IV27 4PN

Tel	+44 (0)1971 511202
Email	stay@visitdurness.com
Web	www.visitdurness.com

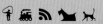

Viewfield House Hotel

This old ancestral pile stands high above Portree Bay with fine views tumbling down to the Sound of Raasay below. Twenty acres of mature gardens and woodland wrap around you, with croquet on the lawn and a hill to climb for 360° views of peak and sea. As for this grand Victorian factor's house, expect a few aristocratic fixtures and fittings: hunting trophies in the hall, cases filled with curios, a grand piano and open fire in the drawing room, Sanderson wallpaper in the dining room. Family oils hang on the walls, you'll find wood carvings from distant lands and a flurry of antiques, all of which blend grandeur with touches of humour. Upstairs a warren of bedrooms wait. Most are big, some are vast, all come in country-house style with lovely fabrics, crisply laundered sheets and sea views from those at the front. Dive into Skye – wildlife, mountains, sea lochs and castles all wait, as do a couple of distilleries. Suppers are on tap – tomato and basil soup, lamb noisettes, chocolate and almond cake with vanilla sauce; there's Highland porridge for breakfast, too. Fantastic.

Rooms	3 doubles, 8 twin/doubles, 2 twins; 1 double with separate bath: £130-£150. 2 singles: £58-£75. Dinner, B&B from £80 p.p.
Meals	Dinner, 3 courses, £25. Packed lunch £7.
Closed	Mid-October to Easter.
Directions	On A87, coming from south, driveway entrance on left just before the Portree filling station.

Hugh Macdonald
Viewfield House Hotel
Viewfield Road, Portree IV51 9EU

Tel	+44 (0)1478 612217
Email	info@viewfieldhouse.com
Web	www.viewfieldhouse.com

Culdearn House

Grantown is a great base for Highland flings. You can fish the Spey, jump on the whisky trail, check out a raft of castles, even ski in Aviemore. Loch Ness is close, as is Royal Deeside, there's golf everywhere and the walking is divine; in short, expect to be busy. As for Culdrean, it stands in a row of five identical houses that were built in 1860 by Lord Seafield, one for each of his daughters. These days it's a lovely small hotel where William and Sonia look after guests with unstinting kindness. There's an open fire and facing sofas in the smart sitting room, panelled windows and a marble fireplace in the dining room, then stylish bedrooms that offer the sort of comfort you'd want after a day in the hills. You get the comfiest beds, the crispest linen, then decanters of sherry, pretty furniture and spotless bathrooms. Back downstairs, William looks after a tempting wine list and 60 malts, while Sonia whisks up delicious four-course dinners, perhaps West Coast scallops, bramble sorbet, fillet of beef, a walnut and maple syrup parfait. Don't miss the ospreys at Boat of Garten. *Children over 10 welcome.*

Rooms	4 doubles, 1 twin/double, 1 twin: £146-£164. Singles from £100. Dinner, B&B from £100 p.p.
Meals	Dinner, 4 courses, £43.
Closed	Never.
Directions	North into Grantown from A95. Left at 30 mph sign & house directly ahead.

Sonia & William Marshall
Culdearn House
Woodlands Terrace,
Grantown on Spey PH26 3JU

Tel	+44 (0)1479 872106
Email	enquiries@culdearn.com
Web	www.culdearn.com

Dalmunzie House

Dalmunzie is quite some sight, an ancient hunting lodge lost to the world in one of Scotland's most dramatic landscapes. You're cradled by mountains in a vast valley; it's as good a spot as any to escape the world. Surprisingly, you're not that remote – Perth is a mere 30 miles south – but the sense of solitude is magnificent, as is the view. As for the hotel, you potter up a one-mile drive to find a small enclave of friendly souls. Interiors are just the ticket: warm, cosy and quietly grand. You find sofas in front of open fires, a smart restaurant for delicious Scottish food, a snug bar for a good malt, a breakfast room with a big view. Country-house bedrooms have colour and style. Some are grand, others simpler, several have ancient claw-foot baths and two are in the towers. There's loads to do: fantastic walking, mountain bike trails, royal Deeside, the Highland games at Braemar, even skiing up the road in winter. As for the tricky golf course, it was almost certainly laid out by Alister MacKenzie, who later designed Augusta National; the famous par three at Amen Corner is all but identical to the seventh here.

Rooms	7 doubles, 3 doubles, 1 twin, 5 four-posters, 1 family room for 4: £140–£240. Dinner, B&B from £85 p.p.	
Meals	Lunch from £4.50. Packed lunch £10. Dinner, 4 courses, £45.	
Closed	Occasionally in winter.	
Directions	North from Blairgowrie on A93. Hotel signed left in Glenshee up one-mile drive.	

Nick Jefford & Jen Gleeson
Dalmunzie House
Spittal O'Glenshee,
Blairgowrie PH10 7QG

Tel	+44 (0)1250 885224
Email	reservations@dalmunzie.com
Web	www.dalmunzie.com

Killiecrankie House Hotel

No Highland fling would be complete without a night at Killiecrankie. Henrietta runs the place with great charm and has spent the last five years pouring in love and money; now it shines. Outside, gardens galore: one for roses, another for vegetables, and a fine herbaceous border. Further afield, you'll find much to please: Loch Tummel, Rannoch Moor and magnificent Glenshee, over which you tumble for the Highland Games at Braemar. Return to the indisputable comforts of a smart country hotel: tartan in the dining room, 52 malts at the bar, views at breakfast of red squirrels climbing garden trees. There's a snug sitting room where a fire burns in winter; in summer doors open onto the garden. Delightful bedrooms come in different shapes and sizes. All are smart with pretty linen, warm colours, chic fabrics and lovely views. Dinner is predictably delicious, perhaps pea and mint soup, Highland venison, sticky toffee pudding. There's porridge with cream and brown sugar for breakfast. Castles, hills and distilleries wait. A great wee place with staff who care. *Minimum stay: 2 nights at weekends. Pets by arrangement.*

Rooms	3 doubles, 5 twin/doubles: £230-£280. 2 singles: £115-£140. Price includes dinner for 2.
Meals	Lunch from £4.50. Dinner included; non-residents £42.
Closed	January/February.
Directions	A9 north of Pitlochry, then B8079, signed Killiecrankie. Straight ahead for 2 miles. Hotel on right, signed.

Henrietta Fergusson
Killiecrankie House Hotel
Killiecrankie,
Pitlochry PH16 5LG

Tel	+44 (0)1796 473220
Email	enquiries@killiecrankiehotel.co.uk
Web	www.killiecrankiehotel.co.uk

AWARD WINNER

Hotel of the Year
Scotland

Entry 274   Map 9

Craigatin House & Courtyard

Craigatin is one of those lovely places where beautiful rooms have attractive prices and hands-on owners go out of their way to make your stay special. It stands peacefully in two acres of manicured gardens on the northern shores of town; good restaurants are a short stroll. Smart stone exteriors give way to warmly contemporary interiors, where beautiful windows flood rooms with light. There are shutters in the breakfast room, which overflows into an enormous conservatory where sofas wait in front of a wood-burner and walls of glass open onto the garden. Big uncluttered bedrooms – some in the main house, others in converted stables – are super value for money. Expect Farrow & Ball colours, comfy beds, crisp white linen, padded bedheads and pretty shower rooms. Breakfast offers the full cooked works and tempting alternatives, perhaps smoked haddock omelettes or apple pancakes with grilled bacon and maple syrup. As for Pitlochry – gateway to the Highlands – it's a vibrant town with lots to do: castles and mountains, lochs and forests, its famous theatre festival. You're on the whisky trail, too. *Minimum stay: 2 nights at weekends.*

Rooms	11 doubles, 2 twins: £95–£105. 1 suite for 2: £122. Singles from £75.
Meals	Restaurants within walking distance.
Closed	Christmas.
Directions	A9 north to Pitlochry. Take 1st turn-off for town, up main street, past shops and signed on left.

Martin & Andrea Anderson
Craigatin House & Courtyard
165 Atholl Road,
Pitlochry PH16 5QL

Tel	+44 (0)1796 472478
Email	enquiries@craigatinhouse.co.uk
Web	www.craigatinhouse.co.uk

Torrdarach House

You're high on the hill with big views south and lovely gardens to enjoy. Susanne and Graeme – an Austro-English alliance – stayed here on their holidays, fell in love with the place, then bought it. It was a clever move – the house was recently renovated from top to toe: new bedrooms, new bathrooms, new everything. The result is this friendly, stylish, nicely priced B&B. An airy sitting room looks the right way – there are comfy sofas, a whisky bar and binoculars to scan the hills. Chic bedrooms come in the same happy style: neutral colours, smart fabrics, textured wallpaper, tartan bedheads. You get blond oak furniture, cute leather armchairs, flat-screen TVs and excellent showers. Downstairs, the breakfast room overlooks the garden, so watch out for red squirrels while tucking into porridge with a splash of whisky or the full cooked works. A drying room with safe storage for bikes and golf clubs is on the way; Graeme is a golf professional and Pitlochry has a good course, so if you need to iron out that slice of yours… Fabulous walking, the festival theatre, and the odd distillery wait. *Minimum stay: 2 nights at weekends April-October.*

Rooms	5 doubles, 2 twin/doubles: £90–£104. Singles from £78.
Meals	Pubs/restaurants 400 yds.
Closed	9 November to 14 February (but open for New Year).
Directions	North to Pitlochry on A9. In town, up high street, past shops, then 1st right into Larchwood Road. Up hill, keep left, then right into Golf Course Road. On right.

Graeme Fish & Susanne Wallner
Torrdarach House
Golf Course Road,
Pitlochry PH16 5AU

Tel	+44 (0)1796 472136
Email	info@torrdarach.co.uk
Web	www.torrdarach.co.uk

Kinnaird Estate

A magnificent 1770 mansion set in 6,000 acres of prime Perthshire countryside. The river Tay passes dramatically below, sheep and cattle graze contentedly, paths behind lead into the estate. The house is sublime from top to toe, grand yet welcoming, a place to feel at home. Most beautiful of all is the panelled drawing room with roaring fire, grand piano, beautiful art and sofas galore. The dining room has original murals. You breakfast in the company of the maharaja of Jaipur (well, his portrait), there's a billiards room with fine views, a snug study, too. Big country-house bedrooms have vast beds, smart wallpapers and colourful fabrics. Those at the front get the view, several have fires, excellent bathrooms come with white robes. The estate owns a couple of world-class fishing beats, so come to try your luck; there's shooting in season, clays, too. Food is delicious (local meat, estate eggs) and you can bring your own wine. Staff are lovely. Five estate cottages tempt you to linger. Fabulous walking and the odd castle wait. House parties are welcome. *Children over 12 welcome.*

Rooms	7 twin/doubles: £140–£160.
	1 suite for 2: £180.
	Singles £120–£160.
	5 cottages for 2–8 (self-catering):
	£560–£1,050 per week.
Meals	Picnic lunch £10.
	Dinner, 3 courses, £35 (not Mon or Tues).
Closed	Christmas.
Directions	Leave A9 for B898 2 miles north of
	Dunkeld. On right after 6 miles.

Guesthouse Manager
Kinnaird Estate
Dunkeld PH8 0LB
Tel   +44 (0)1796 482440
Email   reservations@kinnairdestate.com
Web   www.kinnairdestate.com

Royal Hotel

The Royal is lovely – softly grand, intimate and welcoming, a country house in the middle of town. Queen Victoria once stayed, hence the name. It stands on the river Earn – its eponymous loch glistens five miles up stream – but you're brilliantly placed to strike out in all directions: Loch Tay, Pitlochry, The Trossachs and Perth are close. Those who linger fare rather well. You get a wall of books in an elegant sitting room where two fires burn; newspapers hang on poles, logs tumble from wicker baskets, sofas and armchairs are impeccably upholstered. There's a grandfather clock in the hall, rugs to cover stripped floors in a country-house bar, then walls festooned with beautiful art. You can eat all over the place, in the bar, in the conservatory or at smartly dressed tables in the elegant dining room, perhaps asparagus spears with a poached egg, breast of duck with cabbage and bacon, rhubarb sponge with vanilla ice-cream. Smart homely rooms have padded bedheads, crisp linen, mahogany dressers, gilt-framed mirrors. Bathrooms come with fluffy robes, one four-poster has a log fire.

Rooms	5 doubles, 3 twins, 3 four-posters: £150-£190. 1 house for 4 (self-catering): £585-£890 per week; 2-night stays from £168.
Meals	Bar meals from £6.95. Dinner, 3 courses, £27.75.
Closed	Rarely.
Directions	A9 north of Dunblane, A822 through Braco, left onto B827. Left for town centre, over bridge, hotel on square.

Teresa Milsom
Royal Hotel
Melville Square, Comrie,
Crieff PH6 2DN
Tel   +44 (0)1764 679200
Email   reception@royalhotel.co.uk
Web   www.royalhotel.co.uk

Barley Bree

A few miles north of Gleneagles, a super little restaurant with rooms that delivers what so many people want: stylish interiors, super food, excellent prices, a warm welcome. This is a small family-run affair. Fabrice is French and cooks sublimely, Alison, a Scot, looks after the wine. As for Barley Bree – whisky soup to you and me – it's an 18th-century coaching inn, its name plucked from a Robert Burns poem. Happy locals and travellers from afar come for fabulous Scottish food that's cooked with French flair, perhaps fennel soup with basil pesto, saddle of venison with piquillo purée, tarte tatin with vanilla ice-cream. The restaurant, nicely rustic, has a fire that burns on both sides, while in summer you decant onto a terrace for lunch in the sun. Six comfy rooms have neutral colours, crisp linen, good beds and underfloor heating in neat little shower rooms. The big room, with a claw-foot bath, is well worth splashing out on. There's a sitting room for guests with books, good art, stripped boards and a fire. Don't miss the gardens at Drummond Castle or the Library of Innerpeffray.

Rooms	6 twin/doubles: £110-£150. Singles from £70.
Meals	Lunch from £8. Sunday lunch from £13.50. Dinner, 3 courses, about £40 (not Sunday evening, Mon or Tues).
Closed	Mondays & Tuesdays. Christmas. 7-22 July, 20-23 October, 1-8 January.
Directions	A9 north from Dunblane, then A822 for Muthill. In village on left before church.

Fabrice & Alison Bouteloup
Barley Bree
6 Willoughby Street,
Muthill PH5 2AB

Tel	+44 (0)1764 681451
Email	info@barleybree.com
Web	www.barleybree.com

Creagan House at Strathyre

Creagan is a delight – a small, traditional restaurant with rooms run with great passion by Gordon and Cherry. At its heart is Gordon's delicious food, which draws a devoted crowd, perhaps fillet of brill with plum and damson, local venison with a sloe gin and juniper sauce, then an apple, prune and almond flory with clotted cream. Food is local – meat and game from Perthshire, seafood from west-coast boats – and served on Skye pottery; some vegetables come from the garden. A snug sitting room doubles as a bar, where a good wine list and 50 malt whiskies wait; if you like a dram, you'll be happy here. Bedrooms fit the bill: warm and comfy with smart carpets, pretty colours, flat-screen TVs, a sofa if there's room. Breakfast is a treat; where else can you sit in a baronial dining room and read about the iconography of the toast rack while waiting for your bacon and eggs? No airs and graces, just the sort of attention you only get in small owner-run places. Hens, woodpeckers and red squirrels live in the garden. There are hills to climb, boat trips on lochs, secure storage for bikes. Very dog-friendly.

Rooms	3 doubles, 1 twin, 1 four-poster: £130-£150. Singles £90-£100. Extra bed/sofabed £30 p.p. per night.
Meals	Dinner, 3 courses, £35.
Closed	Christmas, New Year.
Directions	From Stirling A84 north through Callander to Strathyre. Hotel 0.25 miles north of village on right.

Gordon & Cherry Gunn
Creagan House at Strathyre
Callander FK18 8ND

Tel	+44 (0)1877 384638
Email	eatandstay@creaganhouse.co.uk
Web	www.creaganhouse.co.uk

Mhor 84

The entirely benevolent expansion of the Mhor empire has mastered the Midas touch, turning this old roadside inn into the coolest motel in the land. Outside, the glen shoots down to Loch Voil, with mountains to climb and bike tracks to follow. Inside, chic white minimalism mixes with warm Scottish tradition, a perfect blend of relaxed 21st-century living. There's style and humour in equal measure – boarded floors, tractor seat bar stools, curios hanging on the walls, the odd sofa for afternoon tea. Fires roar, cake stands bulge, happy staff weave through the throng delivering fabulous food that you eat at old school tables – porridge with honey for breakfast, sourdough and hummus for lunch, Scotch rarebit, Tyree lobster and plum crumble for dinner. There's live folk music every Thursday – Ewan MacPherson often plays – and a fine selection of malts if you fancy a dram. Simple bedrooms have white walls, contemporary art, small armchairs and honest prices; spotless bathrooms are 1980s originals, all part of the fun. There's a games room, too, with a juke box and pool table.

Rooms	2 doubles, 4 twin/doubles: £70–£80. 1 family room for 4: £80–£110.
Meals	Breakfast from £4.50. Lunch from £3.90. Dinner, 3 courses, £30–£35.
Closed	Christmas Day.
Directions	A84 north from Callander. Through Strathyre, then right after three miles for Kingshouse. In village.

Emer Brummel
Mhor 84
Balhquhidder, Lochearnhead FK19 8NY
Tel   +44 (0)1877 384646
Email   motel@mhor.net
Web   www.mhor.net/mhor84-motel/

Favourite newcomer

Monachyle Mhor

Monachyle is unique – a designer hotel on a remote hill farm that started life as a B&B. Today it's one of the coolest places to stay in Scotland and it's still run by the same family with the children at the helm. Dick farms, Melanie designs the magical rooms, Tom cooks some of the best food in Scotland. It sits in 2,000 acres of blissful silence at the end of the track with the Trossachs circling around you and Loch Voil shimming below. Sheep graze, buzzards swoop, the odd fisherman tries his luck. Inside, there's a cool little bar, a fire in the sitting room, then a slim restaurant that drinks in the view. Bedrooms ooze 21st-century chic: big beds, cool colours, fabulous design, hi-tech gadgets. Bathrooms are equally good, perhaps a deluge shower in a granite steam room or claw-foot baths with views down the glen. Loft-house suites are enormous, but the smaller rooms are lovely, too. Dinner is a five-course feast with beef, lamb, pork and venison all off the farm. Rob Roy lived in the glen, you can visit his grave. The hotel holds a festival in May – fabulous food and cool Scottish tunes.

Rooms	9 twin/doubles, £195-£215.
	5 suites for 2: £265.
	1 family room for 4: £195-£265.
Meals	Lunch from £5.50.
	Dinner, 5 courses, £50.
	Sunday lunch £32.
Closed	Two weeks in January.
Directions	M9, junc. 11, then B824 and A84 north. Right for Balquhidder 6 miles north of Callander. 5 miles west along road & Loch Voil. Hotel on right, signed.

Tom Lewis
Monachyle Mhor
Balquhidder,
Lochearnhead FK19 8PQ

Tel	+44 (0)1877 384622
Email	monachyle@mhor.net
Web	www.mhor.net

Entry 282   Map 8

Pilot Panther

The Pilot Panther is a classic 1950 showman's wagon originally built by The Coventry Steel Company, once renowned as the finest wagon makers in the country. Its journey has been long and rambling, but it has settled in a fine location in the grounds of Monachyle Mhor hotel. The views from your window are of the spectacular loch which seems to change with the weather and provide a new sight every day. Off the main living and sleeping area, which also has the wood-burner, oven and grill, is the double bunk room. The loos and shower are a minute's walk away at the hotel. The great walking and stunning views around the long loch will help you work up an appetite worthy of the hotel restaurant, an award-winning pilgrimage for Scottish foodies. Or you can arrange to have breakfast at the hotel and fuel up before you go. Rather handily, the family also manage the farm, fishery and bakery, which ensures that a good supply of very local produce goes onto the menu. The Panther is both an unusual way to stay at a heavenly hotel, and an experience in itself. *Minimum stay: 2 nights. Book through Sawday's Canopy & Stars online or by phone.*

Rooms	1 showman's wagon for 4: £125–£150. £10 per pet per stay. Max 2. Please arrange with Monachyle Mhor before arrival.
Meals	BYO breakfast, or at hotel, £12.50. Dinner, 5 courses, £50. Sunday lunch £32.
Closed	Never.
Directions	M9, junc. 11, then B824 and A84 north. Right for Balquhidder 6 miles north of Callander. 5 miles west along road & Loch Voil. Hotel on right, signed.

Canopy & Stars
Pilot Panther
Monachyle Mhor
Balquhidder, Lochearnhead FK19 8PQ

Tel	+44 (0)117 204 7830
Email	enquiries@canopyandstars.co.uk
Web	www.canopyandstars.co.uk/pilotpanther

Fortingall Hotel

You're away from the crowds in one of Perthshire's loveliest glens – wild deer roam, buzzards nest, fishermen stand in silent rapture on the banks for the river Lyon. As for this lovely country-house hotel, it sits next to the village church in the shade of an ancient yew tree. In 1900 it was remodelled in Arts & Crafts style, as was the village, hence the thatched cottages. Inside, it's smart but not stuffy, with roaring fires, bold colours, country art, the odd grandfather clock. There's a grand piano in the sitting room, local art in the library, a half-panelled dining room with views up the valley, a cute locals' bar where farmers gather. Bedrooms upstairs have a fresh, country-house feel: padded bedheads, Glen Lyon tweed, sofas in the bigger rooms, spotless bathrooms; those at the front have the view. Back downstairs, you can eat in the dining room or the bar – duck terrine and fillet of beef one night, bangers and mash the next. You can fish, cycle, scale a couple of munros, play some golf or visit the smallest distillery in Scotland. Don't miss afternoon tea.

Rooms	9 doubles, 2 twins: £165–£200. Singles from £110. Dinner, B&B from £145 p.p.
Meals	Lunch from £6.95. Bar meals from £9.95. Dinner, 4 courses, £39.
Closed	Rarely.
Directions	A9, A872 west to Aberfeldy, then B846 north. Left in Coshieville and on right after 3 miles.

Robbie & Mags Cairns
Fortingall Hotel
Fortingall, Aberfeldy PH15 2NQ

Tel	+44 (0)1887 830367
Email	enquiries@fortingall.com
Web	www.fortingall.com

The Allanton Inn

Allanton, population 100. Welcome to the sleepy back of beyond, an untouched corner of the rural idyll that most people skip on their rush north. Well, there's no rush here, just patchwork fields, rolling hills and the river Tweed pottering off to the coast. As for this cute little inn, it's a great base from which to explore. The style is charming, the locals friendly, the prices lovely, the food a treat. It sits on the only street in town with a garden that backs onto open country; in summer you can have lunch in the sun while watching the farmer plough his fields. Inside, home-spun interiors have warmth, style and colour. There's an open-plan feel, the airy bar flowing into a half-panelled restaurant. You'll find a smouldering fire, good art, fresh flowers. Pretty rooms above come with good bathrooms, Farrow & Ball colours, padded bedheads and homemade biscuits. A couple are big, those at the back have the view. Super local food waits downstairs, perhaps hot smoked salmon, rack of local lamb, Tia Maria tiramisu. Local fishing is easy to arrange, there's golf and excellent walking, too.

Rooms	2 doubles, 2 twin/doubles: £75–£95. 1 family room for 4: £100–£130. 1 single: £55–£85.
Meals	Lunch from £6.75. Dinner, 3 courses, £25–£35. Sunday lunch from £12.50.
Closed	Christmas.
Directions	West from Berwick on A6105, then left in Churnside onto B6437. On left in village.

William & Katerina Reynolds
The Allanton Inn
Allanton, By Duns TD11 3JZ
Tel   +44 (0)1890 818260
Email   info@allantoninn.co.uk
Web   www.allantoninn.co.uk

Langass Lodge

Vast skies, water everywhere, golden beaches that stretch for miles. Nothing prepares you for the epic majesty of the Uists, a place so infinitely beautiful you wonder why you've got it to yourself. As for Langass, an old shooting lodge, it makes a great base, not least because Amanda and Niall know the island inside out and can help you discover its secrets. The hotel sits in ten silent acres with paths that lead up to standing stones or down to the water. Inside, cosy interiors fit the bill perfectly: a roaring fire in the bar; watery views in the restaurant; doors onto a terrace for drinks in summer. Bedrooms – warmly traditional in the main house, nicely contemporary in the new wing – are super value for money. Expect comfy beds, crisp white linen, excellent bathrooms, lots of colour. As for the food, it's the best on the island, with game off the estate and seafood plucked fresh from the sea. There's loads to do: kayaking, walking, wild fishing, bird watching. The night sky is magnificent, as are the Northern Lights. Children and dogs and very welcome. Don't miss it.

Rooms	5 doubles; 9 twin/doubles: £95–£145. 2 family rooms for 4: £120–£160. Singles from £75.
Meals	Dinner in bar from £12.95; in restaurant £30–£36.
Closed	Never.
Directions	South from Lochmaddy on A867. Signed left after five miles.

Amanda & Niall Leveson Gower
Langass Lodge
Langass, North Uist HS6 5HA

Tel	+44 (0)1876 580285
Email	langasslodge@btconnect.com
Web	www.langasslodge.co.uk

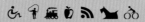

Scarista House

All you need to know is this: Harris is one of the most beautiful places in the world. Beaches of white sand that stretch for a mile or two are not uncommon. If you bump into another soul, it will be a delightful coincidence, but you should not count on it. The water is turquoise, coconuts sometimes wash up on the beach. The view from Scarista is simple and magnificent: field, ridge, beach, water, sky. Patricia and Tim are the kindest people, quietly inspiring. Their home is island heaven: coal fires, rugs on painted floors, books everywhere, old oak furniture, a first-floor drawing room and fabulous Harris light. Homely bedrooms come in country-house style. The golf club has left a set of clubs by the front door in case you wish to play (the view from the first tee is one of the best in the game). A corncrake occasionally visits the garden. There are walking sticks and Wellington boots to help you up the odd hill. Kind local staff may speak Gaelic and the food is exceptional, maybe quail with an armagnac mousse, fillet of Stornoway halibut, orange marmalade tart. A perfect place.

Rooms	2 doubles, 1 twin: £210-£222.
	3 suites for 2 (Annexe): £235.
	Singles from £137.
Meals	Dinner, 3 courses, £43.
	Packed lunch £7.50.
Closed	Christmas & New Year.
Directions	From Tarbert A859 south, signed
	Rodel. Scarista 15 miles on left after
	golf course. W10 bus stops at gate.

Patricia & Tim Martin
Scarista House
Scarista, Isle of Harris HS3 3HX
Tel   +44 (0)1859 550238
Email   timandpatricia@scaristahouse.com
Web   www.scaristahouse.com

Wales

The Dolaucothi Arms

David and Esther's cute little inn sits in a village deep in rural Carmarthenshire. It's an absolute gem, a testament to beautiful simplicity, with lovely interiors that see no need to abandon their period charm for contemporary design. Instead, you find beautiful Georgian windows, original tiles in the bar, then varnished floorboards in the airy restaurant. It's a little like walking onto the pages of a Jane Austen novel, a touch of old-world charm. Pick up a pint of local ale, sink into a chesterfield sofa and roast away in front of the wood-burner; in summer you decant into the pretty garden for a pint in the sun. Excellent food awaits you – homemade soups and pies, pork and elderflower sausages, the best local steaks, sticky toffee pudding. Circular walks help you atone, there's a river at the bottom of the garden, then National Trust goldmines to visit in the village. Bedrooms upstairs are a steal with smart colours, woollen throws and sparkling bathrooms; some have garden views, all get decanters of port. Breakfast is a treat, Aberglasney Gardens are within easy reach. Don't miss Sunday lunch.

Rooms	3 doubles: £75. Singles £55. Extra bed/sofabed £20 p.p. per night.
Meals	Lunch from £5. Dinner, 3 courses, £20. Sunday lunch from £9.
Closed	Monday. Tuesday until 6.30pm. Christmas Day.
Directions	A40 toward Llandovery then right turn onto A482 to Lampeter. After 8 miles, you'll see Pumpsaint sign as you enter the village. Pub is on your left.

David Joy & Esther Hubert
The Dolaucothi Arms
Pumpsaint, Llanwrda SA19 8UW

Tel +44 (0)1558 650237
Email info@thedolaucothiarms.co.uk
Web www.thedolaucothiarms.co.uk

Ty Mawr Country Hotel

Pretty rooms, attractive prices and delicious food make this super country house hard to resist. It's a very peaceful, tucked-away spot. You drive over the hills, drop into the village and wash up at this 16th-century stone house that glows in yellow. Outside, a sun-trapping terrace laps against a trim lawn, which in turn drops into a passing river. Gentle eccentricities abound: croquet hoops take the odd diversion, logs are piled high like giant beehives, a seat has been chiselled into a tree trunk. Inside, exposed stone walls, terracotta-tiled floors and low beamed ceilings give a warm country feel. There are fires everywhere – one in the sitting room, which overlooks the garden, another in the dining room that burns on both sides. Excellent bedrooms are all big. You get warm colours, big beds, crisp linen, good bathrooms. Some have sofas, all are dog-friendly, three overlook the garden. Back downstairs, the bar doubles as reception, and there's Welsh art on sale. Steve's cooking is the final treat: Cardigan Bay scallops, organic Welsh beef, calvados and cinnamon rice pudding. First class. *Children over 10 welcome.*

Rooms	4 doubles, 2 twin/doubles: £115–£130. Singles £75. Dinner, B&B £80–£88 p.p.	
Meals	Dinner £24–£29.	
Closed	Rarely.	
Directions	M4 west onto A48, then B4310 exit, for National Botanic Gardens. 6 miles north to Brechfa. In village centre.	

Annabel & Steve Thomas
Ty Mawr Country Hotel
Brechfa SA32 7RA

Tel	+44 (0)1267 202332
Email	info@wales-country-hotel.co.uk
Web	www.wales-country-hotel.co.uk

The Cors

A bohemian bolthole, one of the best. Nick is a cook, an artist and gardener, his two lush acres a perfect retreat in summer, so come to sip your Earl Grey while the river potters past. Gunnera, bamboo and tree ferns all flourish, so expect a little green-fingered theatre. Inside, a small, personal world of French inspiration – sit in the bar and be swept back to 1950s Paris. Doors open onto a Victorian veranda where roses and clematis ramble elegantly, perfect for pre-dinner drinks in summer. As for the food, you eat accompanied by cool tunes, with busts and paintings all around – perhaps at the front with garden views, or wrapped up behind in claret reds. It's a feast of local produce with an Italian twist: roasted figs with gorgonzola and Parma ham, Carmarthenshire chicken filled with spinach and mascarpone, then a zesty lemon tart. Bedrooms upstairs have a simple, chic style: rugs on bare boards, vintage William Morris wallpapers, pretty pine, bold colours – perfect for the price. Don't miss Laugharne for all things Dylan Thomas. *Minimum stay: 2 nights in summer.*

Rooms	3 doubles: £80. Singles from £50.
Meals	Dinner, 3 courses, from £35 (Thurs-Sat only). Sunday lunch from £17.
Closed	2 weeks in November.
Directions	A4066 south from St Clears for Laugharne. In village right at pub. Over bridge and on right.

Nick Priestland
The Cors
Newbridge Road,
Laugharne SA33 4SH

Tel	+44 (0)1994 427219
Email	nick@thecors.co.uk
Web	www.thecors.co.uk

Penbontbren

You're lost in lovely hills, yet only three miles from the sea. Not that you're going to stray far. These gorgeous suites don't just have wonderful prices, they're also addictive – this is a great spot to come and do nothing at all. Richard and Huw have thought it all through. You get crockery and cutlery, kettles and fridges, you're also encouraged to bring your own wine and to nip up to the farm shop for provisions for lunch. As for the suites, they have big beds, super bathrooms, sofas and armchairs in cosy sitting areas, and doors onto semi-private terraces – perfect for lunches in summer. Potter about and find iPod docks, flat-screen TVs, robes and White Company lotions. Breakfast is served in the big house – the full Welsh works. Incredibly, this was a caravan park once, all trace of which has vanished; in its place, field and sky, birdsong and sheep. Beaches, hills, Cardigan and magical St Davids all wait. Good local restaurants are on hand: lobster from the sea, lamb from the hills. A great place to unwind with discounts for longer stays. *Minimum stay: 2 nights in high season.*

Rooms	5 suites for 2: £99–£120.
	Singles £80–£95. 1 cottage for 7
	(self-catering): £700–£1,150 per week.
Meals	Restaurants within 3 miles.
Closed	Christmas.
Directions	Sent on booking.

Richard Morgan-Price & Huw Thomas
Penbontbren
Glynarthen,
Llandysul SA44 6PE

Tel	+44 (0)1239 810248
Email	contact@penbontbren.com
Web	www.penbontbren.com

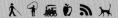

Entry 291   Map 2

Harbourmaster

This is one of those fabulous places where everything hits the spot – the food, the views, the vibe, the style. The hotel stands on the town's quay with Cardigan Bay sparkling beyond. Inside you get that winning combination of seductive good looks, informal but attentive service and a menu overflowing with fresh local produce. The airy open-plan dining room/bar has stripped floors, local art, exposed walls and windows overlooking the harbour. Wind up the staircase to find super bedrooms that come with shuttered windows, lots of colour and quietly funky bathrooms. You get Welsh wool blankets, hot water bottles in winter, flat-screen TVs and DVD players, watery views and tide books. Fabulous suites in the Warehouse next door are worth splashing out on: they're big and stylish with excellent bathrooms. Back downstairs, there are local beers at the horseshoe bar, then great food that's informally served, perhaps half a dozen oysters, a pizza or a steak, Bakewell tart with almond ice-cream. There are bikes to borrow, cycle tracks that lead into the hills, coastal paths that head north and south. *Minimum stay: 2 nights at weekends. Children over 5 welcome.*

Rooms	3 doubles, 4 twin/doubles: £110-£175. 4 suites for 2: £150-£250. Singles from £65. Dinner, B&B £80-£150 p.p.
Meals	Lunch & bar meals from £6. Dinner, 3 courses, about £30. Sunday lunch from £11.50.
Closed	Christmas Day.
Directions	A487 south from Aberystwyth. In Aberaeron right for the harbour. Hotel on waterfront.

Glyn & Menna Heulyn
Harbourmaster
Pen Cei, Aberaeron SA46 0BT
Tel   +44 (0)1545 570755
Email info@harbour-master.com
Web   www.harbour-master.com

Nanteos Mansion

A grand old manor house lost at the end of a one-mile drive, with a small lake, a walled garden and 25 acres of ancient woodland. Views at the front stretch across to nearby hills, four pillars stand at the front door, sofas wait by a wood-burner in the hall. The house dates to 1731, but stands on medieval foundations. It is most famous for the Nanteos Cup – the Holy Grail to you and me – which legend says was carried here by monks from Glastonbury Abbey. A magnificent renovation recently brought the house back to life – electric-shock therapy performed by interior designers. Downstairs, there's a morning room, a sitting-room bar and an elegant restaurant where you dig into Nigel's delicious food, perhaps chilli salt squid, saltmarsh lamb, a trio of chocolate puddings. Upstairs, big suites are grand and gracious, some panelled, others with fine wallpaper, but the rooms are lovely, too, with lots of colour, original art and robes in excellent bathrooms. There's loads to do: rivers to fish, mountains to climb, coastal paths to follow. Don't miss the music room (Wagner visited). Brilliant.

Rooms	14 twin/doubles: £180–£300. Singles from £130. Dinner, B&B from £125 p.p. 1 house for 8: £500.
Meals	Lunch from £7.50. Dinner £32.50–£39.95. Sunday lunch from £23.50
Closed	Rarely.
Directions	Leaving Aberystwyth to the south, take A4120 Devil's Bridge Road, then immediately right onto B4340. House signed left after 1 mile.

Nigel Jones
Nanteos Mansion
Rhydyfelin, Aberystwyth SY23 4LU

Tel	+44 (0)1970 600522
Email	info@nanteos.com
Web	www.nanteos.com

Ffin Y Parc

If you love art, if beautiful things tickle you pink, if you like big old houses stylishly refurbished with a streak of contemporary flair, then you should cancel whatever you're doing next week and head for Ffin y Parc. This is a gorgeous country pad – homespun, quirky, a creative bolthole that sits in 14 peaceful acres. Inside it's an exceptional gallery, not any old gallery showing a little local art, but one that curates some of the best Welsh art, with two artists a month on display – in the conservatory café where you scoff your bacon and eggs, in the airy bar where cool tunes play, and in the big sitting room where you sink into armchairs and watch smouldering logs on the fire. Bedrooms upstairs are equally lovely, in beautiful colours with elegant furniture, more fabulous art and some very fancy bathrooms. Two cool stone cottages wait outside if you want to stay a while. Lunch is served in the café: soups, quiche, perhaps a club sandwich – there are good restaurants further afield and plans are afoot to serve evening meals a couple of nights a week. Hard to beat.

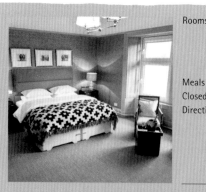

Rooms	2 doubles, 1 twin/double: £135–£165.
	1 suite for 2: £180–£210.
	1 cottage for 2, 1 cottage for 4
	(self-catering): £495–£750 per week.
	Short breaks from £295 & £375.
Meals	Lunch from £5.50.
Closed	January.
Directions	A55, junc.19, then A470 south for 10 miles. House signed left 1 mile south of Llanwrst.

Favourite
newcomer

Roland Powell & Ralph Sanders
Ffin Y Parc
Betws Road,
Llanrwst LL26 0PT

Tel	+44 (0)1492 642070
Email	ralph@ffinyparc.co.uk
Web	www.ffinyparc.com

Escape Boutique B&B

A super-cool boutique B&B with fabulous rooms, attractive prices and some seriously lovely bathrooms. The house stands high on the hill, away from the crowds, a short stroll from the buzz of town and its two-mile sandy beach. This is a 19th-century mill owner's villa and its fine old windows, sparkling wood floors and enormous carved fireplace bear testament to Victorian roots. Other than that it's a clean sweep of funky interiors. Sam and Gaenor scoured Europe for the eclectic collection of colourful retro furniture that fills the rooms – orange swivel chairs, iconic G-plan sofas, beautiful beds wrapped in crisp white linen. Urban Cool, Retro Red, Modern Romance… take your pick. All come with flat-screen TVs, Blu-ray DVD players and iPod docks. Bathrooms are excellent: one room has a magnificent shower for two, another has a copper bath in the room. Downstairs, there's an honesty bar and a fire in the sitting room, while delicious breakfasts are served in the attractive dining room. Excellent restaurants wait in town: try Osborne's for a little glamour or the Seahorse for great fish. *Minimum stay: 2 nights at weekends.*

Rooms	8 doubles, 1 twin/double: £89–£140. Singles from £74.
Meals	Restaurants within walking distance.
Closed	Christmas.
Directions	A55 junc. 19, then A470 for Llandudno. On promenade, head west hugging the coast, then left at Belmont Hotel and house on right.

Sam Nayar & Gaenor Loftus
Escape Boutique B&B
48 Church Walks,
Llandudno LL30 2HL

Tel	+44 (0)1492 877776
Email	info@escapebandb.co.uk
Web	www.escapebandb.co.uk

The Hand at Llanarmon

Single-track lanes plunge you into the middle of nowhere. All around, lush valleys rise and fall, so pull on your boots and scale a mountain or find a river and jump into a canoe. Back at The Hand, a 16th-century drovers' inn, the pleasures of a traditional country local are hard to miss. A coal fire burns on the range in reception, a wood fire crackles under brass in the front bar and a wood-burner warms the lofty dining room. Expect exposed stone walls, low beamed ceilings, old pine settles and candles on the mantelpiece. There's a games room for darts and pool, a quiet sitting room for maps and books. Delicious food is popular with locals, so grab a table and enjoy seasonal menus – perhaps game broth, lamb casserole, then sticky toffee pudding. Bedrooms are just as they should be: not too fancy, cosy and warm, spotlessly clean with crisp white linen and good bathrooms. A very friendly place. Martin and Gaynor are full of quiet enthusiasm and have made their home warmly welcoming. John Ceiriog Hughes, who wrote *Bread of Heaven*, lived in this valley. Special indeed.

Rooms	8 doubles, 4 twins, 1 suite for 2: £90–£127. Singles from £52.50.
Meals	Lunch from £4.75. Bar meals from £9.50. Dinner, 3 courses, £25–£30. Sunday lunch from £15.
Closed	Rarely.
Directions	Leave A5 south of Chirk for B4500. Llanarmon 11 miles on.

Gaynor & Martin De Luchi
The Hand at Llanarmon
Llanarmon Dyffryn Ceiriog,
Llangollen LL20 7LD

Tel	+44 (0)1691 600666
Email	reception@thehandhotel.co.uk
Web	www.thehandhotel.co.uk

Y Meirionnydd

By day you explore the mighty wonders of Snowdonia, by night you return to this lovely small hotel and recover in style. It's one of those places that delivers just what you want; it's smart without being posh, the welcome is second to none, there's great food and the bedrooms are fantastic. You're in the middle of a small country town with a terrace at the front, so sit outside in summer and watch the world pass by. Inside, soft colours and warm lighting create a mellow feel. There's a cute bar with armchairs and games, an airy breakfast room for the full Welsh works, then a smart restaurant cut into the rock, which was once the county jail; the food is somewhat better than it was then, perhaps venison pâté with hot chillies, fillet of salmon with lime and ginger, fresh fruit crumble with lashings of cream. Bedrooms upstairs are gorgeous. Some are bigger than others, but all have the same style: clean lines, cool colours, huge beds, beautiful linen. You get the odd stone wall, an armchair if there's room, then super bathrooms. There's secure storage for bikes, too. *Minimum stay: 2 nights at weekends.*

Rooms	3 doubles, 2 twin/doubles: £75–£115. Singles £65.
Meals	Dinner, 3 courses, £25. Not Sundays in low season.
Closed	One week at Christmas.
Directions	In centre of town on one-way system, off A470.

Marc Russell & Nick Banda
Y Meirionnydd
Smithfield Square,
Dolgellau LL40 1ES

Tel	+44 (0)1341 422554
Email	info@themeirionnydd.com
Web	www.themeirionnydd.com

Penmaenuchaf Hall

This grand old house sits high on the hill with fine views over the Mawddach estuary. It stands in 20 acres of woodlands and formal gardens with daffodils, snowdrops and bluebells running riot in spring and a walled garden that bursts with summer colour. The house has attitude, too. It was built in 1865 for a Bolton cotton merchant, and an open fire crackles in the half-panelled hall, where sofas and armchairs wait. The drawing room is equally grand with mullioned windows that frame the view, cavernous sofas and a grand piano, country rugs on original wood floors. There's an airy restaurant, where French windows open onto to a terrace, so eat al fresco in good weather, perhaps seared scallops, Gressingham duck, apple tart and honey ice-cream. Bedrooms come in traditional country-house style with big comfy beds and warm colours. Some are huge, others have balconies or a new bathroom, all have iPod docks and digital radios. Outside, Snowdon waits, there are 13 miles of river to fish and the fabulous mountain biking trails of Coed-y-Brenin for fun at all levels in the forest. *Please ring for enquiries. Children over 6 welcome.*

Rooms	7 doubles, 5 twin/doubles, 1 four-poster: £180-£270. 1 family room for 4: £240-£270. Singles £120-£185.
Meals	Lunch from £6. Afternoon tea from £7.90. Dinner, 3 courses, £27.50-£45.
Closed	Rarely.
Directions	From Dolgellau A493 west for about 1.5 miles. Entrance on left.

Mark Watson & Lorraine Fielding
Penmaenuchaf Hall
Penmaenpool,
Dolgellau LL40 1YB

Tel	+44 (0)1341 422129
Email	relax@penhall.co.uk
Web	www.penhall.co.uk

Plas Bodegroes

Close to the end of the world and worth every second it takes to get here. Chris and Gunna's home is a temple of cool elegance, the food possibly the best in Wales. Fronted by an avenue of 200-year-old beech trees, this Georgian manor house is wrapped in climbing roses and wildly roaming wisteria. The veranda circles the house, as do long French windows that lighten every room, so pull up a chair and listen to birdsong. There's no formality here – come to relax and be yourself. Bedrooms are wonderful, the courtyard rooms especially good, where exposed wooden ceilings give the feel of a smart Scandinavian forest hideaway. Best of all is the dining room, almost a work of art in itself, cool and crisp with exceptional art on the walls – a great place to eat Chris's divine food; try sea trout wrapped in Carmarthen ham, mountain lamb with rosemary jus, baked vanilla cheesecake with passion fruit sorbet. Don't miss the Llyn Peninsula: sandy beaches, towering cliffs and country walks all wait. Snowdon and Portmeirion are close too.

Rooms	8 doubles, 1 twin: £130–£180. 1 suite for 2: £180. Singles from £112.
Meals	Sunday lunch £22.50. Dinner £45. Not Sun or Mon evenings.
Closed	December-February & Sunday evenings & Monday throughout year.
Directions	From Pwllheli A497 towards Nefyn. House on left after 1 mile, signed.

Chris & Gunna Chown
Plas Bodegroes
Efailnewydd, Pwllheli LL53 5TH

Tel	+44 (0)1758 612363
Email	gunna@bodegroes.co.uk
Web	www.bodegroes.co.uk

Plas Dinas Country House

The family home of Lord Snowdon dates to the 1600s and stands in 15 rural acres with an avenue of oak sweeping you up to the house. Princess Margaret often stayed and much of what fills the house belongs to the family: striking chandeliers, oils by the score, gilt-framed mirrors – an Aladdin's cave of beautiful things. There's a baby grand piano in the drawing room, where you find a roaring fire and an honesty bar, but potter about and find masses of memorabilia framed on the walls (make sure you visit the private dining room). Bedrooms – some with views across fields to the sea – mix a graceful past with modern design. You get four-posters, period colours, bold wallpapers, a sofa if there's room. A cute room in the eaves has mountain views, all have hot-water bottles, Apple TVs and excellent bathrooms, some with showers, others with free-standing baths. Good food waits in the restaurant, perhaps fishcakes with lime and ginger, lamb shank with a rosemary jus, chocolate tart with white chocolate ice-cream. Snowdon is close, as you'd expect, so bring walking boots and mountain bikes. *Minimum stay: 2 nights on bank holiday weekends.*

Rooms	5 doubles, 5 twin/doubles: £89–£199.
Meals	Dinner, 3 courses, £26–£30.
Closed	22 December to 2 January.
Directions	South from Caernarfon on A487. Through Bontnewydd and signed right after half a mile at brow of shallow hill.

Neil Baines & Marco Soarez
Plas Dinas Country House
Bontnewydd,
Caernarfon LL54 7YF
Tel +44 (0)1286 830214
Email info@plasdinas.co.uk
Web www.plasdinas.co.uk

The Crown at Whitebrook

Chris cooks fabulous food. He worked with Raymond Blanc for five years at Le Manoir aux Quat'Saisons, then took the reins at The Grove in Hertfordshire and won three rosettes. Now he's struck out on his own, recently buying this famous restaurant with rooms. It sits in a tiny village that's wrapped up in the Wye Valley. Forest rises all around, bluebells carpet the woods in spring, deer amble by in summer. Outside, there's a dining terrace for lunch in good weather. Inside, smart, airy interiors come as standard, with sofas in the bar, wood floors in the restaurant and good art on the walls. All of which play second fiddle to the food that flies from the kitchen. Much is foraged – hogweed, nettles, wild chervil and bitter cress – most is local with lamb from the valley and beef from Ross. You can eat à la carte or splash out on the seven-course tasting menu, perhaps squab pigeon with rhubarb, Cornish turbot with ground elder, caramelised white chocolate with pink grapefruit. Well-priced rooms have lots of colour, woollen throws, good beds and fancy bathrooms. Don't miss Tintern Abbey.

Rooms	6 doubles, 2 twin/doubles: £115-£140. Singles from £90. Dinner, B&B from £99 p.p.
Meals	Lunch from £19. Dinner, 3 courses, £54. Tasting menu £65. Sunday lunch £34. Not Mondays.
Closed	Mondays. Two weeks in January.
Directions	M4 junc. 24, A449/A40 north to Monmouth, then B4293 south. Up hill. After 2.7 miles left for Whitebook. On right after two miles.

Chris & Kirsty Harrod
The Crown at Whitebrook
Whitebrook,
Monmouth NP25 4TX

Tel　　+44 (0)1600 860254
Email　info@crownatwhitebrook.co.uk
Web　　www.crownatwhitebrook.co.uk

The Bell at Skenfrith

The position here is magical: an ancient stone bridge, a magnificent valley, glorious hills rising behind, cows grazing in lush fields. It's a perfect spot, not least because providence has blessed it with this sublime inn, where crisply designed interiors ooze country chic. In summer doors fly open and life spills onto a stone terrace, where views of hill and wood are interrupted only by the odd chef pottering off to a productive and organic kitchen garden. Back inside, airy rooms come with slate floors, open fires and plump-cushioned armchairs in the locals' bar, but the emphasis is firmly on the food, with the kitchen turning out delicious fare, perhaps seared scallops with cauliflower purée, heather-roasted venison with chestnut gnocchi, marmalade soufflé with whisky ice-cream. Country-house bedrooms are as good as you'd expect: uncluttered and elegant, brimming with light, some beamed (mind your head!), all with fabulous bathrooms. All have sweet views, either of the kitchen garden or the river. Idyllic circular walks sweep you through blissful country. *Minimum stay: 2 nights at weekends.*

Rooms	5 doubles, 3 twin/doubles, 3 four-posters: £110-£220. Singles from £75. Dinner, B&B from £85 p.p.
Meals	Lunch from £5.95. Dinner, 3 courses, around £35. Sunday lunch from £12.95.
Closed	Tuesdays (November-March).
Directions	From Monmouth B4233 to Rockfield; B4347 north for 5 miles; right on B4521; Skenfrith 1 mile.

John Van Niekerk
The Bell at Skenfrith
Skenfrith,
Abergavenny NP7 8UH

Tel	+44 (0)1600 750235
Email	enquiries@skenfrith.co.uk
Web	www.skenfrith.co.uk

Penally Abbey

A small country house high on the hill with views to the front of Carmarthen Bay. Caldy Island lies to the east, the road ends at the village green, a stroll across the golf course leads to the beach. Up at the house, a fine arched window by the grand piano frames the view perfectly, so sink into a chesterfield in front of the fire and gaze out to sea. The house dates to 1790 and was once an abbey; St Deiniol's, a ruined 13th-century church, stands in the garden. There's a terrace for pre-dinner drinks, bluebells carpet the wood in May. Bedrooms are all different: grand four-posters with wild flock wallpaper in the main house; a simpler cottage feel in the coach house next door. Steve's gentle, unflappable manner is infectious and relaxing – don't expect to feel rushed. Elleen cooks in the French style, much of it picked up in the kitchen of a château many years ago, perhaps stilton and walnut mousse, haunch of venison with juniper berries, iced coffee Tia Maria. The Pembrokeshire coastal path passes by outside. Further afield, Narberth, St Davids and Dylan Thomas country wait. *Minimum stay: 2 nights at weekends during summer.*

Rooms	5 doubles, 2 twin/doubles, 1 twin, 4 twin/doubles (coach house): £148–£186. Dinner, B&B from £99 p.p.
Meals	Dinner, 3 courses, £36.
Closed	Never.
Directions	From Tenby A4139 for Pembroke. Right into Penally after 1.5 miles. Hotel signed above village green. Train station 5-mins walk.

Steve & Elleen Warren
Penally Abbey
Penally,
Tenby SA70 7PY

Tel	+44 (0)1834 843033
Email	info@penally-abbey.com
Web	www.penally-abbey.com

Stackpole Inn

This friendly inn is hard to fault. It sits in a quiet village drenched in honeysuckle with a fine garden at the front, a perfect spot for a drop of Welsh ale in summer. Wander further afield and you come to the sea at Barafundle Bay – a Pembrokeshire glory – where you can pick up the coastal path and follow it west past Stackpole Head to St Govan's Chapel. Stride back up to the inn and find interiors worthy of a country pub. There are smart red carpets, whitewashed walls, a hard-working wood-burner and obligatory beamed ceilings. Locals and visitors mingle in harmony, there are four hand pumps at the slate bar and tasty rustic cooking in the restaurant, perhaps deep-fried whitebait, rack of lamb, fresh raspberry brûlée. Super bedrooms are tremendous value for money and quietly positioned in a converted outbuilding. Two have sofabeds, two have velux windows for star gazing. All come in seaside colours with tongue-and-groove panelling, stripped floors, comfy beds, crisp linen and excellent bathrooms. Don't miss Pembroke Castle or the beach at Freshwater West.

Rooms	2 twin/doubles: £90. 2 family rooms for 4: £90–£120. Singles from £60.
Meals	Lunch from £5. Dinner, 3 courses, £25–£30 (not Sundays Oct–Mar). Sunday lunch from £9.50.
Closed	Rarely.
Directions	B4319 south from Pembroke for 3 miles, then left for Stackpole. Through Stackpole Cheriton, up hill, right at T-junction. On right.

Gary & Becky Evans
Stackpole Inn
Stackpole, Pembroke SA71 5DF

Tel	+44 (0)1646 672324
Email	info@stackpoleinn.co.uk
Web	www.stackpoleinn.co.uk

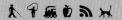

The Grove at Narberth

In the last few years the Grove has emerged as one of the loveliest places to stay in Wales – a cool country-house hotel with one foot in its Georgian past and the other in a contemporary present. It stands deep in Pembrokeshire's beautiful hills with sprawling views to the front and a vast kitchen garden that provides much for the table. Inside, Arts & Crafts interiors come as standard in the main house – an explosion of wood in the entrance hall, a roaring fire in the drawing-room bar, a super-smart restaurant for some of the best food in Wales, perhaps foie gras brûlée with pickled rhubarb, spiced red mullet with a squid risotto, chocolate mousse with beetroot sorbet. Gorgeous bedrooms are split between the main house and converted outbuildings. All are divine, some are just bigger than others. Expect beautiful fabrics, cool wallpaper, crisp white linen, delicious beds. Bathrooms are equally spoiling with robes and heated floors, perhaps a claw-foot bath or a walk-in power shower. The coastal path is close, as is Laugharne, where Dylan Thomas lived, and Narberth, a quirky country town. *Minimum stay: 2 nights at weekends.*

Rooms	14 doubles: £190–£270.
	6 suites for 2: £310.
	Singles from £160.
	Extra bed/sofabed per night: £30 per
	child under 16; £50 per adult.
Meals	Lunch from £7.
	Dinner, 3 courses, £54.
Closed	Never.
Directions	M4, then A48 & A40 west towards
	Haverfordwest. At A470 roundabout,
	take 1st exit to Narberth. Through
	town, down hill, then follow brown
	signs to hotel.

Neil Kedward & Zoe Agar
The Grove at Narberth
Molleston, Narberth SA67 8BX

Tel	+44 (0)1834 860915
Email	info@thegrove-narberth.co.uk
Web	www.thegrove-narberth.co.uk

Slebech Park

An unbeatable position on the upper reaches of the Daugleddau Estuary, part of a 600-acre estate that dates back to 1760. You might think you've washed up at the main house, but this crenellated building originally served as the mill and stables. It stands 50 paces from the water with views of river, wood and sky; the odd boat potters past, migrating birds come to bathe, other than that deep peace reigns. Inside, bedrooms come in different shapes and sizes, but all have contemporary elegance – 21st-century country-house chic. You get padded window seats, warm colours, good art, smart fabrics, a sofa if there's room. Comfy beds are wrapped in white linen, lovely bathrooms come as standard. One room has fine arched windows that open onto a terrace, some in the eaves come on two levels. There's a small bar, then a beautiful restaurant, which is about to extend into a conservatory to make the most of the view. You can also eat on the terrace in summer – perhaps buttered asparagus, sea bream with curried mussels, hot apple tart with toffee ice-cream. Walk it off in stupendous gardens. Divine!

Rooms	14 twin/doubles: £115–£245.
Meals	Light lunches from £8.50.
	Dinner, 3 courses, £25–£40.
Closed	Never.
Directions	M4, then A48 & A40 west. 1st left in
	Slebech (5 miles east of Haverfordwest)
	and drive on left after a mile.

Geoffrey & Georgina Phillips
Slebech Park
Slebech,
Haverfordwest SA62 4AX
Tel   +44 (0)1437 752000
Email   enquiries@slebech.co.uk
Web   www.slebech.co.uk

Crug Glas

If you've never been to St Davids, know this: it is one of the most magical places in Britain. It sits in Pembroke's national park, has an imperious 12th-century cathedral, and is surrounded by magnificent coastline that's dotted with cliffs and vast sandy beaches. As for Janet's wonderful retreat, it's part chic hotel, part farmhouse B&B, stylish yet personal, a great place to stay. The house dates from 1120 and sits in 600 acres of arable and grazing land (they run cattle, grow cereals). Outside, you find lawns and a small copse sprinkled with bluebells, then field and sky, and that's about it. Inside, there's an honesty bar in the sitting room and a Welsh dresser in the dining room, where Janet serves delicious food: homemade soups, home-reared beef, chocolate mousse with clotted cream. Bedrooms are the big surprise: a vast four-poster, a copper bath, old armoires, beautiful fabrics. All have robes in fancy bathrooms, one room occupies much of the top floor, two beautiful suites in an old barn have exposed timbers and underfloor heating. The coast is close.

Rooms	3 doubles, 1 twin/double: £115-£150. 5 suites for 2: £170-£185. Singles from £90.
Meals	Sunday lunch £22.50. Afternoon tea from £12.50. Dinner, 3 courses, about £35.
Closed	22-27 December.
Directions	South from Fishguard on A487. Through Croes-goch, then signed right after 2 miles.

Janet & Perkin Evans
Crug Glas
Solva,
Haverfordwest SA62 6XX

Tel	+44 (0)1348 831302
Email	janet@crugglas.plus.com
Web	www.crug-glas.co.uk

The Manor Town House

Fishguard is quirky – arty and friendly with a folk festival in May and a jazz festival in August. You'll find great coastal walks, sandy beaches and magical St Davids a few miles south. In short, it's much more that an overnight stop on your way to Ireland and, with a happy vibe waiting at The Manor Town House, hard to resist. Chris and Helen escaped London and have taken to their new world like ducks to water. Inside, you're greeted by a couple of gorgeous sitting rooms – stripped floorboards, cool colours, local art, and crackling fires in winter. One has an honesty bar, you get fresh flowers, lots of books, and comfy sofas from which to plan your day. Homely bedrooms have lots of charm: bold colours, beautiful fabrics, the odd antique, super-comfy beds. Those at the back have sea views, perhaps a sofa or a padded window seat, while compact bathrooms do the trick. Breakfast is a treat, there's a garden for afternoon tea overlooking the harbour, and it's a one-minute stroll up the road to Bar 5 for cocktails and The Lounge at No. 3 for the best food in town. Pembrokeshire awaits. Brilliant. *Minimum stay: 2 nights at weekends in summer.*

Rooms	2 doubles, 3 twin/doubles: £85-£110. 1 single: £65-£80. Extra beds: adult £20, child under 16, £15.
Meals	Local restaurants within 100 yds.
Closed	23-27 December.
Directions	M4 west, A48 west, A40 north, then A487 into town. Right at roundabout and on left. Parking close by.

Chris & Helen Sheldon
The Manor Town House
11 Main Street,
Fishguard SA65 9HG

Tel	+44 (0)1348 873260
Email	enquiries@manortownhouse.com
Web	www.manortownhouse.com

Cnapan Restaurant & Hotel

Cnapan is a way of life – a family affair with two generations at work in harmony. Judith excels in the kitchen, Michael looks after the bar and son Oliver has returned to the fold to help them both. It is a very friendly place that ticks to its own beat with locals popping in to book tables and guests chatting in the bar before dinner. The house is cosy and traditionally home-spun – whitewashed stone walls and old pine settles in the dining room; comfy sofas and a wood-burner in the sitting room; a tiny telly in the bar for the odd game of rugby (the game of cnapan, rugby's precursor, originated in the town). There are maps for walkers, bird books, flower books, the daily papers, too. Spill into the garden in summer for pre-dinner drinks under the weeping willow, then tuck into Judith's delicious food: smoked salmon fishcakes, Preseli lamb, banoffee pie with espresso ice-cream. Comfy bedrooms, warmly simple, are good value for money; half have new showers, half are getting them soon. You're in the Pembrokeshire National Park; beaches and cliff-top coastal walks beckon. *Minimum stay: 2 nights at weekends.*

Rooms	1 double, 4 twin/doubles: £60-£95.
	1 family room for 3: £110.
	Singles from £65.
	Dinner, B&B £72.50 p.p.
	Extra bed/sofabed £15 p.p. per night.
Meals	Dinner £25-£30.
Closed	Christmas.
Directions	From Cardigan A487 to Newport.
	1st pink house on right, 300 yds into
	Newport.

Michael, Judith & Oliver Cooper
Cnapan Restaurant & Hotel
East Street,
Newport SA42 0SY

Tel	+44 (0)1239 820575
Email	enquiry@cnapan.co.uk
Web	www.cnapan.co.uk

AWARD
WINNER

Nicely priced

Entry 309 Map 1

Llys Meddyg

This cool little restaurant with rooms has a bit of everything: chic bedrooms that pack a punch, super food in a pine-clad restaurant, a cellar bar for cocktails before dinner, a pretty garden for summer. It's a friendly place with happy staff on hand to help, and it draws in the locals, who come for the excellent food, perhaps brown crab brulée with white crab meat, local pheasant with an oriental consommé, caramelized pear with blue cheese ice-cream. You eat in style with a fire burning at one end of the restaurant and Welsh art hanging on the walls. Chic bedrooms come as standard. They're split between the main house (cool colours, vast beds, funky bathrooms) and the mews behind (rustic, airy and peaceful). All have the same fresh style: Farrow & Ball colours, lovely art, blond oak beds, fluffy white bath robes. In summer, decant into the garden, where a café/bistro opens up for coffee and cake or pizza from a wood-fired oven. Pembrokeshire's coastal path waits for windswept cliffs and sandy beaches. Don't miss St Davids or Laugharne for all things Dylan Thomas. Dogs are very welcome.

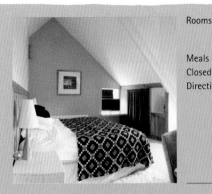

Rooms	4 doubles, 4 twin/doubles, 1 suite for 2: £100–£180. Singles from £85.
Meals	Lunch from £7. Dinner from £14.
Closed	Rarely.
Directions	East from Fishguard on A487. On left in Newport towards eastern edge of town.

Louise & Edward Sykes
Llys Meddyg
East Street, Newport SA42 0SY
Tel   +44 (0)1239 820008
Email   info@llysmeddyg.com
Web   www.llysmeddyg.com

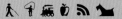

Hammet House

A lovely double whammy here – you're close to the coast, yet lost in Pembrokeshire's beautiful hills. You nip through a grand gate, weave up the long drive, then follow the river Teifi up to this Georgian pile, once home to a Sheriff of London. Outside, gardens drop down to the river, where you can follow a footpath along to Cilgerran Castle. Inside, contemporary interiors have funky furniture sprinkled about – pink and orange armchairs, cardboard trophies, a Banksy stencil in the restaurant – but there's old-world elegance, too, with sofas in the drawing room for afternoon tea in front of the fire. Bedrooms are either 'refurbished' or 'waiting their turn.' Go for the former for lots of style with warm colours, low-slung beds, perhaps a sofa or cow-hide rug, then REN oils and white robes in good bathrooms. The others are simpler with lower prices. Back downstairs, delicious food waits in the restaurant, which opens onto a terrace in summer, perhaps mussels with white wine, venison with parsnip purée, chocolate mousse with walnut syrup. Hills and coast wait for wonderful walking.

Rooms	10 doubles, 1 twin: £145-£220.
	1 family room for 4: £195.
	Singles £95-£145. Child £25.
Meals	Bar meals from £10.
	Dinner, 3 courses, about £35.
Closed	Never.
Directions	Sent on booking.

Philippa & Owen Gale
Hammet House
Llechryd, Cardigan SA43 2QA
Tel   +44 (0)1239 682382
Email   mail@hammethouse.co.uk
Web   www.hammethouse.co.uk

Gliffaes Hotel

A charming country-house hotel that towers above the river Usk as it pours through the valley below. In summer, the sitting room bar opens onto a large terrace, where you can sit in the sun and soak up the view – red kites circling above the water, sheep grazing majestic hills. You're in 35 peaceful acres of formal lawns and mature woodland. Inside, interiors pack a punch. Afternoon tea is laid out in a sitting room of panelled walls and family portraits, while logs crackle in a grand fireplace. This is a fishing hotel, one of the best, and fishermen often gather in the bar for tall tales and a quick drink at the end of the day. Eventually, they spin through to the restaurant and dig into seasonal food (the hotel is part of the Slow Food Movement) – goat's cheese soufflé, lemon sole, plum and cherry crumble… Bedrooms above are in country-house style with smart fabrics and carpets, all mod cons, a sofa if there's room; others are in the coach house annexe. Several have river views, a couple have small balconies, one has a claw-foot bath that overlooks the front lawn. *Minimum stay: 2 nights at weekends.*

Rooms	19 twin/doubles: £112–£265.
	4 singles: £100.
	Dinner, B&B from £90 p.p.
Meals	Light lunches from £5.
	Sunday lunch £22–£29.
	Dinner, 3 courses, £42.
Closed	January.
Directions	From Crickhowell, A40 west for 2.5 miles. Signed left and on left after 1 mile.

James & Susie Suter
Gliffaes Hotel
Gliffaes Road,
Crickhowell NP8 1RH

Tel	+44 (0)1874 730371
Email	calls@gliffaeshotel.com
Web	www.gliffaeshotel.com

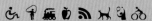

The Felin Fach Griffin

It's quirky, homespun, and thrives on a mix of relaxed informality and colourful style. The low-ceilinged bar resembles the sitting room of a small hip country house, with timber frames, cool tunes and comfy sofas in front of a smouldering fire. Painted stone walls come in blocks of colour, there's live music on Sunday nights, and you dine informally in the white-walled restaurant, with stock pots simmering on an Aga. The food is excellent, perhaps dressed Portland crab, rump of Welsh beef, treacle tart with bergamot sorbet; much of what you eat comes from a half-acre kitchen garden, with meat and game from the hills around you. Bedrooms above have style and substance: comfy beds wrapped in crisp linen, good bathrooms with fluffy towels, Roberts radios, a smattering of books, but no TV unless you ask. Breakfast is served in the dining room; wallow with the papers, make your own toast, scoff the full Welsh. A main road passes outside, but quietly at night, while lanes lead into the hills, so walk, ride, bike, canoe. Hay is close for books galore. Don't miss excellent off-season deals.

Rooms	2 doubles, 2 twin/doubles, 2 four-posters: £118–£165. 1 family room for 3: £160. Singles from £100. Dinner, B&B from £82.50 p.p.
Meals	Lunch from £7. Dinner, 3 courses, about £30. Sunday lunch from £19.75.
Closed	Christmas Eve & Day (evening). 4 days in Jan.
Directions	From Brecon A470 north to Felin Fach (4.5 miles). On left.

Charles & Edmund Inkin
The Felin Fach Griffin
Felin Fach,
Brecon LD3 0UB
Tel   +44 (0)1874 620111
Email   enquiries@felinfachgriffin.co.uk
Web   www.felinfachgriffin.co.uk

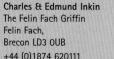

AWARD
WINNER

Hotel of the Year
Wales

Entry 313   Map 2

The Lake Country House & Spa

Deep in the silence of mid-Wales, an old-school country house that looks after you well. Fifty acres of lawns, lakes and ancient woodland wrap around you, there's a spa with an indoor pool, treatment rooms and a tennis court by the lake. Sit in a hot tub and watch guests fish for their supper, try your luck on the nine-hole golf course, saddle up nearby and take to the hills. Come home to afternoon tea in the big, elegant drawing room, where an archipelago of rugs warms a brightly polished wooden floor and chandeliers hang from the ceiling. The hotel opened over a hundred years ago and the leather-bound fishing logs date to 1894. A feel of the 1920s lingers. Fires come to life in front of your eyes, grand pianos and grandfather clocks sing their songs, snooker balls crash about in the distance. Dress for a delicious dinner – the atmosphere deserves it – then retire to cosseting bedrooms. Most are suites: those in the house are warmly traditional, those in the lodge softly contemporary. The London train takes four hours and stops in the village. Resident geese waddle.

Rooms	6 twin/doubles: £195. 24 suites for 2: £240–£260. Singles from £145. Dinner, B&B (minimum 2 nights) from £122.50 p.p.
Meals	Lunch, 3 courses, £22.50. Dinner, 4 courses, £38.50.
Closed	Never.
Directions	From Builth Wells A483 west for 7 miles to Garth. Signed from village.

Jean-Pierre Mifsud
The Lake Country House & Spa
Llangammarch Wells LD4 4BS
Tel   +44 (0)1591 620202
Email   info@lakecountryhouse.co.uk
Web   www.lakecountryhouse.co.uk

Milebrook House Hotel

An old-school country hotel with three acres of gardens that run down to the river Teme. You'll find Wales on one bank and England on the other, so bring your wellies and wade across; the walking is magnificent. The house, once home to writer Wilfred Thesiger, is informally run by two generations of the Marsden family with Beryl and Rodney leading the way. Step inside and enter a world that's rooted in a delightful past: clocks tick, cats snooze, fires crackle, the odd champagne cork escapes its bondage. Beautiful art hangs on the walls, the sitting room is stuffed with books, the bar comes in country-house style and there's food to reckon with in the dining room – perhaps Cornish scallops with a pea purée, rack of Welsh lamb with fondant potatoes, glazed orange tart with mango and praline. A kitchen garden supplies much for the table. You can fish for trout, spot deer in the woods, play croquet on the lawn. Red kite, moorhens, kingfishers and herons live in the valley. Homely bedrooms do the trick, and Presteigne and Ludlow are close.

Rooms	5 doubles, 4 twins: £144.
	1 family room for 3: £172.
	Singles from £79. Dinner, B&B
	(minimum 2 nights) from £95 p.p.
Meals	Lunch, 2 courses, £14.95 (not Mon).
	Dinner, 3 courses, £32.95.
Closed	Rarely.
Directions	From Ludlow A49 north, then left at
	Bromfield on A4113 towards Knighton
	for 10 miles. Hotel on right.

Rodney, Beryl & Joanne Marsden
Milebrook House Hotel
Stanage, Knighton LD7 1LT

Tel	+44 (0)1547 528632
Email	hotel@milebrookhouse.co.uk
Web	www.milebrookhouse.co.uk

The Checkers

Montgomery is gorgeous, a tiny town of Georgian buildings lost in deep country. It has a few things things you'd expect of an ancient county town – a ruined castle and a Norman church – then one you wouldn't – a Michelin star. You find it at this chic little restaurant with rooms that ticks to its own beat. It's a family affair. Sarah and Stéphane met while cooking at the Waterside Inn, then came west to join forces with Kathryn and haven't looked back, a star falling at their feet out of the blue. Inside, interiors date to 1735 and come with original timbers and a vast inglenook. There are sofas in front of the wood-burner, local ales at the bar, but the big draw is the ambrosial food, perhaps roasted scallops with grilled artichokes, local pork belly with caramelised pear, a flawless rhubarb crumble soufflé. Bedrooms are smart and uncluttered with warm colours, good beds, perhaps a sofa. Two have baths, three have walk-in showers. Outside, on the high street, a deli, a gallery and a famously quirky hardware store, but Offa's Dyke waits a mile to the east, so bring your walking boots.

Rooms	3 doubles, 2 twin/doubles: £125–£170. Singles from £105. Dinner, B&B from £100 p.p.
Meals	Lunch (Fri/Sat) & dinner (Tue-Sat) £35–£50. 7-course tasting menu £75.
Closed	Sundays & Mondays. Two weeks in January.
Directions	North from Ludlow on A49. Though Craven Arms, then left onto A489. Right onto B4385 after 15 miles. In town, 2nd left into Broad Street. On right.

Kathryn & Sarah Francis
& Stéphane Boire
The Checkers
Broad Street, Montgomery SY15 6PN

Tel	+44 (0)1686 669 822
Email	kathryn@thecheckersmontgomery.co.uk
Web	www.thecheckersmontgomery.co.uk

Fairyhill

This lovely country house on the Gower sits in 24 acres of beautiful silence with a sun-trapping terrace at the back for lunch in summer. Potter about and find a walled garden, a stream-fed lake, free-range ducks and an ancient orchard. Inside, country-house interiors come fully loaded: smart fabrics, warm colours, deep sofas, the daily papers. There's an open fire in the bar, a grand piano in the sitting room, then delicious food in the restaurant, most locally sourced. Stylish bedrooms hit the spot. Most are big and fancy, a couple are small, but sweet. Some have painted beams, others a sofa or a wall of golden paper. Sparkling bathrooms, some with separate showers, have deep baths, white robes and fancy oils; if that's not enough, there's a treatment room, too. Outside, the Gower waits – wild heathland, rugged coastline, some of the best beaches in the land – so explore by day, then return for a good meal, perhaps scallops with cauliflower and chorizo, Gower lamb with gratin potatoes, baked honey and amaretto cheesecake. The wine list is one of the best in Wales, so don't expect to go thirsty. *Children over 8 welcome.*

Rooms	3 doubles, 5 twin/doubles: £190–£290. Singles from £170. Dogs £10 per night. Dinner, B&B from 135 p.p.
Meals	Lunch, 2 courses, from £20. Dinner £35–£45.
Closed	First 3 weeks in January. Monday & Tuesday, November–March.
Directions	M4 junc. 47, A483 south, then A484 west to Gowerton and B4295 for Llanrhidian. Through Oldwalls, 1 mile up on left.

Andrew Hetherington & Paul Davies
Fairyhill
Reynoldston, Gower, Swansea SA3 1BS
Tel   +44 (0)1792 390139
Email   postbox@fairyhill.net
Web   www.fairyhill.net

Quick reference indices

Wheelchair-accessible
At least one bedroom and bathroom accessible for wheelchair users. Phone for details.

Singles
Single room OR rooms let to single guests for half the double room rate, or under.

Children of all ages welcome

These owners have told us that they welcome children of all ages. Please note cots and highchairs may not necessarily be available.

Quick reference indices

Weddings
You can get married here.

Events

The whole building can be hired for an event.

Quick reference indices

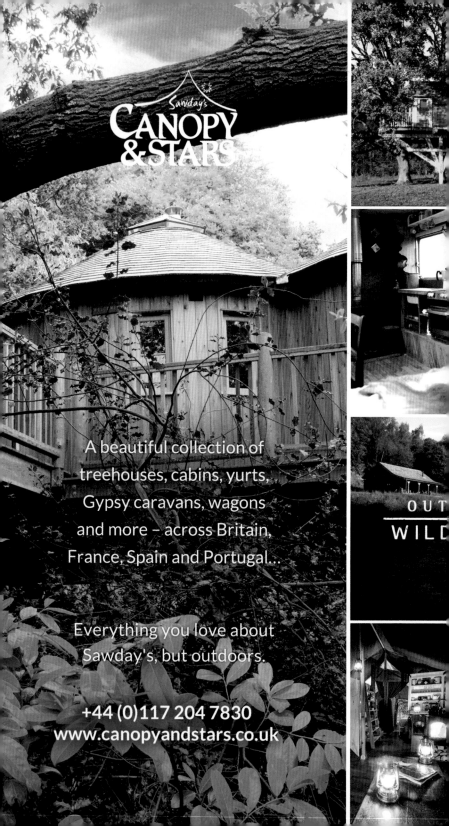

Alastair Sawday has been publishing books for over twenty years, finding Special Places to Stay in Britain and abroad. All our properties are inspected by us and are chosen for their charm and individuality, and with twelve titles to choose from there are plenty of places to explore. You can buy any of our books at a reader discount of 25%* on the RRP.

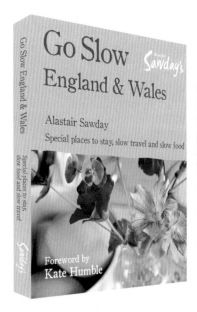

List of titles:	RRP	Discount price
British Bed & Breakfast	£15.99	£11.99
Special Places to Stay in Britain for Garden Lovers	£19.99	£14.99
British Hotels and Inns	£15.99	£11.99
Pubs & Inns of England & Wales	£15.99	£11.99
Dog-friendly Breaks in Britain	£14.99	£11.24
French Bed & Breakfast	£15.99	£11.99
French Châteaux & Hotels	£15.99	£11.99
Italy	£15.99	£11.99
Portugal	£12.99	£9.74
Spain	£15.99	£11.99
Go Slow England & Wales	£19.99	£14.99
Go Slow France	£19.99	£14.99

*postage and packaging is added to each order

How to order:
You can order online at: www.sawdays.co.uk/bookshop/
or call: +44(0)117 204 7810

Alastair Sawday's

'More than a bed for the night...'

Britain
France
Ireland
Italy
Portugal
Spain

www.sawdays.co.uk

Self-Catering | B&B | Hotel | Pub | Canopy & Stars

Photo: The Eltermere Inn, Cumbria, entry 55

Join us

INSPECTED & SELECTED
by
Sawday's
SPECIAL

TIME AWAY IS FAR TOO PRECIOUS TO
SPEND IN THE WRONG PLACE. THAT'S WHY,
BACK IN 1994, WE STARTED SAWDAY'S.

Twenty years on, we're still a family concern – and still
on a crusade to stamp out the bland and predictable,
and help our guests find truly special places to stay.

If you have one, we do hope you'll decided
to take the plunge and join us.

ALASTAIR & TOBY SAWDAY

*"Trustworthy, friendly and helpful – with a reputation
for offering wonderful places and discerning visitors."*
JULIA NAISMITH, HOLLYTREE COTTAGE

"Sawday's. Is there any other?"
SONIA HODGSON, HORRY MILL

WHY BECOME A MEMBER?

Becoming a part of our 'family' of Special Places is like being awarded a Michelin star. Our stamp of approval will tell guests that you offer a truly special experience and you will benefit from our experience, reputation and support.

A CURATED COLLECTION

Our site presents a relatively small and careful selection of Special Places which helps us to stand out like a brilliantly shining beacon.

INSPECT AND RE-INSPECT

Our inspectors have an eagle-eye for the special, but absolutely no check-lists. They visit every member, see every bedroom and bathroom and, on the lucky days, eat the food.

QUALITY, NOT QUANTITY

We don't pretend (or want) to be in the same business as the sites that handle zillions of bookings a day. Using our name ensures that you attract the right kind of guests for you.

VARIETY

From country-house hotels to city pads and funky fincas to blissful B&Bs, we genuinely delight in the individuality of our Special Places.

LOYALTY

Nearly half of our members have been with us for five years or more. We must be doing something right!

The friendly crew

GET IN TOUCH WITH OUR MEMBERSHIP TEAM...

+44 (0)117 204 7810

members@sawdays.co.uk

...OR APPLY ONLINE

sawdays.co.uk/joinus

① Conwy   Hotel **②**

③ Ffin Y Parc

④ If you love art, if beautiful things tickle you pink, if you like big old houses stylishly refurbished with a streak of contemporary flair, then you should cancel whatever you're doing next week and head for Ffin y Parc. This is a gorgeous country pad – homespun, quirky, a creative bolthole that sits in 14 peaceful acres. Inside it's an exceptional gallery, not any old gallery showing a little local art, but one that curates some of the best Welsh art, with two artists a month on display – in the conservatory café where you scoff your bacon and eggs, in the airy bar where cool tunes play, and in the big sitting room where you sink into armchairs and watch smouldering logs on the fire. Bedrooms upstairs are equally lovely, in beautiful colours with elegant furniture, more fabulous art and some very fancy bathrooms. Two cool stone cottages wait outside if you want to stay a while. Lunch is served in the café: soups, quiche, perhaps a club sandwich – there are good restaurants further afield and plans are afoot to serve evening meals a couple of nights a week. Hard to beat.

Rooms	2 doubles, 1 twin/double: £135–£165. **⑤**
	1 suite for 2: £180–£210.
	1 cottage for 2, 1 cottage for 4
	(self-catering): £495–£750 per week.
	Short breaks from £295 & £375.
Meals	Lunch from £5.50. **⑥**
Closed	January. **⑦**
Directions	A55, junc.19, then A470 south for 10 **⑧**
	miles. House signed left 1 mile south
	of Llanwrst.

Roland Powell & Ralph Sanders
Ffin Y Parc
Betws Road,
Llanrwst LL26 0PT

Tel	+44 (0)1492 642070
Email	ralph@ffinyparc.co.uk
Web	www.ffinyparc.com

Favourite
newcomer

⑨ Entry 294   Map 5   **⑩**